Ottawa and the Outer Provinces

Ottawa and the Outer Provinces

The Challenge of Regional Integration in Canada

Stephen G. Tomblin

James Lorimer & Company, Publishers
Toronto, 1995

James Lorimer & Company Ltd. acknowledges with thanks the support of the Canada Council, the Ontario Arts Council and the Ontario Publishing Centre in the development of writing and publishing in Canada.

Canadian Cataloguing in Publication Data
   Tomblin, Stephen
   Ottawa and the Outer Provinces

ISBN 1-55028-477-0 (bound)
   ISBN 1-55028-476-1 (pbk.)

1. Federal-provincial relations - Canada.
   2. Regionalism - Canada. I. Title.

JL27.T65 1995   320.471'049   C95-931467-9

James Lorimer & Company Ltd., Publishers
35 Britain Street
Toronto, Ontario M5A 1R7

Printed and bound in Canada

Contents

Preface

In many respects, this book is a reflection of my academic and life experiences. My fascination with regional integration began while I was a student at the University of Calgary, when Roger Gibbins lectured on the significance of regionalism in Canadian politics. It was the early 1970s and I became enthralled with the topic of boundaries and the federal-inspired Western Economic Opportunities Conference. I then attended Dalhousie University, and with the assistance of David Cameron and Michael Kirby, my attention turned to Maritime Union. Next, while I was attending the University of British Columbia, Alan Cairns and Donald Blake offered me encouragement and invaluable criticisms as I began to explore questions about underdevelopment, boundaries, and space in British Columbia. Finally, living and researching in Newfoundland has provided yet another way of thinking about the regional integration question.

My thinking on the topic of boundaries has changed over the years as a result of these experiences, but I am still struck by the lack of information on this subject. This book is an attempt to rectify the situation.

I am grateful to the many friends, family members, and colleagues who provided me with support, invaluable suggestions, and editorial advice. I wish to express my gratitude to Alan Macpherson, Gunther Hartmann, Karen Tomblin, Gail Murphy, and Jean Barman for all their insight and encouragement throughout the life of the project. I relied on these people for inspiration, and the book benefited from their input. Other colleagues at Memorial University, who are too numerous to name, were also helpful. I would also like to thank Diane Young, Cy Strom, Eileen Koyama, Laura Ellis, and the staff at Lorimer for their generous suggestions for improvement and for seeing the book through to the final product.

Successful completion of the book would not have been possible without the numerous premiers, public servants, cabinet ministers, and others who were willing to be interviewed over the years. And, even though they remain anonymous, I am indebted to them.

Among all my debts, however, I owe the most to my wife Lesley and daughter Leah. Lesley provided encouragement, editorial advice, and was generous with her time. Leah's hugs and early morning visits in front of the computer screen saw me through the project to its completion.

One

Shifting Boundaries and Regional Integration

Canadians are engaged in yet another debate on improving the co-operative spirit amongst the provinces, especially in the Atlantic and the West. The fiscal imperative, another national unity crisis, and Canada's ability to compete in a globalizing economy have all contributed to the rethinking of both provincial boundaries and the role of provincial governments in the 1990s. Canada is undergoing major changes, and Ottawa and some premiers have expressed interest in moving away from a competitive provincial approach to the restructuring of Atlantic and Western Canada.

Complex policy challenges sometimes force us to reorganize institutions in order to generate new ideas and move in new directions — that seems simple enough. However, Canada is organized on a federal basis and lacks an entrenched national identity; thus, premiers have responded in different ways to the regional integration question. Since the 1930s, when regional integration was first introduced, Ottawa and the outer provinces have struggled over territorial integrity.

The debate over the political restructuring of the Atlantic and Western regions on a more integrated basis has always attracted a diverse range of opinions. For decades, each time Ottawa and supporters of the regional paradigm of governance have forced the issue, British Columbia, Newfoundland, Nova Scotia, and Alberta have refused to cooperate, focusing instead on defending their territorial interests.

In fact, the call for cooperation has probably reinforced political competition and state-building as much as it has reduced them. These effects have been strongest in provinces such as British Columbia, which have felt most threatened by these outside forces and which have always had access to political resources for defending unilateral action. Whether this trend continues in the 1990s will depend largely on the environmental conditions facing the premiers.

To understand the divisions created by this issue, we need to investigate the competitive nature of federalist politics and the different forces that shape provincial politics in Atlantic and Western Canada. To this end, we trace the history of struggle over boundaries in British Columbia, the Prairies, and Atlantic/Maritime Canada from the late 1930s to the 1990s.

In a country with divided loyalties and a weakened national government, the regional integration approach provides a means for restraining increasingly independent governments in the West and reducing government costs, while solving the regional disparity problem in the Atlantic region. At least, these are the objectives. However, Ottawa and the provinces supporting the initiative do not have, and have never had, the political resources necessary for implementing the policy. The political leaders of Canada refuse to sing from the same hymn book: instead, they prefer to flex their muscles and work at cross-purposes. They play their part in the political game.

The regional idea has been a political grail for generations. Even though working together to solve problems seems like a good idea, rich provinces such as Alberta and British Columbia do not see much economic logic in further reinforcing east-west ties, especially at the expense of north-south ones.

We must recognize that bad experiences with integrative policies and Central Canadian imperialism have shaped the attitudes in some provinces towards meeting outside challenges. With their growing economic and political power, Alberta and British Columbia will likely be unwilling to sacrifice their own interests. In Newfoundland, nationalism remains a force that could be mobilized under the right conditions. However, the "have-not" provinces in both the Atlantic and Western regions lack the levers of control found in Alberta or British Columbia. As a result, they are more vulnerable to outside forces and trends.

This book explores the idea of regional integration with respect to various elements: the relevance of the issue in Canadian history; the effect of institutional variables, especially the impact of "executive federalism" on the campaign; the impact of past cultural experiences; and finally, the challenge of balancing equity and efficiency principles in a divided policy.

One option for restructuring Canada involves strengthening the regional economies (especially in the Atlantic and the West) and persuading provincial governments to pool and otherwise limit their sovereignty in dealing with new challenges. In the 1990s, the idea of regional integration has reappeared on the national agenda, and again, the premiers do not agree on the merits of the policy. Despite the difficulties in achieving a resolution, Ottawa seems determined to push the issue in response to changing economic circumstances. As clearly stated in *The Liberal Plan for Canada*,

> Liberals favour a new approach. We see strong regional economies as building blocks for Canada. Concerted action and the mobilization of scarce resources are necessary to achieve strong regional economies in this age of international competition and change. One of the most important ways of making this happen is to develop forums for economic cooperation, joint action, and an integrated development on the regional level.

> The different regions of Canada, especially the West and Atlantic, are moving towards common areas of action and development in eliminating trade barriers and developing joint procurement policies, and are looking at cooperative ventures in training, health, trade, and infrastructure development. This move towards economic cooperation can pay major dividends.[1]

Regional integration refers to greater cooperation among provinces through policy harmonization, new forms of association, and communication across provincial boundaries. The intent is to eliminate fragmentation, diminish the authority of provincial governments, and encourage friendly communication between provinces. Proponents of this approach are committed to reducing costly provincial barriers that inhibit the growth of both regional economies and a sense of community. Harking back to the days of Pierre Trudeau, die-hard supporters of the east-west paradigm are concerned that self-governing provinces will see the economic logic of self-sufficiency, especially as Ottawa's powers decline and the forces of the marketplace become more powerful. Hence, from their perspective, we need a new plan for holding the country together that also considers changing economic realities. For a country with a history of conflicting territorial interests, this new approach remains controversial.

This debate arises repeatedly without significant progress toward policy implementation. In this respect, it has much in common with the separatist movement in Quebec.

The Integration Continuum

Regional integration or cooperation can be thought of as an economic, administrative, and political continuum, which, as indicated in the Maritime Union study, takes different forms.[2]

The authors of the report note the differences between informal cooperation and more formal types of integration, which require an assortment of mechanisms for making decisions and implementing joint policies. The Maritime report also discusses three types of union, and this discussion provides us with key insights for understanding the continuum. *Administration union* pertains to joint administration and delivery of programs; *economic union* involves joint planning and the removal of trade barriers between provinces; *political union* requires the elimination of provincial boundaries and the creation of new common political institutions. Even though political union is not a consideration in the 1990s, each of these options has been explored in the past. However, if Quebec separates from Canada, political union may again be on the agenda, especially for the Atlantic region.

The discourse over regional integration and the growing interest in reinforcing common socio-economic structures among provinces are not new. In Atlantic and Western Canada, cross-border relationships have developed over time; however, the lack of common objectives, interests, and institutions has made it difficult for provincial governments to work together. After the Meech Lake Accord and the Charlottetown Agreement, we are all too aware of the limitations of a bilateral federal-provincial structure in achieving fundamental change.

The historical emergence of provincial boundaries has meant that premiers are resistant to outside interference with local powers or a provincial sense of identity, especially in rich provinces. The provincial state has provided a framework for building independent societies and economies that are in competition with each other. Canada is known for its diversity and competitive ways.

Indeed, intergovernmental conflict has been part of Canada's political landscape for decades. As a result, even though regional evolution (and even the establishment of new provinces) has been contemplated in the post-war era, little has been achieved. The Canadian federal system has made it difficult to obtain unanimous support for the project, and, as a result, the status quo has usually survived. Whether this stalemate continues in the 1990s will depend a great deal on economic circumstances and available political resources.

The purpose of this book is twofold: First, we will provide a historical context for the institutional, economic, ideological, and cultural forces underlying the current initiative. Second, we will identify the factors that have worked against integration and link them to new challenges. In the 1990s, conditions have changed and the status quo no longer seems to be an option. On the other hand, the provinces have not agreed to cooperate in strengthening socio-economic linkages along the east-west axis. To be sure, different models might be feasible, especially in Alberta and British Columbia.

For analytical purposes, we will isolate the social, economic, and political ramifications of the discourse over regional integration. The concept has different overtones and implications in different provinces and ideological circles. But what is the nature and significance of the debate? What accounts for the different perspectives? Why does the issue reappear and why do leaders make so little progress towards its resolution? How has the policy process influenced the outcome? What impact will new circumstances have on the current campaign? These questions are crucial to this investigation.

The Concept of Region

To understand the cases for and against greater regional cooperation, we begin by defining *region*. The concept of region seems simple enough and is usually associated with *community*; however, the definition of community also varies. For example, we might incorporate geographical, economic, cultural, or even institutional factors to determine distinctiveness and cross-border homogeneity.

As a result, the concept of region is highly ambiguous, and this uncertainty creates conflict. The Canadian federal system is cursed by the use of many definitions of regionalism, and the self-interests of the politicians affect their responses to such ambiguity. Thus, the concept of Western and Atlantic regionalism, a central tenet of the integration policy, is not accepted in various provinces.

In the real world of politics, government competition and self-interest have motivated leaders to construct their own visions of the world. For decades, Canadians have been confused about competing visions and the stability of provincial boundaries. These factors have complicated the tasks of defining regions and mobilizing public opinion behind a new approach to restructuring.

Canadians remain divided over not only the meaning of region, but also the objective of a regional model; should its goal be to reinforce decentralization at the provincial level or to promote a concept of federalism that recognizes the need to mobilize regional cultures and establish joint problem-solving structures?[3] This conflict has complicated efforts to coordinate regional policy initiatives among provinces. Despite the merits of cooperation, the premiers do not agree on a new model for organizing the country.

Since Canadian politics has always been organized on a federal-provincial basis, some premiers have resisted approaches that involve greater reliance on regions rather than on provinces in dealing with problems. The framing of policy issues and the visions that find expression are greatly influenced by both the institutional structure and the available political resources.

As Simeon indicated, *regionalism*, the behaviour associated with a region, is another confusing concept that has political implications.[4] According to the author,

> we need to be a good deal more systematic both in how we conceive of the phenomenon "regionalism" and how we describe its dimensions and effects. We must first recognize that in no sense is it an explanatory variable: by itself it doesn't explain anything; nothing happens because of regionalism. If we find differences of any sort among regions, it remains for us to find out why they exist; regionalism is not an answer. In this sense, regions are simply containers, whose contents may or may not differ. And how we draw the boundaries around them depends entirely on what our purposes are: it is an a priori question, determined by theoretical needs or political purposes. We can have regions within provinces, or regions made up of groups of provinces, or regions cutting across provincial lines. That we have come to identify regionalism in Canada as being almost synonymous with province is a nice example of the institutional effect I mentioned.

We do so because the provinces are significant political units.[5]

Friesen suggests three basic approaches for thinking about the concept of region.[6] The first deals with physical geographical forces and the impact that landforms have on a community's sense of identity. In spite of the many critics of the geographic determinist approach, the influence of landscape on the way communities define themselves is hard to deny.

The second approach focuses on historical relationships between the heartland and hinterland. Friesen acknowledges that Brodie has been most active in exploring this interpretation of the concept. Brodie states that "regions are seen as part of an interconnected whole in which one regional configuration is largely a function or an expression of another. Regions, following this account, are not arbitrary constructs but effects or consequences of historical relationships."[7] Such a perspective is important because it encourages us to think about relationships between regions, past experiences, and dependencies. Outside attacks on the sovereignty or sense of identity of any community can backfire if there is a history of turbulent relations and a consequent lack of trust between the parties.

Finally, the *imagined* approach to defining regions is based on the view that ideas, perceptions, myths, and visions pull a society together or force it apart (in the case of competing visions). Canadians have always struggled over two such critical issues: the source of regional differences in economic prosperity and the make-up of the country, as equal provinces, five regions, or two nations.[8]

These three approaches are useful because they help to illustrate the various factors that can be used for differentiating communities. The problem of regional definition is not easy to solve. Indeed, given the countless criteria and the diversity of opinion about the number of regions in the country, Simeon's argument is worth reiterating: differences in social and economic experiences are important, but they do not, in themselves, explain anything.[9] These internal cleavages require an institutional focus if they are to be fully recognized or politicized.

In the 1930s, reorganization on a regional basis (and its potential for problem solving) first became an issue. Since then, Ottawa and the outer provinces have engaged in a series of debates over the merits of regional cooperation/integration. Despite the fact that this issue never really disappears, we know little about the concept. From a historical perspective, it is important to understand the reason for repeated attempts to create regions other than those demarcated by provincial boundaries, and the explanation for the ineffectiveness of these campaigns. Moreover, we need to consider the critical factors in the 1990s to determine the likely success or failure of the recent federal government initiative.

We attempt to link the history of failed attempts at integration to the competing territorial, jurisdictional, and economic interests of the governments involved. In the past, the inosculation of intergovernmental arenas and the considerable political resources available to competitors on both sides worked against the drive towards integration in both Atlantic and Western Canada. The system's reliance on unilateral decision making also impeded progress.

Under these conditions, the campaign for regional integration was bound to fail because the process was dominated by political leaders with different agendas, who were operating in a highly fragmented, competitive structure. Other stakeholders were never part of the political process. Clearly, independent state institutions, political party systems, different cultures and objectives, and leadership styles have all contributed to unilateralism. Indeed, our federalist politics was designed to promote provincial separatism. In other words, co-operative regionalism represents an attack on federalism itself, and the system has built-in mechanisms for preserving the status quo.

For example, there is little question that federal spending patterns and, in particular, the obligation to provide financial support for established provincial policies, have obstructed a change in direction. Since any changes required provincial consent, the territorial interests of the premiers were always well protected.

In the past, Ottawa's spending power was used to mobilize support for a more cooperative agenda, especially in Atlantic Canada; ironically, it was an ineffective instrument because other federal transfers helped to reinforce the existing boundaries. As Winters recently argued in his assessment of fiscal relations and Maritime union, Ottawa's spending patterns, "allowed provincial politicians to blithely continue on their path of patronage and power."[10]

The carrot-and-stick approach never seemed to work because the premiers always had the capacity to work at cross-purposes, and Ottawa helped pay the bills. Politicians in Ottawa seeking to use spending power to promote cooperation across provincial borders face this dilemma. Perhaps the trend towards more market-based solutions is a response to this problem. Predictably, if transfers to "have-not" provinces continue to decline, the Atlantic provinces will be forced along the integration continuum. Yet, the considerable autonomy, political resources, and economic interests of Alberta and British Columbia will make it more difficult to forge new east-west ties.

In the 1990s, some circumstances have changed, but others have not. Ottawa will continue to force regionalism onto the public agenda, and, as in the past, some provinces will have concerns about this initiative, albeit each for different reasons. However, unlike the past, decentralization, the fiscal imperative, the decline of state interventionism, and economic globalization will likely push the Atlantic and Western regions in opposite directions.

Our federation has always faced concurrent pressures for integration and disintegration; however, changes in federal spending powers and greater reliance on market-based decisions will likely make it easier to defend a regional cooperative agenda in Atlantic Canada. These poor provinces will have little choice but to work together as transfers decline. The same forces have the opposite effect in the West, where trade liberalization is enhancing the pull of north-south economic and political forces. Especially in Alberta and British Columbia, North American and Pacific Rim trade patterns will provide extra incentive for reducing subsidies for the welfare state, regional development, transportation, and other east-west–oriented policies.

The dichotomous nature of regional integration creates problems. On the one hand, the approach attempts to solve pressing economic development problems without increasing government costs in Atlantic Canada. On the other, it deals with international economic pressures without destroying the logic of economic union in the West. That is, as Ottawa stresses the need for market solutions and self-reliance in Atlantic Canada, support increases for the economic logic of province-building in Alberta and British Columbia and strengthening north-south ties.

The Regional Integration Question in Context

These days, the entire industrial world is engaged in an intense debate over the merits of eliminating boundaries. In Canada, a good deal of tension has been generated over the reaffirmation of the primacy of the marketplace without sacrificing the artificial economic linkages and state policies that have bound us together as a nation. To compound the problem, Canadians have been confused for generations about a sense of identity and geographical boundaries.

Two factors explain why people in different places have responded differently to the challenge of integration. First, people are greatly influenced by perceptions of themselves and of the world around them. Ideas, values, and ideologies, which are rooted in historical experience, provide a guide for those seeking answers to complex problems.[11] These views become permanently embedded in our memories and culture; they help identify community boundaries, relevant and irrelevant issues, and adversaries.

In Canada, provincial cultures have strong foundations.[12] Cultural and ideological differences among provinces help to explain, in part, the lack of a cohesive response to the idea of regional unity. This book presents a brief look at the various provincial cultures and visions that have shaped the regional discourse and attempts to identify their roots.

The second factor influencing responses to the integration model is the institutional context. Based on our discussion of regions, we can conclude that institutions are important, especially when we consider the hinterland and imagined approaches discussed by Friesen. Institutions help us to give meaning to fluctuating socio-economic forces.

Institutions determine the policy actors, the relative influence of borders, the mobilization of support, and the relevant issues. The cabinet-parliamentary system and the emergence of "executive federalism"[13] have had a major bearing on the historical pattern of federal-provincial tensions surrounding the regional integration debate. In this vein, Simeon argued that our executive-dominated system of decision making is comparable to the arrangements that exist among sovereign states in international politics.[14] Such compartmentalization shapes the dynamics of Canadian politics as well as the style and substance of policy debate.

Within such an institutional context, it is not surprising that the premiers have not reached a consensus on the need to embrace a regional agenda.[15] If Simeon is correct in his assumption that the federal-provincial system is comparable to international politics, such a division of political authority among autonomous yet interdependent actors creates a number of political dilemmas. In Canada, the rules of the political game and the power structure reinforce intergovernmental competition and create territorial conflict.

In this study, we assume that the federal-provincial structure (combined with the centre-periphery dichotomy of the economy) has contributed to variation in the perspectives on the merits of integration. In the past, fiscal federalism helped to finance rival state-building initiatives and even supported existing semi-sovereign political units at the provincial level; thus, there was little incentive to reorient Canadian politics towards a regional framework. Even "have-not" provinces were able to remain self-sufficient in the clash over the need to strengthen provincial rather than regional communities within the federation.

Hence, acceptance of the concept of a regional community has always faced a number of obstacles. The lack of regional institutions has undermined efforts to reinforce a sense of identity common to citizens living in different provinces. Without a solid foundation of understanding, shared culture and shared visions, or a common economic interest, challenging provincial models has been difficult. These problems have plagued nation-builders for generations.

The Lure of Regional Integration

Despite widespread views to the contrary, the idea of regional integration has always had supporters in Canada. One of our central tasks is to identify the forces underlying the regional initiative, its proponents, and the reasons for their support. On the other hand, we need to understand why some provinces showed much less enthusiasm for the call for cooperation. Our case-study chapters constitute an attempt to make sense of the determinants of cooperation/competition within the federation.

In the past, a number of national governments have engaged in these regional initiatives, but have never been strong enough to displace continental forces or provincial imperatives. Yet, the issue reappears, attesting to the desire of various federal governments to strengthen ties across provincial boundaries.

Naturally, the federal government has concerns about losing control over development. Moreover, Ottawa may be anxious about competitive relationships between governments and those strong provinces who have less incentive to cooperate.

Alternatively, weaker provinces may support regional initiatives, especially in the absence of internal divisions. Historically, Manitoba and New Brunswick have been the strongest supporters of the regional idea and Ottawa's natural allies. The underlying factor was the basic desire to create a united front in dealing with problems such as the need to share wealth along the east-west axis.

Furthermore, the building of economic partnerships within North America has always yielded benefits. As a consequence, Ottawa has also had to consider efficiency and equity trade-offs in dealing with regional development issues. Since implementation of the First National Policy, Ottawa has found it difficult to subordinate overall economic competitiveness to regional policy objectives. Governments often pursue policies with conflicting goals; this dilemma helps to explain the lack of evolution of the regional idea in Canada. During the past few decades, Ottawa's hesitation in imposing solutions can be attributed partly to jurisdictional problems and partly to concerns about maintaining the country's competitiveness in a global economy.

Since 1867, Ottawa has struggled with what Smiley refers to as the "three axes of Canadian Federalism." According to Smiley,

> there are three particular and continuing problems of Canadian nationhood, each with a jurisdictional-territorial dimension: (a) the relation between Canada and the United States; (b) the relation between the English and French Communities of Canada; (c) the relations between the central heartland of Ontario and Quebec and those Canadian regions to the east and west of this heartland.[16]

From the outset, Canada has faced problems in balancing the forces within the federation. In order to understand the appeal of the regional model and some provinces' opposition to it, we need to determine the relevance of political community and regional underdevelopment to the larger centre-periphery struggle mentioned by Smiley. We must also recognize the different agendas and variations in power of the provinces that vie for control over the political discourse.

The Concept of Province-Building

At the heart of the debate over regional integration is the negative image of province-building.[17] From the start, scholars on both the left and right have heavily criticized the idea of provincialism. Canadian nationalists have always been concerned about self-governing provinces and their negative impact on the national culture and economy. As Cairns indicated, "the greatest mystery for students of Canadian federalism has been the survival and growth of provincial governments, particularly those of English Canada."[18]

Those on the left have characterized decentralization as a threat because it undermines the rise of a unified and progressive society, which is necessary for promoting the national interest against continentalism. For example, both Horowitz and Porter have opposed provincialism for the reason that it hinders the rise of creative or class-based politics.[19] Many left-leaning scholars consider province-building to be the result of the environmental context of political decision making.

Orthodox thinkers have been more concerned about the threat posed to economic competitiveness by institutional duplication and interference. They tend to focus on the role of institutions in shaping the society and economy. Dicey, Schonfeld, and Tarrow, among others, have been guided by the assumption that federalism is inefficient, weak, and too conservative in an era of increasing economic interdependence.[20]

Recently, Cairns coined the phrase *embedded state* in an attempt to understand the obstacles to cultural and institutional change in Canada. Examination of this issue is timely considering the current problems facing the country. He argued that a new pattern of state-society relations has emerged and taken on a life of its own. In the process, he helped to reinforce a negative view of unilateral action, as is clearly evident in the following passage:

> the tighter fusion of state and society engendered in recent decades by activist national and provincial governments simultaneously fragments the state and contributes to the multiplication and increased salience of socio-economic cleavages. The overall Canadian federal state has become a sprawling diffuse assemblage of uncoordinated power and policies, while society with which it interacts is increasingly plural, fragmented and multiple in its allegiances and identities. The more we relate to one another through the state, the more divided we seem to become.[21]

Integration and Trends in Regional Development

Much of the discussion about reversing the trend towards decentralization on a provincial scale has focused on the interest that academic and national political élites have shown in facilitating further homogenization of the country. To interpret this trend, we should briefly consider the influence of development experiences of other countries.

Cardoso and Faleto note that "in almost all theories of modernization it is assumed that the course taken by political, social, and economic systems of Western Europe and the United States, foretells the future for the underdeveloped countries. The 'development process' would consist in completing and even reproducing the various stages that characterized the social transformation of these countries."[22] While Canada is not an underdeveloped country, Canadians have been greatly influenced by the experiences and centralization models of other countries. The fact that in America there were "amalgamations of states into geographical, cultural, economic, or administrative zones," likely influenced attitudes toward the regional idea in Canada.[23] The movement in Europe towards integration has also been an important consideration.

Modernization theories claim that the pressures of economic interdependence and technological change will undermine the socioeconomic roots of provincialism. Based on these theories, a number of prominent academics in Canada have focused on reducing the role of provincial institutions in the policy process.

The "civic culture"[24] perspective has had a dramatic effect on academic research around the world and has influenced this trend. According to this perspective, segmented cultures and economies are closely associated with underdevelopment and political instability. In Canada, the emphasis attached to eliminating provincial boundaries and coordinating regional policy initiatives can be linked to these external models. The central tenet of modernization theory is that integration is a positive force. The popularity of the regional approach has always been tied to the self-interests and power of political actors, and the models they found most useful for defining problems and mobilizing coalitions. In the 1960s and 1970s, the civic culture and modernization theories helped to legitimize the regional initiative. In the 1990s, new economic theories have emerged and they have also been exploited for political purposes.

In addition, the issue of underdevelopment likely contributed to interest in the regional idea, especially in Atlantic Canada. The regional disparity problem has a long history in Canada, and government efforts based on a regional perspective have failed to reverse the trend. We do not fully understand the principle causes of underdevelopment or the strategies that should be adopted to reverse this problem. As a consequence, provincial governments in the island communities of Newfoundland and Prince Edward Island have always found themselves in a paradoxical position: they want to make changes, but not if the result is further marginalization.

This fundamental debate over the principle causes of underdevelopment has significantly influenced the discussion of integration. The diversity of views on the subject has complicated the task of mobilizing support for a policy based on the development/integrative experiences of Europe, the United States, and other industrial societies.

For decades, modernization or orthodox theories have provided ammunition for the attack on provincial structures and policies, especially in the "have-not" Atlantic region. According to these theories, the problems are "internal," and the solutions require forging new economic partnerships, reducing the role of government, and increasing competitiveness by eliminating obstacles to economic opportunity. To many, economic restructuring requires the elimination of political obstacles and the establishment of the policies and structures that will break the cycle. Different versions of this argument have surfaced over the decades, "but they all share a similar orientation: they locate the source of regional underdevelopment within the formal boundaries of the region."[25]

To others, the logic is reversed. Those who blame outsiders for the problem of underdevelopment usually place the reduction of state autonomy at the bottom of the agenda. Radical staples theory, dependency models, and some versions of neo-Marxism focus on underdevelopment as the product of exploitation by outsiders.[26] However, it should be noted that these scholars have tended to be more concerned with national rather than provincial autonomy.

The question of whether regional disparity is caused by internal or external forces is far from resolution. Without a clear consensus on the effects of provincial policies and boundaries on underdevelopment, the issues of integration cannot be resolved, especially given the institutional context. Savoie knew this well when he stated,

> By and large, the economics and politics of pragmatism have shaped regional development programming and by extension federal-provincial relations in the region for the last twenty years. The reasons were varied. Certainly provincial governments have found the theoretical models

explaining the region's underdevelopment to be of little value.[27]

These conflicting views helped to reinforce an incremental and conservative approach to restructuring. Furthermore, Canadian nationalists tended to ignore the effects of their own contradictory interventionist policies. Centralized development schemes and national plans hindered (rather than facilitated) market adjustment to new challenges as much as province-building did. With the changes in response to globalization and the federal government's declining capacity to intervene due to the debt situation, these factors may no longer be as important.

Regional Stereotypes

A major reason for the focus on Atlantic and Western Canada in the regional debate stems from the negative stereotypes that have been inflicted upon both regions as a result of their peripheral status. In other words, the centre-periphery axis described by Smiley has set the context for the issue.

From a historical perspective, Ottawa has shown a strong desire to strengthen cooperative tendencies in the Atlantic and the West. The federal government has focused on strengthening regional unity, encouraging structural change, promoting greater self-reliance, and reducing costs, but in a way that served the national interest. As one might expect, some premiers reacted to this approach with resentment; they had a different perception of their own economic interests, and they were inclined to fight back against their quasi-colonial status. This conflict contributes to the recurring struggle over the integration issue.

Regional stereotypes have drawn national attention to the peripheral regions, rather than to Central Canada. For instance, redrawing the boundaries of Quebec or Ontario attracts little interest, despite the fact that Premier Wells has raised the idea on several occasions. Circumstances may have been different if Ontario and Quebec had not received extra territory and Canada consisted of more provinces.[28] However, given the power of these two provinces, Ottawa is not likely to raise this issue.

Regional stereotypes are also a major factor in the boundary dispute. Atlantic Canada is often cast as a conservative monolith or an economic backwater that needs to be changed.[29] Different standards of conduct have been applied to the citizens and governments of the Atlantic region. In describing this tendency, Young laments that,

> there can also be comfort in the old images of politics in the Maritimes — the snake-oil salesmanship, the rival cliques fighting for the spoils of office, and the politicians who stride across small stages like petty princelings — for these images elicit, especially among Upper Canadians and the more jaded elements of the regional society, that soothing sense of bemused condescension so gratifying to those who can afford to be above the fray.[30]

Even though such images have likely contributed to generalizations about the Atlantic provinces, the efforts of local scholars to refute these stereotypes have probably fuelled the resolve of some premiers to reject a second-class position within the federal family.[31] However, external interest in promoting pan-Atlantic Canadianism has not benefited from these images.

In Western Canada, a similar pattern of negative stereotyping has emerged to the same response by local scholars.[32] Western Canada's image as a place where people are incompetent, greedy, and intolerant has been perpetuated by the print media. According to the *Globe and Mail*, Canada's "national" newspaper, "the West Coast is in no danger of losing its reputation for hosting the zaniest political theatre in the land."[33] In Canada, territorial divisions run deep and limitations are inherent to the institutional structure; hence, in the short term, these negative images have helped to raise the issue, but in the long term, they have made it more difficult for political élites to compromise.

To make matters worse, Central Canada has always viewed the West as a possession. The political framework established by the original 1867 compact provided an opportunity for a business-state coalition to assert its claim of ownership over the western hinterland. From the beginning, it was common to think of the West as a peripheral region. The division resulted from a specific set of historical circumstances; the centre-periphery rivalry that began with the First National Policy was central to this conflict. The idea of integrating the West is a product of history, as is the marked tendency toward revolt in Alberta and British Columbia against actions that threaten local autonomy.

Simeon's Framework

For a complete understanding of the regional integration question, we must determine the institutional factors responsible for the salience of the issue. Moreover, we must investigate the political dynamics that have operated at cross-purposes and prevented the policy from reaching implementation. Thus, we will identify the tensions between provincial and regional aspirations in Atlantic and Western Canada, as well as the role of Ottawa in stressing a regional agenda.

One approach for exploring this issue is to focus on the different political goals, attitudes, and interests of the political leaders. To this end, Simeon's detailed framework for examining intergovernmental relations and decision making is useful. He provides critical insights for understanding executive-dominated structures, institutions, and processes of policy making. This analysis allows us to study the interplay between ideas, institutions, and other forces that have shaped the regional issue over time.

According to Simeon,

> The framework can be stated like this: there is a set of interdependent actors, or partisans; they operate within a certain social and institutional environment; they share some goals but differ on others — it is a 'mixed motive game'; they have an issue or set of issues on which they must negotiate; none has hierarchical control over the others; they have varying political resources; they use these resources in certain strategies and tactics; they arrive at certain outcomes; and these outcomes have consequences for themselves, for other groups in society, and for the system itself.

> The framework also focuses on the interplay between (a) antecedent or background factors, which include the social and cultural characteristics of the federal system as well as the political institutions which define the environment for the decision-makers; (b) concurrent or immediate factors, including the nature of the issues, the goals, and the resources of the actors; and (c) consequent factors, such as the implications for the participants.[34]

In this analysis, we must also broach an important issue in the history of Canadian federalism: the quest to strike a balance between provincial and regional interests. Several questions are relevant to the contemporary discourse: Is such an approach feasible or desirable? Should there be informal or formal cooperation? For example, do we need more formal mechanisms in which premiers give up their unilateral powers and decisions are reached on the basis of consensus? What level of integration should Western or Atlantic Canada pursue in pooling their sovereignties? Should joint administrative units be established to reduce the costs of implementation? Is economic union with formal legal agreements, common development policies, and a joint approach to intergovernmental relations possible? Is full political union the only option because of the various problems associated with these other forms of union? Finally, what are the prospects for change in each region?

Simeon's framework provides a convenient way to understand the debate and the tensions underlying the regional initiative. We will rely on his framework to reappraise past events in addressing the issue in the political climate of the 1990s.

The objective of this book is to situate the Liberal regional initiative in context. In the second chapter, we examine the roots of the discourse by tracing the larger national integration question and the role of previous national policies. To facilitate comparison between the regions, the next three chapters present the roles of socio-economic, political institutions and political culture, and their influence on the movement in the past. In particular, we will focus on why there has never been a consensus on the need to relinquish sovereignty. In this regard, disagreements over the benefits of integration and the persistence of provincial institutions/cultures have always worked against fundamental institutional change.

Some provinces, such as Manitoba and New Brunswick, were more committed to the goals of rationalization and cooperation. These goals were costly in terms of political independence. However, because of their unique institutional/cultural traditions and economic interests, these two provinces were convinced that economic development would suffer in a pluralistic, competitive environment. By contrast, other provinces were unwilling to change direction. In the end, they were unwilling to support any permanent institutional change that might result in more harm than good.

In the 1990s, new forces are pushing Atlantic and Western Canada in opposite directions. While changing the status quo in the West will be difficult, Ottawa may find that Atlantic Canada is now more receptive to a regional agenda. We conclude that it might be worth considering different models for reorganizing intergovernmental relations in each region.

Efforts to restructure the country in response to new challenges will not come easily; institutional change comes about slowly. However, since political institutions are more easily replaced in times of crisis, the current fiscal situation together with the trend toward globalization may provide Ottawa with the opportunity to finally resolve the integration issue in at least Atlantic Canada.

Two

The Quest to Create a Nation

Every country wrestles with the problem of promoting a common identity. It is no different in Canada, even though the context within which policies are formulated and implemented is unique. The same is true at the provincial level, since each community within the federation relies on distinct economic, social, and political structures that give rise to competing territorial interests and conflicts. Our sense of identity at either the federal or provincial level is inexorably connected to disputes over acceptable levels of dependence and self-rule; this connection helps to explain why Canadians are so insular and divided. Thus, we must examine the origins of the regional integration debate by tracing interregional conflicts over previous national policies. These policies were designed to defy geographical and economic logic and to exploit the federal government's control over the hinterland for the purpose of establishing an east-west pattern of communication, transportation, and commerce. The implications of such policies were always centralist; hence the wealthier provinces in the West showed the most resistance to the drive for integration along the east-west axis.

Our federal system has helped to reinforce limited societal identities and clashes between governments over territorial issues. Since 1867, provincial governments have been divided and unwilling to surrender their power, in spite of great pressure to do so. Even if there are advantages to unity on a regional or national basis, there has always been a natural reluctance to it. Black knew this well when he wrote:

> For the Canadian state the politics of federalism are the politics of survival. The continued vigour of her federalism, however, is probably responsible for the stillbirth of Canada as a nation-state; the most conspicuously missing ingredient in this political system has been any over-

arching nationalism. In no other mature country does it seem likely that political figures concentrate so much on the geographic distribution of public power to the apparent neglect of debate over the ends and purposes toward which authority is organized.[1]

In a country such as Canada, the national unity puzzle has always been complicated by extensive socio-economic and political links between regions that are a continent apart and by differences in ideas about the purposes of the federation. A central problem is the lack of a common sense of place or definition that unites Canadians. These differences, which have become more pronounced in recent years, reflect previous political failures in dealing with serious conflicts over regionalism, continentalism, and Anglo-French relations.

Another complication for national unity involves differences in wealth between "have" and "have-not" provinces and the question of who should pay the costs associated with building and promoting a unified Canadian society. Rich and poor provinces in Atlantic and Western Canada have had different agendas and ideas on the need for federal intervention or the call for further disentanglement. If nothing else, this diversity creates a passionate form of politics.

Politics in Canada is difficult to understand because everyone feels threatened by some outside group, and the institutional system reinforces a culture of territorial competition and suspicion. These intense centre-periphery struggles, which are often very polarized, have made it difficult to accommodate conflicting policy objectives and interests. As Bruce W. Hodgins et al. argued, "In the Canadian experience, resistance to central authority has most often been rooted in a bicultural heritage and/or the intense regionalism. In turn, this alienation has encouraged the overall decentralizing trend which began immediately after Confederation."[2]

Whether in 1867 or 1993, Ottawa and the subnational governments have had difficulty agreeing on the best way to promote increased economic interdependence without giving up too much regional or national control over the development process. Every generation of politicians in Canada has faced the problem of finding the most appropriate formula for coordinating industrial development and increasing productivity, while not infringing on the constitutional rights of any of the communities involved. The quest to manage our increasing economic interdependence with the United States and find the most appropriate means for pooling our sovereignties has been a central preoccupation of government in Canada since 1867.

This chapter focuses on understanding the history of struggle over regional development policy in Atlantic and Western Canada. The central task is to determine the influence of past decisions on the different responses of the premiers to the call for effective integration along the east-west axis, but from an Atlantic/Western Canada perspective.

Development and Integration of the Periphery

The First National Policy was a fusion: it was a response to changing circumstances in the international economy combined with the dream of building a separate political and economic structure on a national basis. The project, which was rooted in the desire to unite the country in both an economic and political sense, was specially designed to address industrialization and the threat posed by continentalism to the Canadian industrial centre. As a consequence, the demands for an integrated approach to development were tempered by the need to recognize and accommodate cultural and regional differences in the country.

Since 1867, the Canadian political system has been anchored on the conflicting principles of federalism and parliamentary sovereignty. Such an unusual combination ensured that the tensions between the goals of national and provincial integration would be a salient feature of the federal system. Ironically, the original architects of the system provided an institutional focus for forces exerting a centrifugal effect in every province, even in Ontario. The design of the system essentially guaranteed intense regional conflicts and a divergence of views on the integration question.

To further complicate matters, from the beginning, there was a deliberate attempt to exploit national powers to defend and promote the interests of the industrial centre at the expense of the periphery. Although national integration and development brought benefits to the western and eastern peripheries, there were, at the same time, costs associated with disrupting north-south trade and transferring local control over economic development to a group of élites in Central Canada. In the continuing struggle to create a federal system that was fair and balanced, national policies have done little to shake the power of the old monopoly.[3] Any further attempt to contest provincial frames of reference must consider previous national policies and the tensions between governments over the integration problem.

The alienation of the western periphery began with the original national plan. The intent was to create a region for the industrial centre and to impose a second-class constitutional and economic status on the West. Rather than building a federal system based on the concept of territorial equality, the clear intent of the national plan was to promote the monopolistic interests of the industrial heartland at the expense of the western periphery. Whether the issue was the composition of the Senate, the tariff system, discriminatory freight rates, or control over natural resources, the objective was to put in place a continent-wide development scheme that reinforced the historical hegemony of the industrial heartland over the West.[4] Such an approach guaranteed that the country would remain divided, and it pitted governments in the western periphery against those in the industrial heartland. Although Manitoba benefited more than the other provinces, there was a general feeling that the purpose of the policy was to exploit the West. To explain the resistance to the regional integration option, it is necessary to understand these early experiences, as well as the impact of a social, economic, and political structure that reinforced a provincial as opposed to a regional system.

Given the high stakes and the clear intent of the founders to impose a peripheral status on the West, governments from the region have been concerned about losing control over their economies and societies to outsiders. As Pratt and Richards succinctly stated,

> Within the political framework of the National Policy of John A. Macdonald's Conservative governments, the prairie West was consciously settled and developed as an economic hinterland. This colonialism was no accident of history. It was imposed as an act of policy by the ambitious business-state coalition put together by Macdonald and his associates following Confederation.[5]

The politics of development in Western Canada has no doubt been swayed by past experiences with national policies and by the ongoing centre-periphery struggle for control over the domestic economy. The historical role of politics and the national state in stifling the growth of a diversified economic base in the West, which contributed directly to the problem of underdevelopment, is an important factor that must be taken into account when we examine the integration question. This factor also helps to explain the rejection by many Western Canadians of the notion that underdevelopment should be addressed from an integrated perspective.

The First National Plan was based on a series of interconnected policies that involved the completion of an intercolonial railway, the establishment of tariffs, and the creation of an internal colony in the West.[6] During the first few decades of Confederation, a great deal of attention was placed on reinforcing the control of the centre over the timing, pace, and location of economic development in the western periphery. During this period the extent of national development virtually guaranteed that, once the structure was in place, Ontario and Quebec would have superior political power and enjoy economic advantages that the West would never have. Later on, when conditions changed and Ottawa was more committed to reducing tariffs and dealing with other challenges, governments in Western Canada were naturally suspicious of these actions.[7]

In the interplay between power, politics, and ideas, Canada's early search for answers — no less for the right *questions* — meant a conscious rejection of the American frontier model and the imposition of an alternative framework, which was favoured by élites in Central Canada and enforced by the North-West Mounted Police. The prairies were integrated into the Canadian economic and political structure as a result of the defence of new borders, images, institutions, and priorities that were more a product of the needs of outsiders than an attempt to reflect local preferences. Such conditions were imposed from above, and they met the explicit goals of those Central Canadian élites who felt threatened by a continental economy and the prospect of local self-determination on the prairies. The formation of the North-West Mounted Police in 1873 provided not only the means for dealing with Indians, but also a symbol for constructing a national identity and ideology.

Changes in the economic conditions and needs of Canadian élites, as they adapted to new challenges, resulted in the establishment of the federation and raised questions regarding borders and institutional reconstruction. Stability and legitimacy required new traditions and ways for mobilizing support for a unique Canadian approach to problem solving. With the decline of the fur trade, there was less need for the Hudson's Bay Company or Metis democratic self-government. The prescriptive guide to action, which was dominated by Central Canada, set out to create a more cooperative development plan for the prairies.

The development of the prairies was shaped by its origins as a colony of Eastern Canada. Ironically, the growth of separate provincial boundaries, cultures, and institutions, which have since become an important part of the Canadian experience, was the result of eastern tampering with local traditions. "Initially, the area comprising the provinces of Manitoba, Saskatchewan and Alberta was part of the 'North-West,' a term applied to the great fur region north and west of Lake Superior."[8] Thus, as Kaye and Moodie noted, "The geographically illogical names 'Prairie Provinces' and 'Western Canada' are now widely used to denote the provinces of Manitoba, Saskatchewan and Alberta. Theoretically, Western Canada includes British Columbia."[9] With the passing of control over the North-West from the Hudson's Bay Company to Canada in 1870, a new era began. Such roots help to explain the confusion over boundaries in the country and various attempts to promote new forms of interprovincial cooperation when conditions changed. For a variety of reasons, not the least of which was the threat posed by American expansionism and Metis self-government, outside élites pushed a plan that created separate, yet unequal provinces.

The decision to divide the prairie region along provincial lines was motivated by external considerations. Louis Riel was successful in gaining provincial status for Manitoba in 1870; however, the rebellions of 1870 and 1885 helped illustrate the dangers of granting too much local control.

The Prairie provinces were first controlled by a national policy that was explicitly designed to ensure that the North-West remained divided and controlled. This initial bias (which became fully institutionalized) undermined any possibility of constructing a sense of belonging to a common regional community and led to tension and confusion over regionalism and provincialism on the prairies. Provincialism became the organizing principle and the intent was to ensure that the problems and ambitions of the West did not interfere with Ontario's "Manifest Destiny." This chain of events was sparked by the unilateral imposition of the 1905 Alberta and Saskatchewan Acts. The provincialist approach lessened the dangers of local communities mobilizing as a regional bloc against the national territorial imperative, but it created problems for those advocating integration when conditions changed.

These earlier decisions illustrate the importance of imposed territorial divisions to territorial loyalties and provincial consciousness. By raising the walls of sovereignty and creating a sense of community on a provincial basis, Canada built a divided hinterland. The plan that was designed to isolate and weaken the Prairie provinces made it subsequently more difficult to impose national economic planning priorities. The significant differences dividing the prairies and our "weak state"[10] today can be traced to the initial decision to divide and conquer the prairies.

Furthermore, the original objective of the 1867 program was to gain control over British Columbia, not the plains. The prairies and the wheat economy were not as important as the Pacific region in the early years. From the beginning, British Columbia, while part of the western hinterland, was seen as a separate zone. It was also seen as a prized possession worthy of sacrifice, which had to be controlled for the benefit of the industrial centre. As Fowke indicated,

> The national policy, directed toward the creation of a transcontinental Canadian nation, had as an immediate and critical requirement in its early stages the retention of the Pacific mainland and Vancouver Island. With the lower Columbia River and Puget Sound lost to the United States by the Oregon Boundary settlement, the possibility of locating satisfactory Pacific seaports in British American territory was seriously restricted. The Fraser River and its delta offered the opportunity for land-to-ocean contact but control of the river would be meaningless without possession of the massive barrier provided by Vancouver Island. Pacific mainland and flanking island alike, however, were separated from eastern British North American colonies by thousands of miles of territory, economically empty except for isolated fur-trade posts and the struggling Red River settlement. To hold and secure Pacific frontage for the British colonies it was essential that there be retention and effective occupation of the central plains. The economic imperative of the national policy, as contrasted with its political or territorial requirements, was the establishment of a new frontier of investment opportunity which would be attached commercially and financially to the eastern provinces. Although by no means clearly foreseen in the early decades of the national policy, effective occupation of the central plains as required for the preservation of Pacific frontage

and the doorway to the Orient eventuated in the establishment of the wheat economy.[11]

With the importance of British Columbia to the national plan and the long-term view adopted by the Fathers of Confederation on the requirements for fostering development and enhancing their control over the western periphery, the western premiers became extremely protective of their political control over the entire territory. Although integration with the United States may have been a more economically rational strategy, the creators of the system had other ambitions. From the beginning, political considerations overshadowed economic ones: the entire economic and political structure was designed to impose a hinterland status on British Columbia and the prairies. It also reinforced the idea that these two regions were distinct.

The economic and political framework of 1867 signalled a basic change in British Columbia's economy and society. As a consequence of the new initiative, patterns of commerce, communication and transportation were designed to meet the needs of economic and political élites. This initiative was a deal between élites over the best way to secure and exploit the resource-based economy. Barman argued that "British Columbia was pushed into Confederation, in the end submitting voluntarily on being offered economic plums its leaders could not afford to refuse."[12] This economic compromise between élites had little to do with common bonds or ideas. Future leaders who inherited this struggling staple-based economy would face a number of institutional obstacles in their bid to become more self-reliant and integrated.[13]

Rich frontier societies blessed with economic advantages tend to produce cultures that focus on issues such as entrepreneurialism and they tend to be more resistant to wealth redistribution that interferes with local development prospects. British Columbia has focused on these issues since 1867. A.D. Scott noted that British Columbia, as a more open economy, has always had a different perspective on economic issues and the need to redistribute wealth through the national state. Scott states that "general policy-making on any frontier, of course, is typically more concerned with growth than with efficiency or equality."[14]

In spite of the fact that the industrial heartland in Canada never gained complete control over the resource hinterland from the

Americans, there was a clear attempt to disrupt associational activities which naturally flowed in a north-south direction. The intent was to defend the territorial interests of the centre against cross-border threats. In addition, British Columbia was forced to give up the Peace River Block to Ottawa in order to help pay for the building of a national transportation system.[15] Despite the fact that this land was later returned in the 1930s, British Columbians never forgot the sacrifices made, nor the promises broken, under the original national plan.[16]

As Keith Ralston indicated in his description of British Columbia during Canada's first decade:

> A settled community grew up on the Pacific coast and in the valleys and plateaus of the Western Cordillera which owed next to nothing to any link with the Canadas, and practically everything to its oceanic ties to the rest of the world....It is the existence of this self-conscious community which dictated the nature of the initial struggles within the federation and which called forth and hardened attitudes in British Columbia to the central government of the federation, attitudes basically unchanged to this day.[17]

Under such circumstances, governments in British Columbia have been preoccupied with the integration question and the threat posed by central control. The political economy of dependency that was imposed by the First National Plan had a major impact on the province's political culture. The main problem has been the evolution of an attitude that Ottawa and local élites are not to be trusted. It was no doubt problematic that a plan conceived and enforced in a neo-colonial fashion failed to solve British Columbia's communication and transportation problems. As the relative economic and political power of British Columbia increased and populist leaders on the provincial scene mobilized collectivities on a territorial basis, the politics of Canadian federalism underwent dramatic change.

For British Columbia, Canada agreed "to build a railway within two years, and finish it in ten."[18] By the 1870s, conflicts over the failure to complete the CPR line as specified in the original pact, coupled with other broken promises, led to the rise of a separatist threat.

Emergence of the Eastern Periphery

Ironically, the heartland/hinterland relationship that was clearly imposed on the prairies and British Columbia by the original national plan was endorsed by a coalition of Maritime business and political élites who assumed they would be part of a well-defended industrial heartland. Despite much local opposition by people who felt that the national integration plan would weaken the Maritime economy, the élite coalition was convinced that the plan would create new industrial opportunities for the region: the coalition supported the new form of mercantilism.[19] The élites were willing to take the risk, and they used their monopolistic power to create a new economic and political structure.

After 1867 and during the early settlement of the West, as had been anticipated, the construction of the Intercolonial Railway and the protection offered to Maritime industry by the tariff created various industrial opportunities. The immediate result of the national plan was increased industrial growth throughout the Maritimes. With the rise of new industrial economies and increased consumer demand for local products, new manufacturing facilities were built, and the process of development unfolded as anticipated by the supporters of national integration. It was a time of prosperity and optimism. As Forbes demonstrated,

> Such expansion had been encouraged by the buoyant national economy of the Laurier era. Aided by the protective tariff and favourable system of freight rates, Maritime manufacturers were able to compete successfully with those of central Canada in supplying the settlers of the rapidly growing West. The Maritimers had finally acquired a hinterland which permitted a volume of production necessary for effective competition and industrial survival.[20]

However, as time passed, the bubble eventually burst, and the Maritimes were forced to adjust to being merely another hinterland region for Central Canada. Several factors contributed to the region's sudden marginalization and economic decline. First, the region itself failed to meet the challenges of a new economic order and of changing trade patterns.[21] Second, these internal problems were directly linked to external factors. The new economic order provided little incentive for teachers, skilled labour, and capital to remain in the region. These people were attracted by the greater economic opportunities in Central Canada, the West, and other places in North America. As a result, the Maritimes lost the kind of skilled people required to build new economies. With the rise of the West and changing demographics, the Maritimes witnessed a decline in the number of seats in the House of Commons and saw fewer opportunities to control the process of development.[22] Under these circumstances, the Maritime region had fewer chances to defend and promote its interests. Suddenly, local élites found it harder and harder to prevent outsiders from restructuring the political economy according to their needs.

There are competing interpretations regarding the industrial successes of the Maritimes prior to 1920 and the extent to which national policies undermined further expansion. For example, Wood challenges the dependency thesis, which is based on the assumption that national state policy was responsible for undermining development prospects in the Maritimes.[23] He contends that economic conditions were deteriorating before 1867 and that the constraints created by a pre-industrial class structure — not Ottawa's interference — were the real culprit. Forbes and Bickerton provide an alternative interpretation of regional disparity, which casts Maritimers as victims of outside exploitation.[24]

In any case, despite the early economic success and optimism of local élites, the outcomes of operating within the new economic and political edifice were marginalization and increased dependency on outsiders. National integration and centralization of decision making reinforced the flight of capital and skilled labour to other parts of the country. Local dreams and aspirations were dashed as the integration experiment unfolded. Whether the Maritime economy declined due to internal or external factors is open to debate, but the region clearly did not experience the level of industrial growth witnessed in Ontario.

The consolidation of local manufacturing and financial institutions was the product of many factors. However, as indicated by Forbes, the rapid deindustrialization of the Maritimes in the 1920s could be directly linked to changes that were made to the freight-rate structure, "the loss of a large measure of regional autonomy in the operation of the Intercolonial Railway," and the unfair stereotyping of the rail system as inefficient and a drain on the national treasury.[25] According to Forbes, the negative characterization was unfair because other national projects, which could have been described in similar terms, were not described as such. Forbes has devoted much of his time to examining the nature of Canadian political discourse and to challenging negative images and old stereotypes of the Maritimes.[26]

The freight-rate issue was undoubtedly exploited by the centre to appease the demands of western reformers, while playing the East off against the West. By 1920, it mattered little that the Intercolonial rail system was originally designed to deal with military priorities, and that the federal subsidy was created to ensure that Maritime companies remained competitive in the national economy. Without much influence in Ottawa, Maritime politicians had few opportunities to tell the whole story. It was a sign of things to come.

Time for a New Approach

With the growing power of the West and the threat posed to the traditional parties by the Progressive Party, the federal government had little room to manoeuvre.[27] At this time in Canadian history, Ottawa could ill afford to deal with provinces on an unequal basis, even if their special problems were the direct result of past federal injustices. The federal government was forced to accommodate various problems and divisions at the same time. These were difficult times and MacKenzie King survived by insisting on the need for consensus and by being cautious.

Under these circumstances, Prime Minister King responded to the alienation and disaffection in his customary manner: he appointed royal commissions to deal with the disparity problem while promoting unity within a divided country. Ottawa proved incapable of dealing with the problems that were causing internal strains and divided loyalties across the country. The temptation to deal with the problems facing the Maritimes had to be balanced with the need to address the West's concerns about past unfair treatment. Efforts to deal with the problems of the various regions of Canada did not help the national unity cause. As Careless argued, "Each region had to agree to the prime minister's cash solution of specific claims of other regions before he would accept the settlement of their own."[28] Hence, the West had to agree to the terms outlined by the 1926 Duncan Commission, which was established for the Maritimes, before King would consider appointing similar commissions to deal with western concerns. In this way, one region was played off against another.

Although this pragmatic and expedient style of politics kept the Liberals in power for a number of years, the central problems facing both regions were never addressed. Neither periphery benefited from such a strategy. Without strong leadership, a plan of action, or the administrative structure essential for the development and implementation of an action plan, the country was not well prepared for dealing with the Great Depression. To make matters worse, Canadians lacked a strong sense of purpose or identity.

The market crash of 1929 was a major watershed event. The uneven distribution of wealth within Canadian society and Ottawa's failure to manage economic change created new demands for the federal government and a new approach to economic management.

In pressing for change and a more activist government, reformers on both the left and right began questioning the assumptions of federalism and the free-market system. The depression experience intensified the debate over the benefits of federalism and capitalism, and the combination of protest parties and strong leadership at the provincial level virtually guaranteed that the problems of disadvantaged regions would be high on the national agenda. At the same time, the growing importance of new issues and policy analysis led to the rise of experts as major players.

The depression was especially difficult for the Maritimes and the Prairies. Their lack of an industrial base and their reliance on staples production contributed to their rapid economic decline.[29] Without an advanced welfare state or a system for redistributing wealth between regions, the federal government lacked the planning structure necessary for meeting pressing policy challenges. There was great pressure for increased state planning and for a fresh approach to dealing with the serious problems of regional and income disparity.

With the number of obstacles that confronted Prime Minister Bennett in the early 1930s, incremental tinkering was no longer a viable option.[30] Ottawa finally came to recognize the need for a more integrated approach to federal-provincial relations and state planning. In addition, most governments supported the call to launch the welfare state and adopt a Keynesian approach to economic management.[31] Canadians were seeking new ways to define themselves and a new approach to intergovernmental relations.

Rise of the Second National Policy

An understanding of territorial divisions within the country under the Second National Policy requires that we recognize two elements: the various competing provincial interests, and the extent to which Ottawa, with the support of Saskatchewan, Manitoba, the Maritimes, and a group of economists, tried to redefine the concept of Canadian federalism in a way that directly threatened the economic and political powers of Alberta, Ontario, Quebec, and British Columbia. This time was an important watershed in the history of federal-provincial relations and the integration campaign; national considerations were seen as being more important than federal principles or the needs of supporters of the free-market model. The divisions that emerged during this period provide critical insights for explaining the subsequent difficulties in resolving the integration problem. The solutions that were reached under these circumstances influenced the economy and relations between governments in a significant way.

With provinces pitted against one another in bitter confrontation, Ottawa, with the support of various experts, tried to tilt the balance in her favour. A new era in Canadian politics began when the federal government decided to appoint the Royal Commission on Dominion-Provincial Relations to deal with the pressing issues facing the country.[32] Ottawa responded to a number of seemingly unsolvable problems created by the depression by hiring some of the most critical thinkers in the country to design a new plan for restructuring the federation. These experts were hired to address the problems associated with economic change from a national/integrated perspective.

The appointment of the study was a deliberate attempt by Ottawa to change the policy process and form a more comprehensive, less political approach to problem solving. It was also a clear signal that the federal government wanted experts to participate in the process of problem solving in Canada. As Cairns argued, the establishment of this particular royal commission was important for the rise of a more centralized planning structure, since this commission was "the first one to recruit academics to an extensive research role."[33]

Not surprisingly, a number of premiers voiced concerns about having Ottawa and a group of hand-picked experts in charge of the planning process. The political dilemma premiers faced had as much to do with the internal contradictions of the political structure, as with the threat posed by Ottawa, poorer provinces, and a group of academic élites. These federally appointed experts were naturally viewed as a direct threat to provinces' political independence.[34] For premiers in Alberta, Ontario, British Columbia, and Quebec, granting increased authority over the process of development to a group of experts selected by Ottawa made little sense.

A number of critical insights documented by Owram in his study of experts are relevant to our discussion. First, Owram notes that academic institutions were originally created to deal with pressing societal problems associated with industrialization, urbanization, and global interdependence. The explosion of the social sciences within the last century cannot be fully appreciated unless we take this issue into account.[35] Academics were recruited primarily to deal with these challenges, not to defend the principles of federalism. Every campaign for a more integrated approach to economic and political development in Canada has involved orthodox economic thinkers who believe that change is necessary, but only according to an agenda that calls for transformation of the planning structure. Although the academic community is not a monolith, the impact of various economists who helped to legitimize the assumptions of modernization theory is hard to deny. Ottawa played a key role in mobilizing this kind of expertise against the threat posed by provincialism; Ottawa also exploited these experts and their theories to integrate the nation and legitimize the call for a new process. Modernization theory, with its emphasis on integration, and the rise of a new planning structure controlled at the centre had obvious appeal for Ottawa. As Simeon and Robinson noted when discussing the impact of modernization theory on the second national policy,

> Such sociological trends were reinforced by the logic of the new economic functions which the state would assume. They would require the concentration of financial resources in the hands of central governments. This fiscal power was expected to be "an effective device for control and initiative from the centre" which would "seriously limit provincial autonomy."[36]

Second, Owram notes that, of all the social sciences, economics has had the greatest impact on state planning in Canada. As a consequence, the assumptions, ideas, and interpretations of history held by orthodox economic thinkers have had a major impact on the definitions of problems in the national political arena.[37] Third, academic élites in Canada have tended to be centralist, English-speaking men who were critical of federalism.[38] Given this combination of traits, it is not surprising that some of the premiers had concerns about giving up power.

Despite the benefits associated with the new approach to problem solving, the premiers also had to consider the nature of power within the nation. Ottawa's attempt to impose uniformity and a new approach to managing change was restricted within a federal system with no unified bureaucracy and territorial divisions of power. In 1930, the premiers in the West were pleased that the federal system finally recognized the principle of provincial equality: Ottawa granted the transfer of ownership over natural resources. However, there was a diversity of opinion about Ottawa's real intentions.

The integrationist vision promoted by the Second National Policy created further divisions within the country by setting out to attack the powers of the premiers. As Friesen notes in his analysis of the functional approach to defining regions, these kinds of national policies often backfire. However, Canadian nationalists were encouraged by such developments and they supported the new approach. From their perspective, at least, it made good sense for planners and Ottawa to play a more active role in shaping patterns of economic development in every region of the country. Governments in Quebec, Ontario, British Columbia, and Alberta were more concerned with their own interests. The premiers of these provinces saw such developments as a betrayal of federalism and a threat to their territorial integrity. In the end, as Ottawa pushed harder for national integration, the resistance of these premiers increased.

Even though the experts obviously had much to gain from the exercise, they were also placed in a very awkward position: the task of developing a viable new vision of the country had to take into account competing ideas, myths, and claims. The final policy reflected the great diversity of the country and the struggle to blend together a number of competing principles and concerns.

The specialists faced a number of obstacles in applying the models of social science within a highly fragmented and competitive federal system. Furthermore, these experts were selected because they approached these problems from a national perspective, not a regional or Quebec-based viewpoint.[39] Not surprisingly, the Ontario, Quebec, and Alberta governments indicated that they "did not recognize the authority of the Commission to conduct such an investigation,"[40] and the study, which was a response to the economic problems of poor provinces and which was committed to the goal of national integration, alienated the provinces that were being pressured to make important concessions.

The Rowell-Sirois Commission tackled the issues of economic disparity and the reorganization of taxation powers with a new division of responsibilities. Despite claims from the West and the Maritimes that past national policies had adversely affected their economies, the commissioners decided it would be impossible to measure with any accuracy the costs and benefits of the tariff and other elements of the original national plan.[41]

Hence, they adopted a different approach, and recommended that all provincial debts be assumed by Ottawa, and that a new unconditional subsidy system based on fiscal need be established. This system would guarantee that each province had the monies necessary to carry out their jurisdictional responsibilities. In return, the provinces were asked to give up their title to corporate taxes, income taxes, succession duties, and the original statutory subsidies. The innovative equalization proposal was by far the most significant recommendation to emerge from the study.

As one might expect, the rich and poor provinces collided over the integration option. The call for equal benefits across the country and for increased federal control over the Canadian economy was popular in Saskatchewan, the Maritimes, and Manitoba.[42] As Bickerton noted, the commissioners endorsed the argument, put forward by poor provinces such as Nova Scotia, that national wealth should be shared "on the basis of fiscal need."[43] As a consequence, they rejected the arguments of wealthier provinces and fully recognized how "national integration which tied the country together by East-West bonds of trade and opportunity was weakened as Central Canada and British Columbia felt the direct and competing tug of export demand on their regional resources";[44] they made an obvious attempt to strengthen the centre and meet the threat posed by continentalism and provincialism. The success of this approach depended on Canadians being convinced that it made sense to increase federal powers so that national wealth could be redistributed according to a new integrated plan. With its emphasis on promoting equal opportunities and creating a more integrated national economy through federal initiatives, the Rowell-Sirois study provided Ottawa with much-needed justification to increase federal powers and responsibilities.

Conflicts between Ottawa and "have" provinces over the need to increase federal powers and redistribute wealth between provinces ensured that there would be intense debates at the 1940 and 1941 federal-provincial conferences. The government of British Columbia perceived the Rowell-Sirois study as a direct attack by experts and other Central Canadian élites on the development potential and priorities of the province. The federal study, in attacking the development prospects,[45] had a profound impact on British Columbian politicians' views of experts and the federal government. The decision by Premier Pattullo to walk out of meetings was no doubt the result of alienation stemming from Ottawa's attempt to frustrate his development plans. To understand the resistance to the report, we need to consider not only the impact of federalism on fundamental political relationships in the country, but also the divergence of views on the benefits of integration.

The responses to the report were similar in Alberta, Ontario, and Quebec. Although Alberta was not as wealthy as Ontario at the time, the Social Credit government, because of its distrust of Ottawa and its desire to gain more control over the process of development, showed little interest in expanding federal powers. The plan for increased centralization was also attacked by Ontario's premier Hepburn, who feared that the province could not afford to subsidize services in other provinces. From his perspective, Ontario and Quebec could not afford to help finance government services in other parts of the country.[46] The Quebec government also had concerns about the call to reduce its jurisdictional powers. Although Ottawa was looking for a new formula for pulling the country together, these premiers resisted any change that threatened their interests.

The Rowell-Sirois study was important for another reason: it pushed the idea of Maritime and Prairie integration onto the public agenda.[47] Although the idea received little attention at the time, the study clearly established the issue with Ottawa and a group of orthodox thinkers at the centre, who were perceived as attacking the development priorities of the frontier. The report also helped to reinforce the impression that the concept of regional integration was created to challenge the territorial and jurisdictional powers of the provinces.

With the opposition of these provinces and the outbreak of the war, the focus of the nation shifted from the Rowell-Sirois study to other matters. However, the country was permanently transformed as a result of the experience. In the final analysis, the report helped to set the scene for a more rational and integrated approach to policy making. It also influenced the way governments in both peripheries responded to future calls by Ottawa and the experts for a more integrated approach to economic and social development.

Throughout Canada's history, the struggle over regional integration has featured a passionate debate over the best response to the challenges of industrialism and globalization. Ottawa and the experts preferred to establish a more integrated national structure in Canada, given both the institutional and socio-economic roots of federalism; in response, various premiers assumed the role of defending the territorial interests of their provinces. Ironically, the call for a more integrated planning structure probably triggered further diffusion of power within the federal system, as a number of provinces responded by resisting integration and defending home rule.

The 1940s were a time of great change. The transition resulted from changes in conditions within the policy environment, coupled with the emergence of modern bureaucratic structures in both the public and private spheres. The emergence of professional advisors in business and government was inevitable and can be directly linked to the need to consolidate distant factors of production in a more logical and consistent way. The Second World War brought about a shift in popular ideology, and the trend towards centralization continued.

With the rise of new business management plans, increasing economic interdependence, political optimism, and changing relationships between governments and business leaders, Galbraith coined the phrase, "the new age of technostructure."[48] Technology demanded that science and experts play a more creative role in managing the economy and the state. Federalism, local politicians, and small-scale entrepreneurs were no longer in vogue, and, although the advice offered by experts seemed to matter more than established federal structures, greater emphasis was being placed on excluding political and territorial influences on decision making. The legitimacy of local political and economic institutions — and of federalism itself — was now being questioned by business leaders, experts, and federal politicians. At the time, Laski went so far as to declare that "the epoch of federalism is over."[49]

The depression, the Second World War, and the wielding of national spending power accentuated the federal role in a number of policy fields. Keynesian-inspired social and economic programs were popular with the general public. At the same time, Canada's Second National Policy imposed a heavy cost on the federal system and raised new questions regarding the constitutional or legal basis of the federal structure. Given the experiences of the periphery provinces under the First National Policy and the nature of economic and political power in the country, some premiers had concerns about losing power over the development process through such informal constitutional conventions.

The reconstruction period focused on the need to develop a number of new policy initiatives, based on a more coherent and integrated national industrial strategy. By the mid-1940s, it became obvious that Ottawa was going to take full advantage of the depression experience, the Second World War, and the popularity of Keynesianism to carve out a more dominant role for the federal government. These changes in social policy, labour relations, and federal-provincial relations had a dramatic impact on the growing influence of Ottawa and public servants within the federal system. Such a shift in emphasis was popular with voters, but it also imposed high costs on established federal-provincial structures and norms.

Although the new reconstruction program provided an opportunity to tilt the power balance from the provinces to the federal government, the far-reaching effect was to create an even more fragmented economic and political structure. The great power struggle between Ottawa (and the experts) and the provinces over the next two decades focused on the need for a more coherent and integrated industrial plan for the entire country. However, the pull of continentalism made it more difficult to reinforce common loyalties and interests, and the system ensured that experts were never in a position to challenge the premiers' control over the agenda.

Despite much rhetoric about the need to strengthen national control over the development process, the federal government, instead of producing an independent industrial strategy for the country, actively encouraged American investment and the creation of an even more dependent branch plant economy.[50] At the same time, Ottawa's loyalty to Keynesianism was influenced more by rhetoric than by a real commitment to change based on the principles outlined by the new paradigm.[51]

In the simplest terms, the Second National Policy, which was implemented from the end of the war to the 1970s, reflected Ottawa's dominance and desire to increase federal responsibilities at the expense of the provinces. Ottawa extended her influence and spending power through various policy initiatives in a clear attempt to tilt the balance in her favour. These actions affected federal-provincial relations and transnational interactions across political boundaries thereafter.[52] Although the premiers naturally welcomed the push for a planned economy, they had good reasons to be concerned about Ottawa's increasing power and influence. According to Simeon and Robinson,

> This intermediate response to the problems of post-war federalism was implemented primarily through tax collection agreements negotiated with each province and the extensive use of conditional shared-cost grants from the federal to the provincial governments. This system was, of course, less centralized than that of the quasi-unitary state of the war years. But the federation remained more centralized — in terms of federal control over taxation, share of total government spending and leadership in the development and implementation of new policies — than it had been since Macdonald and the original National Policy.[53]

Ironically, the failure to control transnational flows and interactions under the Second National Policy probably reinforced the growth of distinct, competitive, regional economic zones in North America. Garreau, in his depiction of North America as nine distinct nations, noted that factors such as uncontrolled transnational flows and brisk north-south trade have reinforced the rise of distinct regions within North America.[54] Although the Second National Policy challenged provincial boundaries, Ottawa focused much less on resisting the growth of regional power blocs and defending the boundary between Canada and the United States. These cross-border dependencies and alliances have done little to strengthen the east-west axis. Even more to the point, north-south linkages were strengthened and distinct regional zones became a reality that Ottawa helped to create, but could not control. From the beginning, the Second National Policy dealt more with economic and political problems within Canada than with the problem of American direct investment. By doing so, it may have contributed further to regional and income disparity. At the very least, it enhanced the devolution of power and authority within the federal system by facilitating cross-border linkages in a north-south direction.

Despite these limitations, Ottawa introduced new economic and social policy initiatives during the reconstruction period, and a consensus was achieved on the need to build a more progressive industrial society. These initiatives were outlined in the 1945 White Paper on Employment and Income.[55] Ottawa dominated the agenda by introducing various linked economic and social policies at the 1945 Dominion Provincial Conference on Reconstruction.[56] These nation-centred policies, which were designed to create a peaceful coexistence between Ottawa and the provinces, as well as between labour and capital, probably had the opposite effect.

With the deindustrialization of the Maritimes, the alienation created by the First National Policy in the West, and the proactive continentalist stance of Ottawa from the 1940s on, some premiers were naturally concerned about the lack of control over the development process at the margins. When the federal government failed to defend these interests, provincial premiers began filling the void themselves.

As a result of Ottawa's reconstruction program, most public policy questions have revolved around two issues: the need to avoid the problems caused by the depression and the need to build the kind of linkages and policies necessary for state planning in an advanced industrial society. Ottawa deliberately attempted to restructure the federation and establish the kind of infrastructure and support mechanisms found in other more advanced industrial economies. Yet, by failing to defend the territorial interests of the country against American policy, and by focusing on state-directed economic development, the Second National Policy undoubtedly helped to reinforce provincial attempts to gain greater control over the development process. Over time, as the Second National Policy was implemented and regional power blocs emerged, the tensions between integration and disintegration became fully institutionalized. Thus, the country had even greater difficulties responding in an integrated way to the challenges of change. Federal inaction and the inability to guarantee integrity and autonomy *vis-a-vis* the United States probably reinforced competing trends within the country.

The conflict between province-building and nation-building was certainly not resolved by the Second National Policy; indeed, the policy contributed further to the struggle to balance these competing forces. Such ambiguity provided fertile ground for those entrepreneurial, political actors who were seeking new answers and who knew how to use existing institutions to mobilize coalitions. As one would expect, such entrepreneurialism was manifesting itself at both levels of government.

The Welfare State — A Key Component of the Second National Policy

During the Second National Policy, the country attempted to build a new economy and society based on the industrial model. Ottawa implemented several new policies and gave unions collective bargaining rights in 1944.[57] Another important development was the establishment of an advanced welfare state. As Banting noted,

> The modern welfare state has its roots in the industrial revolution of the nineteenth and twentieth centuries. The transition from an agrarian to an industrial society exposed whole populations to a new and uncertain economic environment, and the industrial wage system left people particularly vulnerable during unemployment, illness, and old age. At the same time, however, traditional social institutions, such as the family and local communities, which had hitherto provided support and protection during periods of economic adversity, were themselves changing in the new urban setting, and were less and less able to cope with the new range of social problems facing the population.[58]

The Keynesian-influenced welfare state performed a number of useful economic and political functions for Ottawa. It offered a convenient way to encourage worker mobility and improve labour relations, while providing a healthier and better educated workforce. The intent of the policy was to provide the income support necessary for meeting the new challenges associated with economic restructuring. The welfare state was designed to serve other purposes as well, and this multifunctional nature created problems that were inherited by later generations.

During the Second National Policy there was much policy overlap and interdependence, especially in the area of social policy. As Simeon and Robinson argued,

> In short, the adoption of new roles for the state was achieved not by the dominance of the central government but by the collaboration of both orders of government, federal and provincial, in the Canadian state.[59]

Social policy was one area where governments, especially in English Canada, embraced the model of cooperative federalism. On the other hand, Ottawa exploited her spending power to influence provincial priorities. However, the fact that some social initiatives like unemployment insurance were federal projects, while others were implemented by the provinces but financed, in part, by Ottawa, ensured that centralization was never fully institutionalized. Ironically, the more Ottawa exploited its spending power to control social policy, the more resources the provinces had access to for empire-building. It was an era of policy overlap, and state-building at both levels. Ottawa's spending power failed to achieve the results predicted by the modernization theorists who worked on the Second Plan. In fact, this policy instrument had the opposite effect.

The original purpose of the welfare state was to provide a hefty dose of government activism to ensure that people would adjust to the challenges of industrialization. However, in practice, it may have had the opposite effect on the periphery, according to Premier Wells, Dr. Doug House, and others involved in the Economic Recovery Commission in Newfoundland.[60] In their new proposal, which calls for fundamental changes to the income security system in Newfoundland, they focus on questioning old ideas and institutions that can be traced to the Second National Policy. They conclude that the welfare state in Canada has undermined entrepreneurialism and has made it even more difficult for marginalized people to adjust to changing economic circumstances.

According to the Economic Recovery Commission, the problem stems from the fact that the implementation of the Canadian welfare state was based more on the need to resolve the regional disparity question than on the need to deal with individual adjustment problems.[61] As a consequence, with concessions such as the decision in 1957 to grant people in the industry special rights to unemployment insurance benefits, the welfare state was both a blessing and a curse. The implementation of such policies made it more difficult for people to adjust to new realities. Although the welfare state provided a source of capital for rural communities, these policies created other problems, such as contributing to the elimination of the cod fishery.

In retrospect, the welfare state, as designed and implemented, probably undermined the market ethos, reduced the incentive for getting an education, deterred mobility, and encouraged people in Atlantic Canada to stay in the old economy.[62] In spite of the rhetoric, the welfare state may have actually contributed very little to the marginalized economies of the eastern periphery. As mentioned, in more recent times, governments in the Atlantic region have tried to come to grips with the myriad of cultural and economic obstacles produced by the welfare state in a quest to rebuild structures according to market-based values.[63] The Second National Policy not only contributed to the debt problem, but it may also have undermined the spirit of entrepreneurialism and self-reliance that existed in marginalized regions in the country. The result of such an approach was an explosion of welfare-dependent economies and societies.

Although there are different perspectives on this issue, few would deny that the federal government fully exploited the welfare state as an instrument of national integration during the implementation of the Second National Policy. Other considerations were always secondary. From a political perspective, income security programs provided a convenient "mechanism for sustaining or enhancing the legitimacy" of the federal level of government.[64] Income programs provided a new vehicle for reinforcing the national identity and mobilizing support for the national state. At the same time, the failure of the policy to deal effectively with the challenges of technological and economic change focused much attention on the inability of the national state to deal with problems in an acceptable way. These kinds of experiences have raised questions about whether an integrated approach is necessarily the best way to deal with new problems and economies. The Second National Policy was riddled with contradictions and inefficiencies.

As time passed, Ottawa was overwhelmed by public demands. Operating in a political system organized on a territorial basis, the government became even more focused on the need to redistribute wealth between rich and poor regions of the country (thus justifying its existence in the eyes of most citizens), rather than using the welfare state for restructuring and industrial growth. Constrained by federal institutions, Ottawa became more preoccupied with using the welfare state as an instrument of nation-building to prop itself up, rather than dealing with other critical regional development issues. In fact, Banting suggested that "[t]he welfare state is a much greater spending priority for Canadian governments than is regional equality."[65] This preoccupation was consistent over time, and it reflected not only the inherent territorial biases of the system, but also Ottawa's refusal or inability to deal effectively with the declining economies of the "have-not" provinces.

Such poor results and misgivings about the adaptability of the welfare state to the challenges of change probably had a negative impact on later attempts to legitimize the need for a more integrated approach to planning.[66] At the very least, the situation raised questions about the efficacy of the national planning process in meeting the challenges of modern industrialization. Under these circumstances, the central authorities eventually had trouble generating much enthusiasm for a more integrated approach to development. It is little wonder that in the 1990s, Ottawa is decentralizing the welfare state.

In light of the preceding discussion, one component of the Second National Plan warrants further discussion, i.e., the history of regional development policy in Canada, which includes the failure of various national strategies to resolve the economic difficulties of underdevelopment. Clearly, the history of struggle over regional development policy is closely linked to the larger regional integration question and thus requires more investigation. The fact that Ottawa's regional development initiatives have been discredited over the years has not made it easier for those preaching the virtues of an integrated approach to development.

History of Regional Development Policy in Canada

It is no coincidence that much of the discussion on regional development in the 1993 Liberal Red Book or plan for Canada is focused on the regional integration question.[67] Nor is Lloyd Axworthy's recent attempt to use his political influence and the western diversification fund to propel the western premiers towards regional integration a new idea or an indication of a new federal attitude towards regional development policy and provincialism.[68] Ottawa has employed such tactics in numerous attempts to use regional development policy as either a lure or a weapon in the struggle over the integration question.

Since 1957, the federal government has made various attempts to address the regional disparity problem. Regional equity considerations became more important when the Diefenbaker government was first elected and the prime minister was obliged to build upon his reputation as spokesman and defender of the regions. Under Diefenbaker, Ottawa forced the regional disparity problem onto the national agenda for the first time. In addition, Premier Frost of Ontario, for the first time in that province's history, endorsed the need for a national plan of action. For the most part, since 1957, Ontario had supported regional development initiatives. The year 1957 was also a critical turning point — at least as far as Ottawa was concerned — in that provincial boundaries in the periphery diminished in value.

With the growing salience of the regional disparity issue in the post-1957 period, policy development went through various phases under the Second National Policy. In the process, Ottawa was forced to deal with the causes and repercussions of territorial underdevelopment in a highly fragmented and competitive political world. With great optimism about the prospect of real change, Ottawa began a journey that took different paths. Unfortunately, those who began the journey were ill equipped for what was to occur; the federal government underestimated the complexity of the regional development issue, as well as the strength of opposing forces.

Initially, the federal government adopted a rural and rather simplistic approach to economic advancement. As a result, little attention was focused on challenging the development priorities of the provinces or involving experts in the process of problem solving. Instead, Prime Minister Diefenbaker kick-started underdeveloped economies with an infusion of federal monies, with the hope that these actions would stimulate new opportunities and increase self-reliance. Not surprisingly, such an approach failed to create productive activity in underdeveloped regions. Critics bemoaned these early experiments as a dismal failure.[69]

Consequently, Ottawa's policy priorities for regional economic development changed markedly. By the late 1960s, nationalist policies became much more rational and comprehensive in approach. Reminiscent of the days of the Rowell-Sirois report that helped design the Second National Policy, Ottawa placed greater emphasis on formulating decisions on the basis of rational arguments and expert advice. Recognizing that Diefenbaker's policies were misguided, the next administration focused on developing a more advanced planning structure.[70] The rural approach, which focused on local control, was now viewed as a failure. In this context, an industrial-based growth-centre strategy suddenly became more popular with federal politicians and the experts who had been hired to come up with new solutions.

By the late 1960s, the federal government became much more aggressive in imposing its solutions, and, as Careless indicated, constitutional constraints were often ignored in the process.[71] A multitude of programs that endeavoured to dictate new policies for the periphery had dubious effects on federal-provincial relations. Such Draconian actions also indicated that Ottawa was more than willing to exploit spending power and the Department of Regional Economic Development to strengthen its dominance over weaker provinces.[72] The federal government's regional development initiatives engendered a new, more complicated system of intergovernmental relations, and some provinces were more vulnerable to attacks than others. Each province had its own agenda to worry about. It was a period of interdependence, conflicting policy objectives, entanglement, and turf wars between territorial actors.

The concept of regional integration was popular with Ottawa and the experts during this stage of the Second National Policy, reflecting both previous experiences with the regional disparity problem and the commitment to adopt a more rational approach. From their viewpoint, it made sense to bank on federal spending powers to quell the rising tide of provincial protectionism, which was seen as inhibiting economic development opportunities in peripheral regions. By the mid-1960s, federal politicians and bureaucrats had much in common as they set their sights on the provinces and developed a more integrated regional development strategy. They attempted to provide an alternative to traditional provincial approaches and to move the federation towards increased integration, albeit based on a regional model.

Ironically, by adopting a more aggressive nationalist approach to the regional disparity problem, Ottawa provoked more intense territorial conflicts. The federal government was guilty of overestimating its own influence over such matters and underestimating the entrepreneurial capacities of the premiers. The provincial governments had much to lose if they did not respond to the challenge posed to their territorial and jurisdictional powers by the federal government, and the Trudeau administration was determined to confront the forces of provincialism and Quebec nationalism within the federation.[73] At the same time, each premier was motivated by different factors. Whereas Ottawa's control of this field of public policy was largely confined to spending power, the federal system ensured that the provinces had the autonomy necessary to ignore these sanctions if they so desired. This combination of factors made it difficult to coordinate policy.

In light of the fact that Atlantic and western Canadians viewed past national policies as being partly responsible for regional underdevelopment, the premiers had many concerns in responding to such demands. By no means were they willing to simply stand aside and let Ottawa dictate policy. As Savoie argued, "Both Atlantic and western Canadians [could] point to a series of specific federal government initiatives to explain the development of central Canada and their own underdevelopment."[74] As a consequence, the premiers did everything possible to ensure that they did not forsake their role as defenders of their respective societies. In the end, the federal government's regional policies met with strong provincial resistance, and by 1973 (just as the Second National Policy was losing momentum), Ottawa was forced to change direction one more time.

Throughout this period, the provinces were relentless in pressuring the federal government to modify its concept of planned change, which was based on orthodox economic theory and national standards. Given the inability of the national state to deal with the disparity problem, there was much pressure to try an alternative approach. By 1973, Ottawa no longer had the will or resources required to impose its views. Acknowledging defeat, Ottawa had little option but to announce that the centralized approach to regional development was about to be abandoned.

Battered and financially drained, the Canadian government finally gave in to provincial pressures and set up a new bilateral system of intergovernmental relations in 1973. With the emergence of General Development Agreements, Ottawa fully recognized that the provinces should be primarily responsible for designing regional development policy.[75] Although this acknowledgement was a great victory for province-building, it was also a sign of Ottawa's inconsistency and inability to manage change. The country had witnessed the dawning of yet another era in Canadian politics.

Rise of the Third National Policy

By the early 1970s, conditions had changed. For one, the Keynesian consensus among state élites disintegrated as a result of the increasing unmanageability of the national economy. As inflation and unemployment rates soared, the Keynesian assumption that the economy could be managed by state planning and intervention was debunked. During the 1970s, monetarism was the dominant paradigm, and anti-interventionist assumptions had greater impact on government thinking.[76]

Another reason for adopting a new approach was the volatile relationship with the United States and the subsequent dilemmas facing Ottawa. When the Nixon administration decided to impose a ten per cent surcharge on Canadian manufactured goods in 1971, Ottawa was under great pressure to reconsider the continentalist policy that had been taken for granted during the Second National Plan.[77] Since Canada did not receive special treatment from the Americans, it was only reasonable that Ottawa would want to reconsider the territorial imperatives of nationalism, provincialism, and continentalism from a different perspective. As a result of these developments, the appeal of continentalism faded temporarily, and the Trudeau administration was provided with extra incentive to introduce another national policy.

Other important issues were the growing deficit problem and the 1973 energy crisis. Regional economic development policy was profoundly affected, as the federal government set out to defend its territorial and jurisdictional interests against foreign multinationals, the United States government, and the provinces. The economic and political costs associated with a province-centred and continentalist approach to energy policy were of particular concern for the Trudeau administration. As Milne noted,

> With energy policy a vehicle for the "new federalism," Ottawa would now assert the primacy of the national interest over the direction of economic policy in energy matters and over economic rent from oil and gas against what it regarded as the lesser resource claims of the producing provinces. Moreover, at least in the sensitive area of national energy supply and development, the Canadian government declared that it could no longer operate comfortably with the existing high levels of foreign ownership in this sector.[78]

The 1970s comprised a period of policy changes, inconsistent experimentation, shifting priorities, and intense competition. The Trudeau government defended the general federal interest against the threats posed by provincialism, Quebec nationalism, and continentalism. For Ottawa, the need to defend the national interest against the forces of continentalism, while striking a new balance between provincialism and Quebec nationalism, created a number of policy challenges. Given the competing forces and contradictory policy objectives that Ottawa had to balance, it is not surprising that these were volatile times.

Despite past defeats, depleting resources, and pressures for further disintegration, Ottawa made one last valiant attempt to mobilize support for the national community in a competitive, but also increasingly interdependent, world. Faced with old dilemmas and new challenges, the proponents of a new national strategy and a different vision of federalism had a sizable task ahead of them: it required not only developing a coherent set of principles for restructuring the federation, but also mobilizing political support for such an experiment within a highly fragmented, élite-dominated political structure. Furthermore, several policy actors with competing interests were involved. The prospects for any national economic planning exercise seemed bleak indeed. On the other hand, the situation provided Prime Minister Trudeau with an opportunity to offer Canadians a conception of national interest that was based on cross-provincial identities, instead of the decentralist ideas that were often espoused by his competitors. It also provided an interesting challenge and a chance for Trudeau to defend his theory of federalism in the real world of politics.

The Pan-Canadian vision or theory of federalism gave Trudeau the means for responding to the challenges of continentalism and provincialism.[79] He fully exploited the Charter and the issue of constitutional reform in a clear bid to alter the country's political dynamic in a permanent and fundamental way. Feminists, natives, multicultural leaders, and other groups suddenly felt empowered, and these new legitimizing forces provided ammunition to tilt the balance in Ottawa's favour. The third pillar of Canadian federalism, the Charter, changed the political dynamic by providing the institutional means for average citizens to defend their fundamental rights against state élites, especially at the provincial level. Suddenly, the constitution belonged to the people, not to the federal and provincial government officials who had always dominated the decision-making process. Such a feeling of Canadian democracy changed the political culture forever; gone was the deference to authority that was a prerequisite for an élite-dominated federal system.[80]

With the rise of a new national political culture, the old traditions of British parliamentary supremacy and executive federalism were being questioned from below. This challenging of traditions had been the original intent of Trudeau's constitutional policy. To ordinary citizens infected with this new populist ethos (especially considering the threats posed by provincialism, continentalism, and Quebec nationalism), it made good sense to expand the role of the national government. Thus began a battle that pitted supporters of Trudeau's federalism against the traditional defenders of decentralization.

The premiers in the periphery, no doubt, expected that Ottawa would intervene in the energy dispute to tip the balance in favour of the centre. Given the lack of Liberal electoral support in the West, Ottawa was willing to change the rules of the game, precisely when the periphery had the opportunity to create new economic linkages using energy resources. In the context of such an opportunity, the federal government wanted to attack the American oil companies and the energy-producing provinces.

In the aftermath of the Second National Policy, the country was forced to deal with new forces and policy challenges. International changes and domestic developments threw into question old ideas, and the tattered balance between the three axes of Canadian federalism, which had been in place since the 1940s, was quickly disappearing. It was time for a new approach to balancing the forces of Quebec nationalism, continentalism, and centre-periphery relations. For Trudeau, these volatile times were also an opportunity to question old assumptions about what he saw as government-dominated federalism. Based on a strategy of unilateralism, Ottawa attempted to restructure the federation according to Trudeau's more homogeneous, citizen-centred, liberal-democratic, integrated vision.

Ottawa introduced a number of federal initiatives that pitted supporters of the new Pan-Canadian vision of federalism against the traditional supporters of province-building under the Third National Plan. The Trudeau government consistently pushed for a new model of federalism, whether it was applied to the National Energy Plan, constitutional reform, institutional reform, the need to regulate foreign investment, or the promotion of regional integration in Atlantic or Western Canada. This model was based on the need to strengthen national unity while reducing American dependence and preventing further decentralization. Such a moral crusade was a direct attack on political rivals, who were driven by other ambitions and visions. To add insult to injury, Trudeau often presented his vision as one based on reason and condemned alternative plans as simply being products of emotion.

The Third National Policy reflected Trudeau's desire to challenge the conflicting principles and visions that had always divided the political system and replace them with a more coherent theory of federalism. The intense battle led to major confrontations with Trudeau and his team of superbureaucrats on one side, and the American élites and provincial governments on the other.[81]

Trudeau's ambitious attempt to restructure the economy and political system was more confrontational than the previous national policy. Explicitly, the third plan attempted to determine the perceived causes of deindustrialization and disunity, and establish a new economic and political structure. As Leslie stated,

> The more interventionist role of the federal government, visible in many discrete decisions apparently intended to promote national development, permits one to postulate that a third national policy was beginning to take shape during the 1970s. National development, though it may incidentally involve allaying the discontents of disaffected regions, classes, or ethnic groups, is more emphatically concerned with creating or restructuring an integrated national economy through the agency of a powerful state apparatus. In aiming for this goal the federal government showed itself at times ready and even eager to challenge the power of provincial governments and to provoke considerable interregional conflict.[82]

As far as the affected premiers were concerned, Ottawa was again preparing to exploit national policies to defend the interests of the centre against the periphery provinces. A number of the premiers in Atlantic and Western Canada were, naturally, angry at what they saw as another attack on their resources and an attempt to impose a new system of colonialism on their people.

In the 1970s, the federal government attempted to initiate the development of a more mature and integrated national economy, organized around new principles. The new strategy reflected changing political concerns about the dangers of continentalism and provincialism, and, with this in mind, Ottawa devised a plan for containing those forces seen as threatening the general interest. The elaborate scheme included tax reforms and the National Energy Policy, as well as a new regulatory agency for monitoring foreign investment. The primary objective was to increase national powers.

Hence, in the early 1970s, the government attempted to reform the federal tax system by increasing the tax load of the resource sector, while providing various tax incentives for the manufacturing sector to encourage growth. When Ottawa finally decided to increase federal regulatory powers over aspects of oil and gas sector activity, the periphery provinces naturally felt singled out. Regional alienation was fuelled by the federal government's differential treatment of various sectors of the economy. The establishment of the National Energy Program in 1980 further reinforced the view that the hinterland regions and their natural resources were being exploited by the economic and political centre.[83]

The introduction of the National Energy Policy had a major impact on feelings of regional alienation. Trudeau's aggressive bluntness (in combination with controversial reforms) touched off a barrage of hostile feelings. Few people in the western periphery applauded the fact that energy profits were now going to be drained from Alberta to subsidize exploration in frontier regions controlled by Ottawa; nor did they like the prime minister's intolerance for those who disagreed with his policies.[84] To make matters worse, the Atlantic provinces were outraged that Ottawa considered offshore areas as part of her frontier, and they refused to give up any jurisdictional powers over these oil and gas resources. According to Leslie, the new development strategy was viewed in Atlantic and Western Canada as a "central Canadian strategy," rather than a national one.[85]

The need to defend and promote the national interest was undoubtedly reflected in two other policies. First, in an obvious bid to respond to the threat posed by continentalism, without driving out foreign capital completely, the government decided in 1973 to regulate foreign investment through the creation of the Foreign Investment Review Agency.[86]

Second, in another attempt to reduce the power of the premiers over economic activity within their own borders, Ottawa fought for a new provision in the constitution that would eventually eliminate various provincial trade barriers. Such a policy was no doubt appealing for a federal government committed to the goal of integration; however, some premiers perceived this policy as yet another attack on their autonomy by a hostile competitor and thus resisted.

In the context of a fragmented federal system, Ottawa was becoming more impatient with the provinces and their determination to work at cross-purposes with federal policies. Frustrated at every turn by provincial state élites, Ottawa was in a no-win situation. By the mid-1970s, the federal government had a very crowded agenda, and regional development was not the only problem facing the country. As a consequence, the Trudeau government retreated for a while and spent less time fighting the provinces in policy fields that were not a top priority.

As mentioned, the first sign of Ottawa's growing disinterest in controlling patterns of regional development by direct action was the establishment of a bilateral system of decision making based on the General Development Agreements (GDAs); regional development was no longer a top government priority. As a result, regional development programs never received a large share of the federal budget, in comparison with, for example, social policy programs. Besides, there were other more effective ways for controlling patterns of economic development and mobilizing support for the east-west axis. Ottawa logically preferred the option of solving market problems through the elimination of provincial regulations over the development process; this goal could be achieved by creating more porous provincial boundaries and by encouraging integration.

In the area of regional development, the federal government faced the significant problem of finding the best way to accommodate provincial equality and economic efficiency, while recognizing the competing claims of the provinces. At the same time that Ottawa was attempting to gain greater control over economic development in other policy fields, there were obvious attempts to be more flexible when it came to dealing with regional development policy. It made little sense to attack the provinces in every policy field, especially in a low-priority area such as regional development.

A New Agenda

In 1981, to the surprise of many observers, Trudeau's national development strategy had to be aborted. The federation was not responding well to the challenges of economic change or external pressures, and the Trudeau government had little option but to change its strategy. As Leslie argued,

> The new strategy aimed, like the earlier one, to strengthen Canadian manufacturing industry but presumed that the most effective way of doing so was to link manufacturing directly to development of resource industries.[87]

The intent was to consolidate the resource and manufacturing sectors while reinforcing a pattern of economic development that took into account the country's comparative advantages. The megaproject approach to remaking Canada provided a fresh opportunity for building a national consensus on economic strategies and a last chance to gain control over the development process based on state-directed national industrial policy.[88] Despite the valiant effort, the high-stakes gamble failed. With the unexpected decline in oil and gas profits in the early 1980s, the national policy was officially dead. The determination to defend the east-west axis had also died. Interventionism as an option for the federal government suddenly disappeared. "By 1984 Liberal leaders had lost faith in their capacity to predict the future and reconcile regional economic differences."[89] Industrial policy was no longer an option.

Suddenly, the federal government did not have the resources or political will to defend the national community against the contending forces of continentalism or provincialism. In the 1970s, Ottawa attempted to gain greater control over the process of economic development, while integrating policy formulation and implementation based on a new national plan. In the 1980s, market forces and transnational influences changed the country in a fundamental way. In a climate of great change, the national government was losing both control over the process of economic development and the ability to defend its territorial and jurisdictional interests.

Mexico witnessed a similar weakening of commitment to defending a national industrial policy at exactly the same time; thus, these changes were likely influenced by continental/international pressures.[90] During this period, North American politics underwent revolutionary changes, and we should not ignore the impact of outside subnational forces on national boundaries and state actions. We need to understand the influences of transnationalism in North America on the underlying political dynamic and the goal of national/regional integration.

By the early 1980s, Trudeau was disillusioned with interventionism and the task of devising a new national plan. He was forced to deal with a recession and a fiscal crisis. Under such circumstances, it was questionable whether the public would stand for another round of feuding over the best approach for remaking the country. It was time for another royal commission and a new approach for the country.

Conceived in the context of a changing North America, when traditional boundaries, institutions, ideas, and policies were being questioned, the Macdonald Commission was established in 1982 to chart a new course for Canadian federalism. In recognizing the limited role of state intervention in an age of increasingly global politics, the authors of the report made no real attempt to develop a new national strategy. Rather, they focused on the elimination of economic and political boundaries, the restructuring of the welfare state, regional development, and other policies based on changing external conditions. As Leslie noted,

> The Macdonald report, while confirming the need for drastic change in Canada's economic structure and the orientations of economic and social policies, inverted the suppositions that seem to have informed its mandate. It put forward, not a redesigned national policy for Canada, but the most comprehensive condemnation of the very idea of a national policy ever contained in a Canadian public document. It proposed no strategy or program for economic development except to facilitate adaptation to changing world market conditions, whatever future course they might dictate.[91]

At a time when governments were losing control over boundaries and the processes of economic and political development, the Macdonald study acknowledged that,

> While we have indicated a number of directions in which we think it likely that the future will take us, including the increasingly competitive international environment and the prospects of more modest growth than the economy experienced in the golden age of the 1950s and 1960s, we have not attempted to predict the future in detail. Anyone who has had responsibility for policy making since the beginning of the 1970s would recognize that such precise prediction is unrealistic.[92]

By the mid-1980s, free trade and the continentalist option replaced the Third National Policy as the first priority of the national government. At the centre of the decline of national state intervention was the failure of past initiatives and the lack of recognition of the high costs associated with preserving the economic and political under-pinnings of an integrated national economy. Consequently, the continentalist option was placed firmly on the public agenda, with less focus placed on the jurisdictional and territorial interests of the national government. Most of the commissioners of the study thought that the country had no other options, particularly given the chaotic political circumstances and the economic crisis facing the national state. Many felt that national political élites no longer had the resources or autonomy necessary for meeting the realities of the 1980s. Remarkably, the old Canadian political and intellectual nation-centred traditions vanished in response to changing circumstances and new challenges. The consensus achieved by the academics involved in the commission was an important watershed in Canadian history, marking a new orientation in statecraft in the country. As a consequence, the pull of the east-west axis weakened.

Suddenly, the debates over shifting boundaries and the implications of border regions and transnational influences were front and centre. The changing socio-economic and political context described in the Macdonald Commission forced the academic community to finally deal with an area of research that had been generally ignored. It was the dawning of a new era when Canadians were forced to come to grips with a changing North America.[93] On the other hand, the findings of the report helped legitimize a new approach to governing. It was the time that saw the rise of a new paradigm of governance.

Implementing the Policy

When the Mulroney government was elected in 1984, the new administration inherited not only the old dilemmas and paradoxes, but also the new definitions and solutions put forward by the Macdonald report. The regime change was complete, and there was a new opportunity to transform the federation guided by a different set of assumptions.[94] The debate on the impact of transnationalism on ideas, culture, institutions, and patterns of association had begun with a bang. With a new mandate, the Conservative government seized the opportunity to push for a market-based economic development plan and free trade with the United States. During this restructuring process, boundaries were less important and old assumptions and policies had to be transformed in response to the challenges of globalization. An entire range of policies, from welfare reform to deregulation, pulled Canada further and further into the North American orbit.

With the rise of Mulroney's leadership, the United States model for development was no longer resisted. The continental trade initiative provided the motivation for questioning old assumptions from the Macdonald study about the welfare state, regional development, constitutional reform, macroeconomic management, industrial strategy, and the need for state regulation. The report indicated that the costs and inefficiencies associated with national state planning had to be eliminated if the country wanted to be an effective participant in the larger, more competitive North American marketplace. These modifications clearly influenced patterns of economic and political development in the country, as well as the nature of Canadian political discourse.

The Mulroney government attacked the notion of universality, scrapped the National Energy Program, called for the deregulation of the economy, reduced federal transfers, restructured the unemployment insurance system based on the market ethos, and reduced regional development funding.[95] A new kind of balance between continental, national, and provincial interests had emerged.

Even the new Liberal government sees the need for less state intervention. Ironically, the party that in opposition fought many of these changes has now become the catalyst for fundamental restructuring based on changing realities. In contrast, the New Democratic Party suffered great losses in the 1993 election, in part, because their definitions and solutions were seen by voters as being irrelevant in an age of shifting paradigms and boundaries. It is an era when state autonomy is limited by fiscal realities.

These changes in the relationship between nation-building and continentalism also had a significant effect on the socio-economic and political character of provincialism. With the decline in federal spending power and the decision not to exploit policies in defence of Ottawa's territorial and jurisdictional powers, the Mulroney government placed less emphasis on disrupting continental integration and provincial patterns of association. Inevitably, the removal of such support for the east-west axis changed the political dynamic within the federation in fundamental ways.

Several provinces have shifted their attention to defining and solving economic problems based on the new realities of globalization. Rather than dealing with these issues on a national basis, provincial governments across the country are increasingly recognizing that they need to play a more direct role in the realm of international politics.[96] Given the transnational linkages for trade and investment that exist between the United States and various regional economies in the country (coupled with the growing debt crisis), it is not surprising that such a shift in national policy has directly influenced the relationship between the other two fundamental axes of Canadian federalism. Nor is it surprising, under these circumstances, that the various regions have found it more difficult to achieve a national consensus on key economic development issues.

Despite the National Energy Policy, the welfare state, the Foreign Investment Review Agency, and earlier national policies, Canada has been pulled closer and closer into the American trajectory. As a consequence, national ties have weakened and policies have been increasingly influenced by American norms and the needs of a continental, market-driven society. North-south ties have been reinforced and new linkages established as the impulse for economic integration and policy harmonization have gained strength over the years. Gradually, the requirements of a continental, market-based economy have overshadowed the need to control the processes of national development.

In several respects, these trends were reflected in the constitutional wars fought over the last decade. In particular, the Mulroney government rejected the Trudeau vision of the country and tried to replace it with a more decentralized version.[97] Both the Meech Lake Accord and the more recent Charlottetown Agreement were clear attempts to weaken the power of the national government, while providing Quebec nationalists and other forces exerting a centrifugal effect with more of an institutional focus. Ironically, by basing the proposed constitution on the need to balance these potentially conflicting forces, rather than on a national vision as Trudeau did, Mulroney strengthened the roots of disunity in the country.

In the end, both constitutional initiatives were defeated, partly because they failed to provide a national vision or acceptable new formula for balancing charter rights, federalism, native rights, and parliamentary government. Mulroney's neoliberal vision of state-market relations was supported by a number of state and academic élites; however, the attempt to further decentralize power, based on the enlightened self-interests of the players involved, was soundly rejected by the voters in the 1992 referendum.

Cairns stated, in his assessment of the Meech Lake round,

> The provincializing outcome was facilitated by the Mulroney bargaining style, which appears to put a higher premium on getting agreement than on the substance of the agreement reached. Certainly in this constitutional round the federal government promoted no national vision, nor did it seek to strengthen a pan-Canadianism derived from the Charter. This absence may be partly attributed to a bargaining process that suggested that a federal government assertiveness requiring provincial government concessions would simply have made agreement impossible. Given the very strong desire of the federal government for an agreement, the provincial governments held most of the bargaining chips. On the other hand, there is little evidence of the existence of a Mulroney vision of a national community that was suppressed as a statesmanlike gesture in support of the higher objective of bringing Quebec into the constitutional family.[98]

To understand the importance of national developments in the determination of patterns of regional and continental integration, we must bear in mind that national policies do influence the other two axes in Canadian federalism. From 1867 to 1993, the debate focused on the best way to balance continental, national, regional, and provincial interests within a political system based on the contradictory principles of federalism, parliamentary government, and in recent times, native self-government and Charter rights.

Conclusion

The unity-disunity conundrum, which deals with the problem of balancing economic efficiency with competing forces such as Quebec nationalism, continentalism, and individual rights, is central to the integration question in Canada. At various stages in Canadian history, the policy question of the extent to which a national framework should be used to blend these contradictions has arisen again and again. Invariably, it has been difficult to impose a coherent vision within a political and economic system that is highly fragmented.

The consensus achieved in each of the national policies was based on the desire to strike a new balance between these competing forces, while adjusting to both domestic and international pressures. While democracy thrives on debate, national unity does not. Each time the federal government has tried to formulate new ways for resolving problems, it has faced many obstacles on the path towards national reconciliation.

Given the contradictions in the three national plans, the different expectations reinforced by each plan, and the new political and economic forces within the Canadian federal system, it is not surprising that each plan has contributed to regional and intergroup rivalry within the country. The frustration and conflict that arose in the debate over the integration question provide a background for understanding the history of struggle over the regional integration question in Atlantic and Western Canada.

Three

The Atlantic Region of Canada

Imagine the advantages of a united Atlantic region with a total area comparable to that of Ontario: a diverse landscape and economy, common institutions, and the determination to deal with mutual problems arising from external challenges, according to the needs of local people. However, we live in a federation with multiple contradictions where there is ample opportunity for mischief making. Atlantic Canadians share problems but each province is also the product of distinct institutional and cultural experiences. In the final analysis, our institutional structure, which placates parochialism, also reinforces a style of competitive statecraft that displays internal divisions and ambiguities in the worst way.

To facilitate comparison on the regional integration question and to understand the distinct experience of each province, we will introduce the socio-economic forces and political institutions that operate within the region. We take the position that different kinds of forces and experiences shape how communities define themselves; this position will guide our discussion of the three case studies. Physical geographical forces, previous historical relationships, and myths or images influence one's sense of community or definition of region. The source of an idea and the person trying to impose change also make a great deal of difference. Our institutions instinctively tend to resist the ideas put forward by outside competitors. This resistance has certainly been seen in the struggle over integration in Atlantic Canada.

The integration campaign in the eastern periphery has a long controversial history and there have been various plans put forward over the years. At the same time, there has always been an uneasy tension surrounding the issue. Those who have initiated the debate on the best way to respect the autonomy of each province, while achieving real policy coordination, have often done so reluctantly. Perhaps appropriately, this concern was first expressed by the authors of the Rowell-Sirois Commission report who saw no problem with raising the regional idea but refused to go much further. According to the authors of the study,

> Throughout Canada the view seems to be widely held that the cost of government might be materially reduced by a reduction in the number of provincial governments. It is frequently suggested that economies would result both from the cash saving in the dead weight cost of government, and from a reduction in the wasteful expenditures of government through the reduction in the number of spending units. In addition, it may also be suggested that the union of certain of the present provinces might, by pooling economic risks, improve their general credit and thus enable them to borrow money at lower interest rates. But union of the provinces is not a simple matter. In addition to its financial consequences there are broad political implications. These include both an increase in political stature, which may be obtained at the expense of some loss in intensity of local political life, and a change in the outlook of the citizen who is asked to forgo some traditional local loyalties or at least to merge them in a loyalty to the larger political entity.[1]

It was certainly an understatement that there would be political implications associated with those who pushed for a regional agenda or plan. Over the years various plans have been proposed for restructuring the region. During the 1950s the accent was on informal cooperation. Such an approach was sensitive to provincial political processes and institutions while providing an opportunity for the premiers to meet and discuss common problems and concerns.

During the 1960s and 1970s, political union and the establishment of more formal mechanisms such as a European-style Commission, a Joint Legislative Assembly, and a Council of Premiers were hot topics in the Maritimes. By this time, Newfoundland had lost interest in the project. In the end, only the Premier's Council survived. By the late 1980s, Newfoundland joined the club again and premiers turned their sights on coming up with a new cooperative vision. In the 1990s, the Atlantic premiers have gone a long way in eliminating trade barriers and initiating joint planning. Despite various political obstacles, these premiers have gone further than any others in promoting integration through the promotion of various cooperative activities.

We noted in Chapter One, in the section dealing with Simeon's framework, that reaching a consensus on any policy issue is difficult when the stakeholders involved play for different audiences, possess different resources, pursue dissimilar goals, and operate in different institutional and cultural settings. A major problem confronting proponents of integration is that the Atlantic provinces, despite common economic problems, are not homogeneous. Furthermore, the process of negotiation has always been dominated by the premiers; few citizens are even aware of the issue. As a result, the local citizens are not psychologically or intellectually prepared for the kinds of changes that might be imposed on the Atlantic as a consequence of the fiscal imperative, the Quebec question, and new forces in the West.

To fully appreciate the struggle to solve problems resulting from changing circumstances in any society, we need to recognize the interplay between power (external limits) and culture (internal limits) and its effect on decision making. Power refers to external controls over behaviour or autonomy, i.e., the capacity to influence the definitions of problems and their solutions.[2] Political culture refers to political attitudes that shape behaviour internally.[3]

Premiers, in resolving conflicts over the best approach to dealing with new challenges, cannot ignore external considerations and the intense competition for political control between the federal and provincial levels of government. Provincial governments have a vested interest in remolding dependencies within their boundaries and thereby increasing political autonomy and power. Indeed, the territorial and jurisdictional interests of the governments are reinforced by the institutional characteristics of Canadian federalism. To complicate matters, the premiers must also consider the social and cultural characteristics of their communities, the extent of political consensus possible for any definition of a problem and the costs associated with forming or changing that level of consensus. Finally, in the context of the 1990s, the premiers cannot ignore the fact that if they choose to make their relationships more conflictual than integrative (or cooperative), the conflicts could eventually destroy the system. All of these factors complicate the struggle to find new policy guides for coping with environmental changes.

The call for integration has been an intense, emotional issue for the governments of Atlantic/Maritime Canada because it directly affects culture, traditional economies, and nearly every aspect of daily living. Marginalized peoples in the eastern periphery want to meet the challenges of change, but, like others, they oppose relinquishing all power over economic and political development to outsiders. As a consequence, the integration question has been approached with caution. Understandably, Atlantic/Maritime Canadians want to improve their economy and resolve the problem of underdevelopment; however, there is a natural fear of losing even more control over the process of development to outsiders.

Old experiences and divisions cannot simply be ignored with the rise of changing circumstances or a new paradigm. In spite of common challenges and pressing problems, governments in the Atlantic/Maritime region have found it difficult to agree on the need for a common regional framework. Thus, it has been difficult to change the political dynamic within Atlantic Canada.

Few researchers have investigated the reasons for Atlantic/Maritime Canada's division over the idea of regional integration. With the cod fishery virtually eliminated as a result of federal government mismanagement, it is perhaps appropriate to reconsider why some local communities view integration as an intrusive force. In this chapter, we explore these feelings of insecurity in order to improve the scope of our understanding of a complex issue. Clearly, there are different outlooks on the integration question, inside and outside the region, and until we examine these differences, it will be difficult to find common solutions.

Also critical are the process and institutional structure that have always permitted governments in the region to adopt an independent approach to problem solving. From a strictly jurisdictional perspective, it is unlikely that the Atlantic/Maritime premiers would have gained anything by abandoning the principle of provincial equality. When we consider the historical context of the organization of the federal system, what was at stake, and the power of the premiers, it is no wonder that little has been achieved in terms of solving common problems and removing provincial obstacles. We must recognize the internal and external forces that affected both the definition and the administrative delivery of regional policies.

Competing Perspectives on the Integration Question

Several factors have restricted the growth of regional economies in Canada. These constraints, in part, are a product of the federal structure itself. Indeed, provincialism has survived because provincial actors operate in separate worlds: they play for different audiences, they have access to different resources, and their responses to problems or new policy challenges are guided by inherited policies, assumptions, and past experiences. These policy traditions, deeply embedded in the political culture, and reinforced by province-centred bureaucratic structures and political party systems, have made it difficult for premiers to deal with issues from a regional perspective. Inherited arenas used for resolving conflicts and meeting the challenges of change have naturally reinforced an incremental and insulated approach to decision making in all regions of the country. The federal system was designed to preserve and encourage local control over economic and political development, and to ensure that the founding provincial cultures were not assimilated or threatened by outside influences. From this perspective at least, the original federal design has been a great success.

All of the provinces, including the Atlantic/Maritime provinces, are separate and competing entities struggling for advantage within a larger economic and political order. Each provincial society has been conditioned by a different combination of forces and historical experiences, and each has its own interests to worry about. A central fact in Canadian politics is that each province must rely on its own experiences and institutions in making sense of changing circumstances.

Newfoundland

Newfoundland stands out as a province like no other. Organized around a dual economy, Newfoundland has a history that is littered with old scars and competing visions from earlier governments' attempts to strike an appropriate balance between integration and self-reliance. The questions of integration and whether it is worth sacrificing home rule for industrial capitalism have a long, tumultuous history within the province. The fact that Newfoundlanders have been divided on these issues, since they rejected the 1867 integration option helps us understand their strong opinions and fully appreciate what is at stake.

Examination of the history of struggle over integration in Newfoundland, prior to 1949, also reveals the importance of early cross-border associations in the drive for a regime change. Malcolm Macleod showed that a long history of close economic and social connections, joint policies, and even a common currency (after the bank crash of 1894) pushed the Newfoundland and Canadian societies towards a common path. Demonstrating the importance of these cross-border experiences, Macleod concludes:

> The union arrangement decided upon in 1948–9 was an extremely important step in this lengthy, on-going chronology of Newfoundland's integration with Canada. It was not the last step, nor the first, and did not much affect Newfoundland's various links with the rest of the Atlantic region, already well-established. Confederation when it came was therefore no sudden, postwar phenomenon. Since the late 1800s Newfoundland has been going through a process whereby it accepted, and promoted, the pull of continental connections.[4]

Although the movement to Canadian integration was successful, it was a painful experience for Newfoundlanders. Since then, Newfoundland governments have had difficulty overcoming internal divisions and maintaining a cooperative approach to federal-provincial relations.

Few issues arouse as much passion among Newfoundlanders as regime change. As Summers argued, it did not help that "the interests of British bond holders and Canadian banks held sway over the maintenance of a democratic regime"[5] during the 1930s. Moreover, the 1933 Amulree Report legitimized the rise of the commission government in 1934 by attacking the integrity of the Newfoundland political system.[6] During this time other governments in Canada faced similar economic circumstances.[7] Yet, such characterization likely made it easier to impose change. Summers concluded, "In the post-World War II period of political adjustments and British dollar shortages, the interests of the British government in eliminating the cost of the maintenance of Newfoundland's administration led to Newfoundland's movement out of the British domain into Canadian jurisdiction."[8] Hence, things change, yet they stay the same. In the past, external dependency undermined Newfoundland's capacity to control its own development; future regime changes will likely be determined to a great extent by external forces. Internally divided, Newfoundland's bitter politics have provided an impediment to local attempts to gain control over the development process.

For a large percentage of the population, entering the federation in 1949 and attempting to refashion the community on the industrial model was a mistake. Prior to the 1970s and the rule of the Small-wood administration, the critics of integration were generally weak and divided. There were few opportunities to mobilize these forces against the premier. The defeat of the Smallwood government in the early 1970s ushered in a new era, and the Conservative government attempted to refashion the community under the influence of a different diagnosis and set of prescriptions.[9] This attempt was an obvious bid to increase local control over economic development and change the political discourse according to a different agenda.

Newfoundlanders fall in two camps: those who support and those who oppose integration with other industrial societies. Those voters who originally supported the policies of Joey Smallwood, or who now see Clyde Wells as being more in touch with the needs of the Newfoundland people, have tended to be more open to industrialization and new economies.[10] With the current state of the Newfoundland economy, the collapse of the fishery, and the plight of those now dependent on the welfare state, the divisions over the integration question have intensified in recent years. To fully comprehend the struggle over regional integration in Newfoundland, we need to establish the historical context of the debate.

The history of Newfoundland is scattered with competing visions of various prophets who promised to pave the way for a more prosperous, independent society, but failed to deliver. These past failures and unfulfilled expectations have most likely heightened ideological and territorial divisions within the community and made ordinary people more cynical of visionaries. Newfoundlanders have often been seduced by reformers and the promise of economic and political change.

William Coaker, Robert Bond, Richard Squires, the Commission government, Joey Smallwood, and Brian Peckford have all attempted to remake the society according to competing visions.[11] Unfortunately, none of these experiments has succeeded in reversing the problem of underdevelopment. When we take into account the differences between the various development strategies, and their impact on the mobilization of new competitive forces within the community, it is not surprising that reaching a consensus has posed problems.

For generations, Newfoundlanders were ruled by a thinly disguised autocracy controlled by the merchants of St John's. Alexander and Ommer noted that much of this history was dominated by a conservative élite who failed to provide the institutional support and policies necessary for erecting a sovereign and self-reliant economy.[12] For most Newfoundlanders, these old lessons of history provide a painful memory of what might have been, and a reference point for interpreting and responding to current issues.

Despite much fanfare, none of the previous economic evaluations, proposals, and strategies have lived up to the idealized mythology of Newfoundland as a vibrant, prosperous, and self-reliant society. One problem was the leadership; another was the reliance on development strategies that never seemed to work.[13] No doubt, unrealistic expectations and old tales associated with Newfoundland's mystical image have made it difficult for those seeking sensible solutions. Regardless, Newfoundland's society and economy have remained underdeveloped and dependent, and the memories of old regimes and policies have made it difficult for those seeking public support for new initiatives.

As indicated in a recent commissioned study on employment and unemployment, Newfoundlanders may not have benefited much from previous federal development initiatives. Ironically, this study concluded that various national state policies in Canada may have actually contributed to the problem of underdevelopment. These contributions include inhibiting labour mobility and reducing the motivation for education, while weakening the effect of the market ethos on the Newfoundland culture.[14] Although the benefits of industrialization were generally recognized by the authors of the report, in the end, they concluded that such a policy "in many ways [was] inappropriate for a small, peripherally located society distant from the marketplaces of the world."[15]

Historically, Newfoundlanders' approach to the regional integration question has been influenced by their own experiences. This history includes the relative independence of the inshore fishing community, a differentiated economic base, the impact of rural development associations and the fishermen's union on the organization of rural peoples,[16] and previous experiences with change under the Commission and Smallwood governments; it is little wonder, then, that the people of Newfoundland remain divided on the issue. It is these internal divisions that have prevented Newfoundland from restructuring. Regardless of which government has been in power, leaders have had few opportunities to mobilize enough public support to change economic, social, or political objectives in a significant way. On the contrary, governments, despite great ambitions, have been forced to play a game that does not change very much.

A further complication is that, for generations, Newfoundland was isolated. When pressured to deal with new forces that directly threaten current definitions of provincial, regional, and national communities in North America, Newfoundlanders often focus as much on old battles and romantic images as they do on current changing realities. Considering the power of these mythical images in Newfoundland folklore, it will not be easy to achieve a consensus on the regional agenda, especially if the focus is on internal problems rather than on the need to defend provincial interests.

Prince Edward Island

The citizens of Prince Edward Island face the regional agenda informed by a different set of assumptions. They are attempting to respond to the pressures of global interdependence, yet are still divided on whether to sacrifice a distinct way of life for industrialization, urbanization, bureaucratization, and environmental destruction; thus the integration question has posed a number of riveting dilemmas. As in Newfoundland, provincial state actors and the citizens of Prince Edward Island derive their meaning of the debate from past experiences, myths, images, and the inherited structures. Within any society, old institutions, processes, and ideas provide a foundation for interpreting and confronting new challenges.

Previous leadership contests in the Island community have focused on whether the structures, policies, and norms of outside industrial-based societies provide a useful model for economic restructuring. Inevitably, those who both reflect and lead public opinion have faced difficulties in reaching a consensus on an approach to global restructuring that does not destroy a unique way of life.

Given the variety of interests and perspectives involved, coupled with the lack of regional divisions or ethnic distractions, Islanders, perhaps more than other Atlantic Canadians, have focused much of their attention on the costs and benefits of modernization, urbanization, and planning. The debate over integration and the best way to balance these competing forces, therefore, is not new. Quite simply, Prince Edward Islanders face the challenge of determining the best formula for preserving local independence and their distinct culture without sacrificing economic prosperity.

The image or myth of a self-reliant garden paradise within a society that has, in reality, been highly dependent on outside economic and political interests, has not made the choice any easier. The "Garden Myth" — that Prince Edward Island is a society consisting of independent farmers — has been defended and even promoted by the Canadian federal system, and its origin can be traced back generations.[17] According to Milne, "the idea of an independent rural, and prosperous Prince Edward Island has been a constant preoccupation of Island politicians. With the possible exception of Alexander B. Campbell's early years (1966–71), Island politicians have returned again and again to this vision."[18] The persistence of such a powerful image has no doubt been reinforced over the years by a unique interplay between ideas, institutions, and processes.

This inclination to respond to outside pressures by relying on a mythical vision has no doubt restricted the opportunity to break new ground and forge new relationships within the region. Despite this, the image has provided a convenient way for any politician seeking power to mobilize public support. Such a powerful and lasting image has probably made it more difficult for those who want to challenge old-fashioned ways of defining policy issues. At the same time, it has provided a convenient safety valve and a sense of pride for a marginalized people who are naturally concerned about becoming disenfranchised.

Some of the paradoxes found in Newfoundland are also present in Prince Edward Island. Despite the changes that have accompanied modernization, the threat posed by planners and outsiders to the development process has remained a constant concern for those who depend on the myth of an independent garden paradise for insight. For Walter Shaw, Angus Reid, and even Joseph Ghiz, the persistent image of an independent rural community has provided a convenient way to mobilize voter support across the Island.[19] Such an approach to problem solving has probably also inhibited the drive for integration on a regional scale.

Ironically, attempts to deal with "internal problems" of the Island community, such as underdevelopment, have met with suspicion of outsiders and their motives. Operating within a territorial political system, local leaders have had little incentive to endorse a regional approach to restructuring. Indeed, the spirit and power of the garden myth have helped to engender a direct confrontation between the ideas of reform and more traditional community values.

Unfortunately, Ottawa and outside experts have not been very effective in dealing with these kinds of concerns over the decades. The 1969 Development Plan, which was designed and implemented by outside experts, did little to reduce local anxiety.[20] If anything, the local apprehension over restructuring was exacerbated by Ottawa's insistence that the job had to be done by outsiders. As Dyck noted, "Islanders had the feeling that a group of highly educated officials, ignorant of local circumstances, had moved in and taken over. Some even doubted whether the premier and cabinet continued to have any control."[21]

In response, new political forces have emerged in Prince Edward Island as more and more people imbued with the garden myth have become better organized. Future attempts at restructuring will be forced to deal with these new realities, such as the emergence of environmental groups with their own agendas, who oppose the industrial model.

Prince Edward Island has its own unique history, embedded memories, and policy traditions; thus, its citizens have their own views on the underdevelopment problem. The provincial state and the unilateral system of decision making have naturally reinforced a "we" versus "they" approach to the integration question. In this context, territorial considerations have remained a central concern for all stakeholders.

New Brunswick

The drive for integration was interpreted differently in New Brunswick. In the 1960s, the Robichaud government devoted considerable effort to mobilizing public support for revolutionary "internal" changes. The government also focused on erecting the bureaucratic infrastructure required for central planning that would thrust the system forward in an attempt to meet new challenges.[22] There is little question that the New Brunswick government helped legitimize Ottawa's interference and blatant disregard for the constitution.[23] The initiatives introduced in the province during the 1960s and the Liberal premier's positive attitude towards intergovernmental cooperation helped to both define underdevelopment as an internal problem and provide an opportunity for Ottawa to become more active in the region. To exacerbate problems, it became more acceptable — even fashionable — for planners and outsiders to reinforce old images of the region as an economic backwater and underdeveloped culture. These events gave momentum to the reform movement, provided a glimpse of the planning culture that was sweeping industrial areas of the country, and changed the political dynamic in New Brunswick in a significant way. As a result, the culture was transformed and New Brunswick's state planning system became the most focused, integrated, and motivated in Atlantic Canada. There were few political sideshows or attempts to work at cross-purposes with Ottawa.

Several factors explain the magic appeal of such a policy in New Brunswick. The ethnicity issue involved the need to equalize opportunities for the Acadians who formed one-third of the population in the north. During the 1960s and 1970s, New Brunswick was attempting to ensure that everyone had equal access to public services and equal opportunity to develop and prosper; thus, the ideas of integration and central planning became popular.[24]

Such priorities were also affected by the lack of dominance by one industrial or urban centre. Under such circumstances, New Brunswickers in outlying regions perhaps had less reason to fear central planning and industrialization than Newfoundlanders or Nova Scotians. The dynamic in New Brunswick politics has always been very different from that in other regions, and the province has established a well-deserved reputation for being innovative and open to experimentation.

Another consideration unique to New Brunswick was its close proximity to Quebec, which facilitated exposure to the Quiet Revolution. The reorganization and positive changes witnessed in Quebec probably added to the appeal of centralism and industrialization. The image of rural living and the garden myth were less attractive in such a context. In their place, the vision of a more vibrant and self-reliant industrial economy gained widespread popularity. Both New Brunswick and Ottawa were greatly influenced by the changes introduced in Quebec during the 1960s.[25]

Such a vision required a leader with entrepreneurial skills who could change the political landscape and grasp the opportunities that were presented at the time. That leader was Louis Robichaud. He himself was a product of an undeveloped rural community who was also well acquainted with the costs of an outdated planning structure. Robichaud spent much of his public life convincing others of the benefits of eliminating boundaries and the need for a new market-based industrial strategy for both New Brunswick and the region. He was premier from 1960 until 1970. Once in power, he took full advantage of the opportunity to force his ideas onto the public agenda, and he introduced revolutionary changes. With support from Ottawa, Robichaud built a more modern bureaucracy, recruited an entire echelon of reform-minded planners, and abolished old institutions, including local rural governments. By doing so, he effectively destroyed the institutional basis for the rural myth and made it very difficult for any future politician who opposed such a plan of action.

Nova Scotia

Nova Scotia has always approached the integration question from a different perspective. A comparative analysis of the campaign for a pan-Atlantic Canadian development strategy provides the opportunity to question an assumption, often raised in the literature, i.e., that richer and more advanced provincial societies are more open to changing old institutions in accommodating new economic forces. Such a misleading, negative image of poorer provinces is not reflected in the history of struggle over regional integration in either periphery.

On the basis of the "stage" theory of development, the orthodox model, or even the "civic culture" view of the world, the scholars have exaggerated the extent to which more advanced societies embrace change and new industrial models.[26] In reality, as witnessed in the case of British Columbia, wealthier and more industrial societies who have the power often resist models developed by outsiders. Nova Scotia has shown this resistance over the past three decades. The combination of this power to resist and the internal divisions over the integration question has made it difficult for the government in either British Columbia or Nova Scotia to embrace a new model.

Indeed, political engineering sometimes lacks appeal, particularly when there is no immediate crisis to disrupt old patterns of association. Intellectual debate over the integration question was never as compelling in Nova Scotia as it was in New Brunswick — at least in government circles. The new political discourse had strong appeal for planners and central agency types, but not much impact on the traditional state élites who continued to dominate the policy process in Nova Scotia until the 1990s.[27] In their search for a common approach to restructuring involving multigovernment partnerships, the premiers, each operating under different conditions, found it difficult to develop a community of common interest. As far as established élites in Nova Scotia were concerned, it made little sense to rock the boat and sacrifice power.

Future battles emerged against this backdrop, which featured a major division of opinion between competing provincial élites over the regional integration question. One of the great illusions displayed in the Canadian political literature is the characterization of Nova Scotia as the province with the most progressive thinkers in the region.[28] Over the years, Nova Scotian politicians have been consistent in resisting modern reforms and denying planners the opportunity to wrest control of the development process from their hands.

Interestingly, as in the case of British Columbia, Nova Scotian premiers over the years have consistently opposed handing over significant power to those imbued with the planning ethos. This opposition is reflected in the fact that the province "has a proportionally smaller bureaucracy than her neighbours."[29] Nova Scotia has certainly not been an agent of change in the region, with regard to upgrading municipal structures, reforming university operations, improving the system of land registration, or reducing patronage practices of political parties. Without the intellectual support necessary for stimulating debate and experimentation, the old élites and institutions remained as permanent fixtures in the provincial state for generations. For decades, old provincial state élites relived the regional integration debate, using a strategy of defensive conservative defiance. Each successive generation of political élites dug in its heels and resisted the call for change.

By the end of the Buchanan years, it had become clear that future Nova Scotian governments would have little choice but to pay more attention to reforming the political system. It is remarkable that the system survived as long as it did, especially considering the climate of opinion within the federation during the 1960s and 1970s, and the pressure that came from outside the region to restructure institutions. These events had a major impact on the encounter over the integration question.

To fully appreciate Nova Scotia's more conservative governing philosophy and resistance to change, we need to consider several factors. For example, as mentioned previously, in societies not experiencing an immediate economic or political crisis, politicians are less inclined to hand over significant powers to experts. Nova Scotia did not bottom out, as New Brunswick did in the early 1960s, and as a consequence, the issue of reform lacked the same sense of urgency. During economic restructuring, when local citizens are losing control over the process of development and are thus feeling vulnerable, such conditions create a dilemma for local élites. When forces push industrial societies towards integration, there are also pressures to defend local autonomy.

In the case of Nova Scotia, the cultural, political, and ideological setting was different from that in New Brunswick; by refusing to reform institutions and hire more planners, the politicians themselves were able to play a more significant role in defining problems and implementing solutions. As a consequence, more attention was placed on defending the territorial and jurisdictional interests of the provincial government than on providing a new vision influenced by the planning ethos.

Another explanation for Nova Scotia's stance is that the province has always led the region in terms of economic growth and has had greater influence in the nation's capital. As a consequence, the élites in Halifax had less reason to support change, especially if it meant giving up resources or losing power.[30]

Central planning based on a regional formula has been viewed differently in Halifax.[31] Political élites fear that regionalization might reduce federal monies going directly to Halifax and that Nova Scotia might end up subsidizing the restructuring of poorer provinces; thus, it is not surprising that provincial leaders approached the regional integration question differently.[32] The Nova Scotia government, until recently, operated in a manner similar to the Smallwood administration in Newfoundland.

The government had no planning structures and was blessed with a conservative group of élites; under these circumstances, there was less need to change the way problems were defined and increase the role of planners in the policy process. From the élite perspective at least, the government had little incentive to develop a new policy community based on a regional abstraction.[33] The reform of political and economic institutions simply did not have the appeal that it did in New Brunswick, and restructuring the political culture, upgrading institutions, and mobilizing public support for a new kind of regime were not priorities.

Public debate in a province already divided over the provincial integration question (as clearly seen in the history of struggle over municipal reform) rarely focused very much on the regional integration question.[34] Nova Scotians have a unique political culture, and a history that has enhanced local pride. As a consequence, politics and economic life tend to revolve around provincial and national issues, not regional ones.

Just as it has not been easy for Britain to embrace institutional changes at the European level, richer provinces in Canada have generally resisted giving up provincial powers. The combination of a sense of superiority, a lack of strong bureaucratic traditions, internal divisions, and inexperience with institutional crisis has worked against the call for institutional change in these kinds of societies.

In the context of Nova Scotian politics, a common and more rational pan-Atlantic approach to economic and political decision making has never had much appeal. These ideas were seen as being imposed by New Brunswick and planners and there were other factors that had to be appraised.[35]

Pressures toward economic and political disintegration are influenced not only by the organizational forms that help to define policy issues, but also by internal conditions. With a more conservative political culture and a history of domination by one industrial centre, Nova Scotia found little support for increased centralization in peripheral regions such as Cape Breton. From the élites in Halifax to the marginalized peoples in outlying areas, resistance to the centralization of power has been strong. Paul Brown, in his dissection of Nova Scotian political culture, found that those advocating a common approach to problem solving in the province operate within the context of a divided society.[36] Politically, regional integration represented an attack on old symbols of both pride and humiliation, and, with the survival of old élites and the traditional rhetoric of Nova Scotian politics well into the 1990s,[37] there were no easy solutions.

History of Struggle over the Integration Question

The issue of adopting a pan-Atlantic Canadian approach to problem solving first arose on the Atlantic/Maritime political scene during the early 1950s. Since that time, the debate has evolved through many stages as various interests competed for power in different arenas. The roots of this debate lie in the analysis offered by the experts involved in the Rowell-Sirois Commission study; however, these principles and standards were applied in a more progressive era in Canadian politics.

In the following section, we review this history to identify the reasons for the difficulty in achieving a consensus on the regional integration question. The origin, character, and impact of the struggles over regional development, provincial autonomy, and regional integration have been generally ignored in the literature. It is time to examine the meaning and consequences of shifting boundaries at the margins.

Due to differences in community power and competing assumptions about the benefits of integration, the pan-Atlantic Canadian campaign has always been controversial. For supporters of the movement, integration provides an opportunity to correct underdevelopment by eliminating internal market problems. For critics, the drive for integration represents a grab for power by outsiders and planners, and an attack on democracy, local culture, the principle of provincial equality, and rural development. Such differences of opinion have made consensus difficult to achieve.

In the competitive world of Canadian politics, where the members of the federal family are usually divided over key issues, the Atlantic/Maritime governments have faced great pressure to work together and solve common "internal" problems. Beginning in the early 1950s, as a result of the challenge to restore the Newfoundland economy to regional standards, greater emphasis was placed on developing a more uniform approach to restructuring the entire region.

The crusade was no doubt swayed by the admission of Newfoundland into the federation in 1949. Such a change in policy orientation in Ottawa was the culmination of a number of factors; however, the ambition to build an entirely new economy and society in Canada's newest province was a major determinant of future events.[38] The roots of the struggle go back to the days when Joey Smallwood used to brag about the benefits of restructuring.

Regional integration began as an innocent attempt to effect voluntary change. Territorial integrity was not at issue when the Maritime Board of Trade met in 1951 to discuss common concerns. Nor were there centralist zealots seeking new powers and a different kind of political discourse. At the time, business leaders were the main catalysts pushing for changes in policy orientation within the region. Indeed, the first historical meeting that dealt with a new approach to regional development was simply a response to economic and technological demands.

In 1953, all four Atlantic premiers and various business leaders met at a round-table discussion to deal with a series of policy issues and problems. Without outside distractions, there was strong support for the development of a new regional approach; the four premiers originally endorsed the bid for increased regional cooperation guided

by the concerns raised by the representatives of the business community.[39]

By far the most significant result of the discussion was the creation
of the Atlantic Provinces Economic Council (APEC), a permanent
non-governmental research body.[40] The idea was first put forward by
the Maritime Board of Trade in a clear attempt to rationalize problem
solving and reduce the role of politics in setting priorities, while
increasing the role of planners within government.[41]

The creation of APEC and the idea of a meeting where the Atlantic
premiers could discuss common problems were influenced by an
earlier New England experience.[42] Each successive generation of
stakeholders had to deal with the dilemmas associated with the overwhelming ideological dominance of American liberal-democratic
thinking. From the start, the regional integration question was influenced by orthodox economic considerations and American values.
Indeed, patterns of intergovernmental relations in the United States
were becoming increasingly more integrated and national in scope.[43]
Hence, the regional integration model, with its New England influence, was a clear reflection of changes and forces within North
America.[44]

The rise of APEC as a policy actor provided economists with an
opportunity not enjoyed by other scholars. At the time, business
leaders placed a premium on the need to generate policy-relevant
analysis; thus, the ideas of a number of classical economists stayed
on the agenda on a permanent basis. Others later regretted this decision, which virtually guaranteed the marginalization of other kinds
of experts. These early developments set the stage for a major ideological, territorial, and jurisdictional struggle among Ottawa, planners, and the premiers. Once APEC was in place, the battle lines were
clearly drawn, and the debate evolved within the territorial and ideological limits set by these earlier decisions and organizational forms.
For those who would later inherit these old structures and definitions
of the problem, the debate would take on new meaning. One camp
supported restructuring according to orthodox economic theory; the
other camp defended and promoted local control over the development process. Various premiers over the next few decades would
attempt to deal with the issue under different circumstances.

Early in the game, there were competing perspectives on the best
way to balance the forces of integration and disintegration. While
APEC officials were busy organizing joint economic conferences
with the New England Council,[45] and the publisher of the *Atlantic*

Advocate was proposing that "Quebec should formally join the Atlantic Provinces and become our leader and champion,"[46] the so-called Atlantic revolution was gaining support in Ottawa. Economists in the region were discussing the benefits of building new cross-boundary linkages, a more autonomous regional economy, and a new relationship with New England.[47] In 1956, in Bar Harbour Maine, officials from APEC, the New England Council, the Atlantic premiers, and the New England governors held a meeting for the purpose of creating new cross-border associations.[48] Transnational influences and the need to reduce the impact of national, provincial, and state boundaries were popular themes for economists even then. On the other hand, although revolutionary thinking was becoming more popular with the federal government, economists, the media, and some provincial officials, there were also signs of internal divisions over the issue.

During the 1956 conference of the Atlantic premiers, Premier A.W. Matheson of Prince Edward Island made it clear that he was upset by the opening statement made by Premier Flemming of New Brunswick, who appeared to fully embrace the idea of political union. Given the national media support and the confusion over the purpose of the conference, Premier Matheson wanted to make it very clear that he did not support the general union of the Atlantic provinces — even if others did.[49]

Incidentally, the original meeting of the Atlantic premiers in July 1956 was a response to the challenge put forward by Prime Minister St Laurent. The prime minister helped spark the discourse by indicating that he felt it was time for the four provinces to start working together to solve common problems.[50] When he made the statement, St Laurent indicated that his government was committed to resolving the regional disparity problem, but that the Atlantic premiers must take on the responsibility of developing a common game plan. The drive for integration entered a new phase: the premiers were now being pressured by economists and Ottawa alike to develop a common regional policy for reversing the history of underdevelopment. This task was no longer a voluntary or local affair.

To complicate matters further, the federal government had initiated talks with officials from APEC. Meanwhile, the media in other regions were quickly mobilizing national support for the political union option.[51] Territorial and ideological competitors went out of their way to defend their interests and visions; it was a sign of things to come.

During these early meetings, the premiers, indignant at being singled out and no doubt concerned about the direction of the debate, began raising old concerns and shifting attention to the influence of past national policies and external factors on the problem of under-development. Within the context of a debate where outsiders were attacking the traditions of provincialism and calling for revolutionary changes, the premiers were naturally overwhelmed. Given these cir-cumstances, it was not surprising that some of the premiers had an interest in providing an alternative definition of the underdevelop-ment problem.

One focus of attention at these meetings was the need to address old claims regarding the handing over of valuable western and north-ern territories to the other provinces. As the premiers indicated in their discussion of the regional disparity issue, past province-building initiatives in Ontario, Quebec, and other provinces created new opportunities that were never shared with the eastern periph-ery.[52] With British Columbia's call for expansion into the Yukon, the four Atlantic premiers were naturally concerned about the conse-quences of such a policy for their region in the future.[53] While Pattullo and W.A.C. Bennett used the extension of Ontario and Quebec's northern boundaries to justify British Columbia's five-re-gion vision of Canada, the Atlantic premiers discussed the impact of not being in a position to share these resources on a national basis. Other issues included transportation policies (in particular, the nega-tive impact of the 1927 Maritime Freight Rates Act on the region), problems with national fisheries policy, tariff structure, energy, and other policies that the premiers maintained had helped create the problem of regional disparity in the first place.[54]

The premiers faced a number of dilemmas. Even though they welcomed the fact that regional disparity was on the national agenda, they feared losing control over policy decision making to outsiders. In particular, questions were raised about the effect of these policies on rural communities. Given the experience of Newfoundland with restructuring in the mid-1950s, the premiers expressed a growing concern about the consequences of moving people out of rural com-munities to industrial areas. While resettlement originally was a provincial affair, by 1965, Ottawa provided federal support for the experiment.[55] According to Copes, the settlement program "had the purpose and effect of reinforcing a pattern of population movement that followed the rational or natural pressures of social and economic change."[56] There was no consensus on the need to abandon the rural approach to economic development, especially with few guarantees that the gamble would ever create a better way of life. In the end, each of the premiers had to make a decision based on his province's own needs, past experiences, and expectations. No doubt influenced by institutional, cultural, and structural factors, as well as their own agendas, the provinces had to consciously attempt to make fundamental changes in provincial-style regimes due to external pressure.

In an institutional system organized on a territorial basis, these inherited arenas of federalism and parliamentary government did not make it easy for premiers to deal with problems from a regional or national perspective. Indeed, there was little incentive to focus on internal problems or to blame local people for the problem of regional disparity. Instead, politicians relied on a defensive expansionist policy and framed the issue in a way that reinforced provincial autonomy and local norms. The real challenge for those in favour of regional integration was to find the means to overcome institutional obstacles within the region.

As one might expect, Newfoundland, in being a new province, was somewhat isolated and approached economic development problems from a unique perspective. In the view of at least one historian, Newfoundland never had much interest in the economic development objectives of the First National Plan. According to Blake,

> By the time Newfoundland joined with Canada, the policy objectives of the federal government had changed radically from what they had been in the early years following the original union in 1867. The heyday of rapid industrial development fostered by successive federal governments under Sir John A. Macdonald and Sir Wilfrid Laurier had long passed. The National Policy had been largely displaced by the social policies of the federal government after the Second World War. While Macdonald promised in 1867 to build a strong, vibrant economy, Prime Minister Louis St. Laurent promised in 1949 equality of opportunity and social benefits for all while maintaining full employment in a strong economy. As the economy prospered throughout most of the 1940s and 1950s, the federal government was concerned with improving the lives of Canadians. This shift in federal policy meant that the benefits accruing to Newfoundland from Confederation were radically different from those that its Maritime

neighbors had hoped for nearly eighty-five years earlier. The Maritimes had opted for union in large part because it promised great economic opportunity. For a short period at least, their goals were realized. Newfoundland, on the other hand, never demanded economic development, its people were never promised it, and Newfoundland never received it. Instead, it was promised greater social benefits, and it is in the area of social welfare policy that Newfoundland gained, in the short term at least, from confederation with Canada. By 1949, the promise of confederation no longer had the same meaning it had had in 1867, and this affected the nature of Newfoundland's integration into Canada.[57]

By the early 1960s, the Smallwood government's enthusiasm for an integrated approach to problem solving was clearly waning. No doubt influenced by the experience of the McNair Commission (which included John Deutsch, a leading economist and proponent of effective integration, who later headed up the Maritime Union Study), Smallwood was growing more and more frustrated with outsiders and, in particular, the findings of those experts involved in this controversial study.[58]

The McNair Commission, which Smallwood helped select, was established in 1957 for the purpose of resolving the old controversial federal-provincial dispute over the meaning of Term 29. Since the study took a critical view of his government's priorities and policies, Smallwood lost much of his enthusiasm and affection for those intellectuals who were supposed to provide advice on Newfoundland's sacred journey into the land of industrialization. The reputation of "Uncle Ottawa" and various experts involved in changing economic and political relations in the region was quickly tarnished as a result of this clash. Term 29 was an ambiguous clause in the original Newfoundland-Canada Agreement that described the process whereby specific details could be negotiated at a later date. According to this clause, Ottawa would appoint a commission for the purpose of determining the nature of federal assistance necessary to raise the standard of provincial public services to a national level. The original agreement reflected the government's desire to push the province towards effective integration, but offered few details on the direction of the policy or the source of funds for such restructuring.

Predictably, Smallwood was very displeased with the report's recommendation that the province should receive only $8 million a year until 1962. To make matters worse, Ottawa fully endorsed the ideas put forward by the experts. Since the premier was hoping to receive at least $15 million in compensation, these events formed a major turning point in the integration campaign. Smallwood no longer wanted to work cooperatively with Ottawa and the intellectuals who had previously helped to legitimize the campaign for assimilation within the country. Imposition of a new agenda on Newfoundland was difficult enough; Smallwood found it unacceptable that these costs would be provided to a great extent by the local economy.

During this time, the premier fully exploited the integration issue for the purpose of increasing his popularity in the province. The premier's decision to use his entrepreneurial skills to take on these outside political competitors, who were conveniently cast as villains and cheats, virtually guaranteed popular support. Gwyn argued,

> As for Smallwood, quite apart from political exigencies, he was spoiling for a fight for the sheer joy of it. By 1959, he had run out of worth-while political opponents in Newfoundland, a frustrating circumstance for a man who could say after a gruelling campaign: "That's over, now I suppose I have to get back to work." In time-honoured political tradition, Smallwood also needed a political enemy abroad to distract attention from his difficulties at home. Had Diefenbaker not existed, Smallwood very likely would have been forced to invent him.[59]

The dispute between Smallwood and APEC, over the licensing of a regional air carrier, no doubt raised another flag about the dangers of granting economists the opportunity to interfere in government affairs. The Newfoundland government was clearly incensed at what it considered to be "APEC's intrusion into Newfoundland affairs in backing the application of Maritime Central Airways for a license to serve Newfoundland territory in opposition to the recommendation of the Newfoundland Government in support of Eastern Provincial Airways' bid to develop its services as regional carrier."[60] In response, Smallwood removed Gordon F. Pushie from the position of vice-president of APEC; gradually, the premier was becoming more suspicious about the threat posed by outsiders. Oddly enough, while

Newfoundland was rapidly losing interest in the project in the early 1960s, an opposite trend was growing in New Brunswick.

Push for Reform in New Brunswick

In reaction to the economic and institutional crisis that it faced in the 1960s, the New Brunswick government initiated a massive restructuring experiment. Such a substantial regime change was both a watershed and a source of inspiration for those seeking a more integrated approach to economic and political development in Atlantic/Maritime Canada; it has remained so ever since.

Indeed, with the elimination of rural governments and the erection of modern bureaucratic structures within the province, New Brunswick was a Mecca for reformers and a shining example for others to emulate. If nothing else, these changes ensured that the government had access to the institutional means necessary for bringing about fundamental change. Reformers who were committed to the idea that underdevelopment was an internal problem had a great opportunity to experiment and transform economic and political relations. From their point of view, it was an occasion to champion the cause of regime change within Atlantic/Maritime Canada.[61]

The rise of the Liberal government in 1960 under Louis Robichaud was a godsend for those seeking fundamental change within the region. With the backing of Ottawa, the reform-minded premier set his sights on re-examining the historical role of government institutions in relation to economic disparity at both the provincial and regional levels.[62] Despite the opposition of the other premiers, Robichaud felt it was time that the provinces not only worked together in reforming institutions, but also collaborated closely with the federal government in devising an industrial plan for the entire region. A new discourse and struggle over competing agendas began.

These differences emerged at Robichaud's first meeting of the Atlantic premiers in 1960. As Stanley noted,

> On September 21, Premier Robichaud met with Premiers Stanfield, Shaw and Smallwood in Halifax at the annual Atlantic premiers' conference. He rather startled his colleagues by stating "if somebody donated $100,000,000 to the Atlantic provinces tomorrow for planned redevelopment, we would not know what to do with it." It was an emphatic way of pointing out the need for the provinces

to draw up an "integrated program which would provide a faster rate of economic growth." Robichaud reminded his associates that all plans should be integrated with national policies and he urged the Atlantic premiers, as a body to "force the federal government to adopt policies consistent with a balanced economy...including diversification of industry."[63]

The Byrne Commission and the Equal Opportunity Plan

One of the premier's first chores in setting priorities for the new government was to establish several commissions for the purpose of gathering information and mobilizing support for a regime change. Undoubtedly, Premier Robichaud's determination to set a new course and change the agenda was reflected in the decision to first appoint the Byrne Commission in 1963, and then implement the Equal Opportunity Plan, as recommended by the study.[64] The Byrne Commission was by far the most important inquiry ever sponsored by the government: it provided a site for initiating a new dialogue and for convincing people that the status quo was indefensible. The call for a more modern industrial plan for both the province and the region intensified as the premier provided both a platform and a set of institutions that ensured there would be a new political discourse.

The Byrne Commission was important to the cause of reform in several ways. First, in a conscious effort to impose a new direction, the government recruited experts from outside the province to work on the study.[65] This strategy ensured that the arguments required by the government to legitimize a new action plan were set in place. It also sent a message to reformers in Ottawa and elsewhere that New Brunswick was committed to real change. To be successful in promoting a new direction, the province needed federal assistance and outside experts for the implementation of the plan. In addition, when economists with international reputations were brought in, few people were prepared to question their research or recommendations. Thus, the job of mobilizing support for a new agenda was much easier later on.[66] The authors of the report provided a well-researched document that offered several logical conclusions and recommendations. The report provided a new vision for New Brunswick: it called for the abolition of rural governments, and for centralization of health, education, social welfare, justice, and other general services. It also argued that the province needed to reform the tax system and create more modern decision-making structures if it wanted to raise the standard of government ethics.

The report also focused on finding ways to ensure that the experts themselves were in charge of the design and implementation of new reforms. In the final analysis, the authors of the report strongly recommended the creation of new administration commissions to make sure that critical decisions were made by reformers and that decision making was not based on political/partisan considerations.[67] The intention was to depoliticize decision making and increase the role of experts in the policy process.

An unusual recommendation — the idea of economic and political union of Atlantic Canada — appeared at the end of the study. The concept was influenced by the experiences of New Brunswick, and the authors had reached the conclusion that it made good sense to expand the experiment on a regional basis. With this background, it was not surprising that some of the ideas raised in the Byrne Commission later appeared in the Maritime Union Study. As Byrne concluded at the time, "admittedly one can envision many objections, but union would dictate a more authoritative voice for the Atlantic area within Canadian Federalism, and, if any significance is to be given present portents in Canadian affairs, then a united voice in seeking what many believe to be at least our manifest economic betterment."[68]

Even though Robichaud refused to establish the new commissions recommended by Byrne, several of the other ideas were endorsed. Establishment of the Equal Opportunity Plan required a total of 130 bills.[69] A new discourse in both the province and region had been created.

The Equal Opportunity Program had four primary elements: "the need to respond to federal initiatives,"[70] the aspiration to abolish rural governments and reform other local institutions, the need to build a more modern planning system, and the commitment to economic growth, "especially through manufacturing development."[71]

These were interesting times in New Brunswick politics. With the leadership of Robichaud, encouragement from Ottawa, and the support of some of the best planners in the country, there was a feeling of optimism that a new approach might succeed in finally solving the regional disparity puzzle.[72] At the same time, these new agents of change and their emphasis on planning as a basic ideological cornerstone probably made it more difficult to convince other premiers of the need for fundamental change. One striking feature of the struggle over integration that created tensions and reinforced competition was the rising power of New Brunswick superbureaucrats, who were committed to defending their ideas against territorial power brokers within the region.

Union on a Regional Basis

The crusade for political reform and economic transformation, which was led by the technocrats in New Brunswick, the Atlantic Provinces Economic Council, and outside political competitors, reached a new apex in 1964. Yet, despite the fact that there was finally a site for the new discourse, those who supported integration as a means for reversing underdevelopment on a regional basis faced a number of obstacles.

The idea of regional integration provided a convenient new strategy for regional development, as well as a formula for restructuring intergovernmental relations within the region. For the most part, Ottawa worked behind the scenes trying to persuade the premiers that it was time for real change. Premier Robichaud noted, when discussing Prime Minister Pearson's views on the topic, that "he was all in favour of reducing the number of provinces, because it was reducing the number of jurisdictions with which the Federal government would have to deal or negotiate."[73] Robichaud also indicated that Jean Marchand, the Minister of the Department of Regional Economic Development and his deputy, Tom Kent, were big supporters of the idea.[74] Under such circumstances, those divergent interests who resisted central reform initiatives had concerns about Ottawa's interference. In addition, they viewed the New Brunswick politicians not as reformers, but rather as agents working for more powerful external interests. Robichaud's call for a study on amalgamating the four provinces in 1964 posed a clear threat to territorial integrity, but the premiers were forced to respond. The integration initiative was immediately rejected by Smallwood, who lost all interest in meeting with the others to discuss common problems. When Prince Edward Island premier Shaw opposed the initiative, there was real concern that the study would never even get off the ground. However, with a change of government in Prince Edward Island, and the rise of a more progressive leader, the momentum shifted in the other direction (at least as far as the Maritimes were concerned). As a consequence, in 1968, the Maritime premiers agreed to establish a study to investigate the merits of economic and political union.[75]

In light of the environmental considerations and Smallwood's contradictory policies, the integration option was rejected in Newfoundland. While New Brunswick was determined to eliminate rural governments, Smallwood was busy setting up a new local government infrastructure. In fact, the number of local governments in Newfoundland actually doubled in the late 1960s.[76]

The Smallwood government was operating within a federal system that provided generous transfers with few conditions and thus had little reason to endorse the new initiative. Rather than embracing Byrne's vision of an Atlantic union, Smallwood chose a separate path for Newfoundland. Yet, given past experiences and the fact that general services were already centralized, it would have been difficult to convince voters of the need to reform the economy and society according to the New Brunswick model. At the very least, the attempt would have been a major political gamble.

Furthermore, Smallwood, unlike Robichaud, refused to build a sophisticated planning structure. There was no site for mobilizing new forces of reform or contesting the autonomy of elected officials. His approach to decision making was incompatible with the needs of planners, and as a result, he focused more often on being pragmatic and surviving in a divided community than on moving the province in a single direction. Such an approach was to a great extent financed with federal transfers.[77] An enduring theme during Smallwood's leadership was the need to keep priority setting within the hands of the premier. Not surprisingly, his style of leadership did not help the reform movement.

Ironically, the Newfoundland government often worked at cross-purposes with Ottawa; Newfoundland's policy decisions were based more on politics than on any overall plan, industrial or otherwise. The lack of coherent policy worked against the needs of industrial capitalism.The Economic Council of Canada argued that, while Smallwood's transportation and resettlement policies reinforced the growth of industrial areas, "other government policies on taxation, and transfer payments tended to have the opposite effect by restraining the migration of people from the outports to the urban system."[78] In the context of a fragmented yet generous federal system, Ottawa and the other supporters of reform were ill equipped for dealing with opposing premiers.

Maritime Union

With Newfoundland's lack of interest, Byrne's vision of Atlantica remained but a dream. Curiously enough, there was still hope for Maritime integration. Passive acceptance of changing realities during the time when Quebec was threatening to separate and Ottawa was threatening to cut transfers[79] meant that there was good reason to endorse the project; the premiers faced great pressure to support the study. In the end, the premiers reached an agreement on the need for further study. However, they were also fully aware that regardless of the findings of the experts, nothing could be changed unless they all agreed. The unilateral system of decision making virtually guaranteed that the premiers remained in control and that provincial institutions provided a base for mounting a counter-offensive. Federal dependence did not circumscribe the power of the premiers to defend their interests, as long as their unilateral powers remained intact.

The Maritime Union Study was committed to examining possible advancements in the economy and improvements in the quality of services that could be achieved through union. As in the case of the Equal Opportunity Program, there was a solid pledge to aggregate power, redraw borders, and increase the role of planners in the policy process, in response to federal initiatives to stimulate new forms of industrial activity on a regional basis.

The ideological debate over the issue of underdevelopment has always been contentious, and the appointment of John J. Deutsch to the position of special advisor was a sign that the work would have a market-based slant. Deutsch, who had completed two commissioned studies for Premier Robichaud, served as chairman of the Economic Council of Canada and was one of the best-known orthodox economic thinkers in the country.

Even more illustrative of the power of the orthodox camp was the appointment of Frederic Drummie to the position of chief coordinator for the project. Drummie played a major role in designing and implementing the Equal Opportunity Plan, and he had chaired Robichaud's Office of Government Organization. Frederic Arsenault, who also worked in the New Brunswick government and later became a member of the board of the Atlantic Provinces Economic Council, served as secretary of the study. The study was very much a New Brunswick project, which created problems later on — especially in Nova Scotia.

With its emphasis on investigation of the challenges facing the region from an orthodox viewpoint, the study mounted an impressive attack on rural development and the problems created by a territorial system of decision making. The report was critical of traditional government practices, the refusal to introduce new planning infrastructures, rural cultures, and the political obstacles inhibiting industrialization and change. The authors concluded that if the premiers were serious, and if they supported the need to centralize populations, "to move out of the agricultural, fishing, and rural based industries," and to promote the growth of "new and expanding industries," the economic problems of the region would be resolved — and very quickly.[80] The authors, who were greatly influenced by the rise of the European Common Market initiative, endorsed a logical extension of the orthodox economic experiment in New Brunswick.

The 1970 Maritime Union Report defended the view that economic and political reform was inevitable — with or without provincial support. The report maintained that if the premiers continued their old practices and resisted the drive for modern government, Ottawa would either lose interest or impose its own solutions.[81] These agents of change wanted to see the rise of a more entrepreneurial culture. In adopting the arguments that they did, the authors of the report tended to blame local people and reinforce old stereotypes about the region. In a nutshell, it was assumed that regional disparity was an "internal" problem. The solution was to change the cultural and institutional setting and thus solve the problem.

The study concluded that full economic and political integration was necessary, with a clear warning to the premiers that administrative and economic union would not work unless the existing competitive system of power-sharing was completely eliminated.[82] As discussed in Chapter One, the report presented integration along a continuum. It was concluded that substantial administrative and economic integration was unlikely if these decisions were left to each province. In pursuing their mission to create a new site for changing the political dynamic within the region, the authors, influenced by the integration project in Europe, recommended the establishment of three new political structures.

First, a Commission staffed with experts would ensure that there would be a non-political site for dealing with complex issues and facilitating the move towards effective integration. The authors of the study assumed that unless the premiers were willing to hand over power to these technocrats, real change was unlikely. Second, the authors suggested that a council of maritime premiers and a small secretariat be installed. Third, they recommended that a joint legislative assembly be created in order to legitimize the important decisions. These suggestions were based on the European integration model and growth pole theory.[83]

Growth pole theory also inspired the establishment of the Department of Regional Economic Expansion in the late 1960s. It was based on the assumption that economic growth or prosperity was associated with the building of large industrial/urban centres.[84] Hence, great emphasis was placed on creating the conditions necessary to promote development or growth poles in Atlantic Canada during the 1970s. It was a popular theory at the time.

When the study was first made public, there was much optimism that new cross-border associations were about to be realized. Given the political climate at the time and the finding that "84% of the English-speaking Maritimes up to 45 years of age were favourably disposed to a full Maritime Union,"[85] the status quo was no longer an option. On the other hand, it was an issue that few people knew much about.

Yet, circumstances had changed. Nova Scotia premier Robert Stanfield and Louis Robichaud were gone by 1970. Premiers Hatfield and Regan inherited a project that was not of their creation. In the context of a highly competitive, adversarial political party system, the premiers naturally questioned the initiatives they had inherited. Besides, the rhetoric and the assumption of the orthodox economic thinkers that a Maritime union would improve industrial opportunities were supported by little hard evidence.[86] On faith alone, the premiers would have found it difficult to simply abandon old traditions and provincial powers. David Cameron, in his assessment of the Maritime Union Study, states that "the problem in attempting to evaluate these arguments is simply that we have no basis for comparison, and must accept or reject them on the basis of belief, rather than knowledge."[87]

The debate over whether underdevelopment was influenced more by internal or external factors was not resolved in the union study, and, as a consequence, the premiers faced a major dilemma. While the report helped legitimize Ottawa's efforts to undermine the threat posed by rural development and provincialism, the premiers were left to decide whether to accept the call to hand over new powers to these forces of reform.

In confronting this major dilemma, the premiers, each with a reputation for being a progressive thinker, also had to consider the consequences of sacrificing their territorial and jurisdictional powers. It would be difficult to win support for the relinquishing of more control over the development process to Ottawa and a group of non-elected experts, especially from within the cabinet.[88] The premiers faced a battle over territorial integrity, as well as an ideological debate over what role, if any, the provincial state should play in addressing the problem of underdevelopment at the margins.

From a provincial perspective at least, resisting the push for a growth pole strategy and an integrated approach to economic and political development was a good idea. These leaders, elected to serve three autonomous and distinct communities, would naturally be suspicious of any call to eliminate existing economic and political structures. In the eyes of the new premiers, Ottawa and other supporters of reform must have appeared arrogant in their willingness to ignore the traditional strengths of the local economy and invoke a scheme that further undermined local control over the development process. It was a big gamble.

Confronted with such demands, the premiers attempted to gain control over the experiment early on in the struggle by refusing to sacrifice their powers to outsiders. They responded to the challenge posed by the emerging new orthodoxy by designing the new intergovernmental machinery in a way that virtually guaranteed protection of their territorial and jurisdictional interests. The key was the premiers' refusal to replace the confederal power-sharing system with the new regional sites recommended by the authors of the report. A confederal system is based on the idea that nothing is done unless all agree. It is a form of partnership that leaves the decision-making powers and initiating powers with the political leaders. Hence, any effort to promote regional integration can be vetoed by one premier.

In 1971, the premiers had little problem endorsing the establishment of the Council of Maritime Premiers, a number of regional agencies, and even a secretariat, but they did not reach a consensus on the commission.[89] New Brunswick premier Hatfield at first seemed to support the idea. However, the other premiers rejected the concept. The Nova Scotian government, in particular, had concerns about sacrificing its territorial and jurisdictional interests and handing power over to a group of experts; Nova Scotia was simply unwilling to give up power in the way that the New Brunswick government proposed.

From the beginning, the nature of the entire policy process guaranteed that nothing would be done unless all three provincial governments were in agreement. In this way, unilateralism and the powers of the premiers were well defended, as were the interests of rural communities against the threat posed by planners, the federal government, and the industrial model. The assumptions, approaches to development, and systems of implementation were based on distinct jurisdictions and experiences, and the premiers refused to allow experts the opportunity to develop an alternative strategy. The key was maintaining control.

In the process of formulating and implementing policies for regional economic development, the three governments depended on the cooperation of Ottawa. Given the high stakes, and the danger of being perceived as uncooperative, a major reason for establishing the council was that it provided an opportunity for lobbying for extra funds. The premiers were fully aware that Ottawa supported the project, and they were willing to provide new money for what was considered a worthwhile cause.[90] It was an opportunity that they could not afford to pass up. At the same time, there were benefits in working together on common projects. With provincial sovereignty never at risk, the premiers had little reason to fear the regional partnership. There was never a danger of having anything imposed by outside interests so long as the premiers remained in charge. As noted, this was a concern raised by the authors of union report.

Ironically, the multigovernment partnership lacked a common vision or integrated strategic planning system: its primary intention was to defend provincialism and local communities against external threats, while attracting new federal funding. The factors that influenced the different reactions to the integration question in the three provinces probably consisted of the historical experiences of each province, pragmatism, leadership, and the level of commitment to a nonpolitical approach to problem solving. These differences became institutionalized on a permanent basis, and, as the provinces tried to cooperate through these new regional structures, they became further divided.

The extent to which New Brunswick tended to focus on endogenous factors, and Nova Scotia, on exogenous ones, certainly made it difficult for the premiers to achieve a consensus on the rationalization of economic and social matters according to a common industrial plan.[91] Even the hiring of Frederic Drummie to work in the Nova Scotian government in the early 1970s failed to change the dynamic or discourse in Nova Scotia. Drummie failed in his mission to mobilize support for a new dynamic approach to strategic regional development planning, and he lasted for only a short period of time.[92] As a member of the "New Brunswick mafia" and part of the "New Brunswick Expansionary Imperialism" movement, Drummie was unable to turn things around.[93]

These differences in governing philosophy made cooperation and regional planning across jurisdictions very difficult indeed. In the end, New Brunswick was forced to play the game according to Nova Scotia's rules, with the hope that everyone would eventually see the benefits of sacrificing provincial powers to promote the growth of a more industrial and integrated regional economy.

Even though the paradigm of the intergovernmental experiment has been used in a number of projects over the years, the fact that all decisions require unanimous consent has certainly had an effect on the multigovernment partnership. Furthermore, the ideas presented in the original union report have been reworked to serve the territorial and jurisdictional interests of the premiers who dominate the process.

Ironically, throughout the 1970s, the Council of Maritime Premiers went to great lengths to distribute offices and programs on a provincial rather than a regional basis. Meetings were often held in small communities, and a municipal training program was created in an attempt to ensure that local communities were in a better position to defend themselves against outside attacks.[94] The structuring of the regional confederacy to "reflect and represent the integrity of the respective provinces"[95] created new kinds of obstacles and incentives for those who later sought integration on a regional basis.

The Integration Debate in the 1970s

With the growing debt problem and the decline in the popularity of Keynesianism, the premiers were steadfast in their resolution to remain equal players. Conflicts between nation-builders and province-builders intensified as some of the premiers opposed the federal government's determination to impose solutions unilaterally. Predictably, the federal government faced a backlash: as Ottawa pushed harder for integration, the provinces' resistance increased. It was an exercise in futility.

In the face of these developments, the premiers were under constant pressure to compromise provincial powers for the good of the general regional interest. With supporters including Tom Kent (one of the most powerful federal planners in Ottawa), APEC, the Maritime Provinces Board of Trade, and other business organizations, the orthodox camp was well organized.[96] In accepting that the regional disparity issue was primarily an internal problem, these groups were constantly pushing the regional agenda.

Nevertheless, the premiers were in control of the process, and they had the political capacity to defend a provincial agenda. As assimilationist pressures intensified, the premiers responded by refusing to sacrifice their provincial institutions, culture, and separate identities. Despite the Trudeau government's determination to challenge provincial powers, the premiers in every region of the country responded by guarding their control over their respective economies and societies. The 1970s were a period of province-building as governments squared off to defend their turf against Ottawa and outside interests; it was an expensive political game that went nowhere.

In Newfoundland, the emergence of a strong anti-Smallwood social movement in the 1960s and the subsequent rise of a new style of political leadership in the 1970s certainly presented new impediments for the supporters of effective integration.[97] The Conservative Moores and Peckford governments' commitment to managing the province's resources and reducing structural dependency provided additional obstacles for the integration movement. Politicians could no longer mobilize voters by simply raving about the benefits of economic and political integration, as Smallwood had. The mood change was the result of broken promises coupled with the rise of new economic and political forces within the community.

By the 1970s, more and more Newfoundlanders began to question the models of integration and industrialization. The Conservatives gained power because they succeeded in convincing voters of their ability to redesign society and the economy. While such a change in orientation created much excitement, it was always open to question whether the new government party had the resources or autonomy necessary for confronting Ottawa, local conservative-minded business élites, and the realities of assimilation in an era of industrialization and increasing interdependence.

The province's dependence on federal transfers and on a poor, but still market-based, economy made it difficult for the reformers to gain greater provincial control over the process of development. These inherent contradictions and the lack of resources, in the end, restricted the provincial government's capacity to direct economic development and mobilize forces around a new vision. At the same time, these problems probably frustrated the drive to promote effective integration within the region. Despite the difference in rhetoric, few things had actually changed. Internal divisions between St John's and the outport communities have also retarded provincial restructuring initiatives over the decades. As a result, governments failed to attack Newfoundland's structural problems for a quarter of a century. Political incentives for discussing economic renewal have remained, but politicians have preferred to maintain the status quo.

However, the Newfoundland government introduced several significant changes in defending the provincial border and the ideas of rural development against external influences. First, it transformed the government machinery, upgrading the executive and bureaucratic branches and hiring new talent to increase the policy capacity of those who favoured small-scale enterprise and local community development. These planners faced the task of reorienting policy according to the needs of the rural-based Newfoundland economy. The province-builders who were hired to defend the nationalist or dependency version of underdevelopment against outside orthodox thinkers were "entrepreneurial in their approach both to politics and administration."[98] As Doug House noted, in his assessment of some of the key players in the Peckford government, "In their dealings with outsiders, particularly those who wield power over Newfoundland society, they tend to adopt a confrontational stance, whenever they feel that Newfoundland's interests are at stake."[99] Even though the government had accomplished little in terms of solving Newfoundland's chronic economic weaknesses, it had at least changed its political style.

The second significant change was that Ottawa, ironically, shouldered much of the cost associated with erecting these new provincial institutions. The creation of the Department of Rural Development, the emergence of the Newfoundland and Labrador Rural Development Council, and the mobilization of thousands of rural residents through regional development associations changed the political discourse in the province in a significant way. Within such a context, the government had difficulty responding to pressing policy challenges, especially those involving the need to restructure the fishery.[100] This difficulty was due in part to intergroup rivalries and internal divisions that were further complicated by these new linkages. With the increased power of rural Newfoundlanders to insulate themselves and create new myths and images, any plan that was based on the modernization/integration perspective had little appeal. Old internal divisions became more institutionalized.

The third important change was that the provincial government during the Peckford years further distanced itself from the vision of a united Atlantic Canada put forward by the orthodox camp. In the early 1980s, in a determined bid to refute the image of Atlantic Canada as a separate zone, the Peckford government refused to even recognize the concept.[101] In addition, the government attempted to undermine the influence of the orthodox perspective: it decided to quit APEC altogether and establish a rival provincial body. Such a change provided a new site for defending an alternative development strategy based on the needs of rural Newfoundland.

The question of external control and sovereignty gave Peckford the opportunity to push another agenda. This aggressive approach and concern for provincial control over economic development had a major effect on the bid to develop an industrial strategy for the entire Atlantic region. In the broader context, the message was that the flexibility of the federal system made it possible to work at cross-purposes.

Despite the problems created by province-builders, the drive for effective integration continued, albeit in a different form. By 1979, Ottawa had decided to pull out all federal funding for the Council of Maritime Premiers' integration project. The experiment had failed to achieve its goal of integration, and it made little sense to pour federal monies into a structure built upon contradictions. Besides, Ottawa had received little credit and much abuse for trying to resolve the regional disparity problem in this way.

In contrast, as in the past, APEC continued to play a key role in keeping the integration debate alive throughout the 1970s and 1980s. With the support of prominent members of the private sector and other community leaders, the council continued to focus on the benefits of integration and cross-border cooperation.

In these two decades, it is likely that Ottawa's inconsistent policies and refusal to play hardball influenced the outcome. Given the other forces within the federation, Ottawa, understandably, moved with much caution. No matter how popular the concept of regional integration may have been in other parts of the country, Draconian methods could have backfired. The federal government was fully aware of the pitfalls of forcing a regional approach on the premiers.[102] The preferred option was always to persuade the premiers of the advantages of adopting an alternative approach.

The 1970s and 1980s were full of ambiguities and contradictions as federal policies changed frequently in a volatile environment. Even though the pan-Atlantic concept was part of an overall federal development strategy, it was hard to deny that Ottawa's new General Development Policy was a victory of sorts for province-builders. This victory was an indication that the provinces, not Ottawa, were winning the battle to control regional development policy. Political entrepreneurialism seemed to pay dividends, at least at the provincial level. As Savoie indicated, "From an Ottawa view, not one of the GDAs pointed to an overall development strategy. They supported rural development if a provincial government favoured it, or tourism projects, or highway construction. Simply put, no one could discern a central and coherent purpose in any of the GDA strategies."[103] Since Ottawa was inconsistent, the premiers found little incentive to support the elimination of provincial powers and boundaries. Ironically, whenever Ottawa tried to become directly involved in regional development policy, the situation became even more complicated. These policy initiatives not only increased provincial dependence on federal funds, but they also helped to create an even more fragmented Canadian federal system. The parameters of the struggle were determined by contending interests and the political resources available for defending existing boundaries. The problem was that Ottawa helped finance both sides of the struggle. As the debt continued to rise, more critics began questioning whether such a system of fiscal federalism was sustainable.

Integration in the Context of the 1990s

The debate over regional integration has not changed very much over the decades — only the players have. Yet, the concept of integration and the debate over its implementation have taken on a new shape in response to new forces and realities. Ottawa seems less committed to the regional development policy sphere, and, given that provincial institutions in Atlantic Canada are heavily subsidized by federal monies, the premiers will likely have little choice but to abandon some of these old provincial sites. As a consequence, they may eventually lose the institutional capacity required to defend their territorial and jurisdictional interests against outside influences. It is hard to play in a game without marbles.

Even the Ontario government has recently been complaining about the costs of equalization and the need for greater self-reliance.[104]

Ottawa no longer has the money for solving regional development problems, and the threat of shrinking federal transfers is now a permanent reality. These changing circumstances have created new problems for the Atlantic/Maritime premiers and raised new questions about previous attempts to frustrate the growth of new economies.

Another factor has been the rise of a new style of leadership in Newfoundland. More outward looking than either Moores or Peckford, Premier Wells has been more confident of the benefits of change and the need for a less interventionalist approach to problem solving. Reformers can no longer exploit the powers of the provincial state for the purpose of protecting the traditional Newfoundland economy and society, and then expect Ottawa to pay half of the bill. In 1989, Premier Wells decided it was time to rejoin the Atlantic Provinces Economic Council; he also attended a meeting of the Council of Maritime Premiers the same year.[105] These events were a great victory for the orthodox camp and those supporting the drive for new partnerships.

The McMillan Report

The current campaign for Atlantic/Maritime integration began in 1988 with the decision of the Maritime premiers to hire yet another orthodox thinker to revisit an old question. This time it was Charles McMillan, a well-known expert on economic efficiency and key policy advisor to Prime Minister Mulroney. Again, the continuing economic disparity problems and the threat posed by shrinking federal transfers in a period of economic restructuring were sufficient to generate such interest. The hiring of McMillan also sent the prime minister the message that the premiers were fully committed to making changes based on the priorities of the federal government. Given the threat posed by the decrease in federal transfers, it made sense to hire someone close to the prime minister to investigate ways of revitalizing the experiment in interprovincial cooperation, reducing trade barriers, and establishing a new agenda.

Implicit in the literature and media commentary on the current debate over integration is again the unsubstantiated assumption that by eliminating trade barriers and consolidating the provincial economies, a higher level of industrial growth will eventually be achieved.[106] With our attitudes anchored more on faith in the marketplace than on concrete evidence, it is little wonder that we are entering a new era of ideological and paradigmatic conflict over the elimination of trade barriers and the reduction of state power at the provincial level.[107] Predictably, the premiers have responded by adopting an incremental and conservative approach to a complex issue. From their perspective, it makes little sense to give up provincial control over the factors of development until there is more evidence that such a strategy would stimulate a mutually beneficial pattern of economic growth. Hence, despite the emergence of new forces and changing circumstances, the struggle has not changed substantially over the decades.

In an environment where there is even greater pressure from the outside to facilitate the market adjustment process, there is a natural fear that such an approach may not work. In the end, despite the confidence of reformers, there are no guarantees. Incidentally, not every economist from the orthodox perspective is convinced by the arguments presented by McMillan and other reformers. For example, Jim Feehan, a well-known economist from Newfoundland, in a recent assessment of Atlantic economic integration and trade theory, concluded that "the evidence and theory imply that any gains can be expected to be extremely small."[108] The premiers are fully aware that once these powers to regulate the marketplace are given up, it would be difficult to reclaim them. Without consensus on the nature of the regional disparity problem and on whether market-oriented policies are part of the problem or the solution, the premiers involved in the process have faced many challenges.

The debate over integration in the 1990s has focused on the need to revitalize interprovincial cooperation and find new ways to eliminate trade barriers and build a more prosperous and competitive economy. The task outlined for McMillan by the Maritime premiers was much more specific than that of the 1970 union study, and political union was never an issue. McMillan was hired to examine "the Council's role, operations and operating capabilities now and in the future."[109]

It was obviously significant from a political standpoint that province-building was never McMillan's focus. The fact that the 1990 study was much less analytical than the 1970 report was also an advantage for the premiers. McMillan's forty-six-page document was based more on wishful thinking than on well-documented evidence. The lack of empirical evidence, in the end, probably strengthened the power of the premiers to control the agenda as they had in the past. The premiers again responded to outside pressure for change by first hiring an acceptable orthodox thinker for advice, and then by defending their political interests. Again, the key was adopting an incremental approach and making sure that the premiers maintained control over the process.

Interestingly, the McMillan report also played on the fear that Ottawa could no longer subsidize the many costs associated with provincialism and that, whether the premiers liked it or not, "there is not overwhelming evidence for a strong federal desire to make Atlantic Canada a focus of policy priorities."[110] Focusing attention on the realities of globalization and changes within the federation, the study makes a passionate and obvious bid to convince the premiers of the need for working together to build a more productive and efficient industrial economy. It is argued that, in these times of great economic and political uncertainty, there is little to be gained by adopting old ways of thinking; government-led economic development is no longer considered to be an option.

No doubt influenced by the mandate he was given and by the fact that much of the information for the study came from members or colleagues of the Council of Maritime Premiers, the author adopted a much more pragmatic view of province-building. He also challenged old stereotypes and negative images of politics and politicians in the region. Rejecting the view that the Atlantic premiers are more parochial than those in other regions, the author acknowledged the appeal of provincialism and concluded,

> These issues are not idle political concerns. They point to the historical basis of provincial equality, the legitimate suspicion of "solutions" imposed from the outside, the understandable fear of creeping "outsidism" that provinces will lose their capacity to guide their own future. The model of cooperation proposed in this study is not one of extremes. Maritime union is a non-starter.[111]

In a clear attempt to achieve a new balance between provincialism and regionalism, the McMillan report fully acknowledged the realities of competitive federalism. Given the natural propensity of premiers to defend their powers and territory, and the extent to which the "Council has suffered from the complex that it was the bastard child of Maritime Unionists,"[112] McMillan fully endorsed an incremental approach to change. By fully recognizing the right of the premiers to control the process of development, he hoped that the four provinces would see the advantages of working together in eliminating trade barriers and developing an industrial strategy for the entire region.

McMillan's concern over outsiders imposing their views on the region brought him to the conclusion that there is only one solution: region-building is possible only if province-building flourishes. It is truly remarkable that an institution designed by reformers to stimulate change has become the defender of the status quo. Ironically, as we try to further integrate the state, we become more divided.

In the end, as in the first union report, McMillan also recommended the need to establish an advisory board of experts to "help the Premiers establish a collective strategic agenda."[113] In an obvious effort to increase the influence of experts over the process, the report endorses the idea of lessening the power of elected politicians. Such entrepreneurialism on the part of the politically oriented expert who fathered the report was reminiscent of the Maritime Union Study.

However, one significant extension was the recommendation that Newfoundland should be involved in the renewed regional experiment in interprovincial cooperation. With the change of leadership, McMillan attempted to build new links across the entire region. The thrust of this new approach was to provide the preconditions for the rise of a regional development strategy for Atlantic Canada.

Reaction of the Premiers

The discourse of regional politics changed somewhat after the release of the McMillan report: the premiers made a concerted effort to come to grips with new forces and problems. In the context of restructuring in the 1990s, fewer and fewer people are confident that governments are capable of managing the economy. New questions have also been raised about past approaches to regional development and the need to revamp the council in light of changing circumstances. Moving away from a highly fragmented system seems like a good idea, but the premiers have also had to consider the far-reaching implications of restructuring.

Unlike the economists involved, the premiers have to consider the non-economic effects and implications of the regional integration option: how would rural communities in Newfoundland, Cape Breton, or Prince Edward Island be affected? If the premiers embraced the concept, how would the other parts of the country respond? Would Ottawa further decrease federal transfers to the region? How would such a change influence federal-provincial relations? What are the long-term prospects in terms of the east-west axis? Would the integration of the regional economy create a new dynamic in North America and reinforce decentralization? Is Atlantic Canada competitive or large enough to hold its own in a globalizing economy? Is there a danger that Atlantic Canada might be absorbed into a larger borderland region? These kinds of concerns have to be considered.

The parameters of interprovincial cooperation have changed in the 1990s, and all four premiers responded in a positive way to the call for change. The Maritime premiers acknowledged that "The forces and momentum of provincialism are formidable. Consensus comes slowly in the absence of a unifying crisis."[114] Whether the crisis was real or a fabrication of outsiders remains an open question.

Some things, however, have not changed. Before the federal election in 1993, the Maritime premiers and their caucuses met with Jean Chrétien, the leader of the federal Liberal Party, to convince him that they were serious about working together to solve common problems. In doing so, they persuaded him to promise that if he formed the next government, transfers to the provinces would be "guaranteed for three to five years."[115] As a consequence, province-building was defended by the Council. The premiers were more determined than ever to be in charge and to ensure the survival of provincial institutions and programs.

Armed with the McMillan report, the premiers were in an even better position to defend the current system of decision making. The premiers have not endorsed the establishment of a commission or advisory board for developing a common industrial strategy, and, as a consequence, they are very much in control of the recent experiment in regional integration. Despite the new problems and forces that need to be managed, the provincial institutions remain intact for the most part.

Some progress has been made in the elimination of trade barriers. This progress is not surprising in an era of new global forces, given the restructuring of the Keynesian welfare state, and the fact that governments everywhere are relying less on state intervention to solve economic problems. At a historic meeting, the three Maritime premiers and 46 ministers attempted to build upon the success of the 1989 common procurement agreement between the same premiers.[116] The accord was applicable to bids on government contracts for goods under $25,000, construction tenders under $100,000, and designated services over $50,000.

The federal and Newfoundland governments were granted observer status at these meetings. The subsequent Atlantic procurement agreement will be phased in over a three-year period.While Premier Wells received much criticism from some labour and business groups, the Newfoundland government recognized the need for such an agreement in an era of free trade and global competition.[117] As state powers are being dismantled and the entire industrial world appears to be removing trade barriers, the commitment to a more integrated regional economy can hardly be construed as a radical policy.

At the same time, such initiatives might be misconstrued in other parts of the country. For the governments involved, the trend toward transnational regional integration weakens the east-west axis, and further erosion of a sense of national community could have a negative impact on Atlantic/Maritime Canada. One of the dangers of extensive region-building is the creation of regional blocs within North America. Even though the premiers dislike being told what to do, they are not blessed with strong provincial economies; hence, they would prefer that Ottawa continue to play an important role in economic development. The Atlantic provinces would have much to lose if the north-south axis were further reinforced and economic decision-making powers at the centre were further undermined. Thus, the Atlantic premiers tend to be stronger supporters of national, not regional, solutions.

It is too early to predict how far this particular experiment will proceed; nevertheless, progress has been made in health care, the environment, science and technology, energy, education, and other areas of public policy.[118] One area that has been a flashpoint is fisheries management: Premier Wells was outraged by Ottawa's plans to develop a regional approach to managing the fishery in Atlantic Canada. He found such an approach unacceptable, preferring instead a joint management system.[119] If this alternative was not feasible, Premier Wells preferred the status quo. Given the current fisheries crisis and the long history of frustration with previous management plans, a regional system may never be acceptable in Newfoundland. In fact, Ottawa has reinforced provincialism in recent times by changing its position on regional management and by endorsing the idea of erecting separate boards for restructuring the fishery on a provincial basis.[120] Reaching agreement on some policy questions will definitely be more difficult for the four governments involved in this experiment in regional cooperation. As in the past, Ottawa's interference in provincial affairs will very likely have both a positive and a negative impact on the drive for integration. Within a system of competing principles, visions, and forces, change will not come easily.

Conclusion

The foregoing analysis on Atlantic/Maritime integration indicates that the premiers have responded in significantly different ways to the call for integration. If nothing else, such evidence contradicts the popular image of Atlantic Canada as a conservative monolith and refutes the view that patterns of economic and political development in the region have been moving in a common direction. Furthermore, appearances are often deceiving: there is little in the history of struggle over regional integration to support the view that wealthier and more industrial societies are the first to recognize the advantages of eliminating boundaries and reducing local autonomy. Finally, even at a time of rapid economic transformation and stifling economic dependency, one should never underestimate the capacity of the premiers to survive and defend their interests against outsiders.

Four

The Prairie/Western Regions of Canada

The Prairie region evokes different, even contradictory images: beautiful landscapes and open frontier; resource hinterland; farmers organizing wheat pools or protest parties in their struggle for greater local control against eastern-dominated banks, railways, and manufacturers; right-wing religious fanatics who are more influenced by American ideas than Canadian ones; the Winnipeg General Strike and the traditions of radical trade unionism; class struggle and the emergence of the social democratic movement in Canada; and blue-eyed sheiks more concerned with generating profits than sharing the wealth with other Canadians. The western periphery, which consists of Manitoba, Saskatchewan and Alberta, is all of these things and more. The provinces share certain characteristics but they have distinct political histories and their patterns of state-building and protest politics are diverse. These conflicts have made it difficult for those who support integration of these diverse forces into one regional community.

Imagine a western region of wheat fields and majestic mountains, with common institutions, a vibrant culture, and no borders. Is such a dream possible in a federation where provincial institutions provide incentives for defining problems and mobilizing group conflicts on a provincial basis? The resurgence of the regional integration debate in Ottawa (as Canada enters into the larger process of economic integration in North America) has rekindled old feuds over competing visions of federalism. Increasingly, the question is being posed: Does it make sense to operate in separate worlds where cultures and discourses are defined largely in terms of provincial institutions and interests? As in the past, outside pressures will provide the incentives for embracing or rejecting the option of east-west integration. A further complication involves the suspicion that Ottawa and the planners are again trying to impose on the "have" provinces a definition of integration that will reinforce the sharing of wealth along the east-west axis. Legitimate questions are being raised about the possible consequences of again embracing such an approach to restructuring in the West, especially as far as wealthier provinces such as Alberta and British Columbia are concerned.

The primary objective of this chapter is to consider the challenge of integration as understood in the West. The chapter is divided into two sections: The first section contains an assessment of the provincial differences that divide the region. The second deals with region-building initiatives; as such, it is intended to be an inquiry into the various ideas, institutions, and underlying processes that are pertinent to the contemporary discourse. Throughout, emphasis is placed on understanding the various assumptions and forces that reinforced a common sense of western alienation, without creating a communal identity or purpose for everyone involved. With diverse histories and few shared cultural and institutional experiences to draw upon, the call for effective integration along the east-west axis symbolizes different things to different governments in the West.

There are several pertinent issues that are central to the debate: Does it make sense to organize the policy process, the way we define problems, and the means we employ to deal with them, on a regional basis? Are there common social, economic, and political forces moving the provinces in the region in the same direction, or is this discourse simply an attempt to impose an outside agenda? What impact have established provincial élites and institutions had on these cross-border influences in the past? If it is true that socio-economic forces are becoming more powerful than institutional ones, when one takes into account the rise of globalization, transnational influences, and other cross-border trends, what does this tell us about the power of either national or provincial state élites to control future developments in North America? Who would benefit most from regional cooperation? Does it make economic sense to push the east-west agenda as opposed to a policy of continentalism? And what impact, if any, have opposing bureaucratic and populist traditions had on the movement? These and other issues are clearly relevant to the regional unity debate in the Prairie/Western regions.

Previous attempts to build stronger regional economies provide us with an excellent opportunity to analyze the various dimensions of the discourse and to place it in a historical and comparative context in the West. The problem of securing support for regional cooperation has been complicated by the constitutional, social, and economic order: furthermore, not everyone agreed on priorities or had a common vested interest in supporting the project. Nor has a consensus on the possible internal and external implications of such an approach ever been achieved.

Diverse institutional and cultural traditions in the West have reinforced multiple contradictions, competing assumptions, and myths about the country. The way we react to challenges is greatly influenced by historical experiences and our system of values, beliefs, and assumptions about the outside world. When we consider the various images and distinctive forms of populism produced in the West, it is no wonder that the premiers (who play for different audiences and inherit very distinct policy traditions) would find it difficult to reach a consensus on the integration option. The reality is that Western Canada has few shared cultural and institutional traditions to build upon. Provincialism and state-building have reinforced an incremental and insulated approach to problem solving and community-building. Even though the Prairie provinces share concerns and feel cut off from Central Canada, there is no consensus when it comes to dealing with complex policy issues. These ideological, socio-economic, and institutional elements of each province's community history have created different kinds of expectations and assumptions about the region and country.

Unlike the Maritimes, there has never been an opportunity in the West to sketch out the kind of plan set out in the Maritime Union Study. Even though Ottawa has over the decades tried to reinforce the building of regional economies and cooperative tendencies between these provinces, there has simply been less opportunity to develop a blueprint for action. For obvious reasons, there was never much interest in launching a study in the West as far as Alberta or British Columbia were concerned.

On the other hand, as we shall see, in 1965, the three Prairie provinces began meeting under the auspices of the Prairie Economic Council. These meetings lasted until 1969, operated on a sporadic basis, and accomplished little. British Columbia Premier W.A.C. Bennett scoffed at the idea of such interprovincial cooperation and never attended. In 1973, the Western Premiers Conference replaced the Economic Council. The new NDP government in British Columbia ended the province's isolation and the premiers have met on an annual basis ever since. Even though they have established ministerial task forces to investigate certain problems, there has never been much attention placed on sketching out the kind of integrated plans as proposed for the Maritimes in the 1970s.

Manitoba: Is it Part of the West?

Manitoba has little in common with the other provinces in the West. When we consider differences in demography, economics, and institutional experiences, as illustrated by the Manitoba government's "[throwing] all of its weight behind the Rowell-Sirois Commission recommendations for a centralized federation,"[1] it becomes evident that this province is very different from Alberta and British Columbia. Greatly influenced by the original centralist vision, Manitoba has always had a distinct view of the country.

Governments in Manitoba have, for good reason, been more open to any solution that promoted the east-west axis and the sharing of wealth between provinces. Not blessed with the rich natural resources found in Alberta or British Columbia, the province has tended to rely more on the agricultural sector and old imposed federal integrationist policies. As Phillips indicated, the Manitoba economy "is still largely reliant on agriculture and the transportation, manufacturing and financial service industries that developed, initially at least, as backward, forward, and finally demand linkages of the staple, or export, agriculture of the Prairies."[2] Such a diverse economic base, which can be traced to the time of the original national policy, has created a very different kind of political dynamic and discourse in Manitoba.

Manitoba began as the designated transportation centre of the new periphery and, as a consequence, had more in common with Central Canada than with the other provinces:

> Winnipeg's strategic geographic position as gateway to the West was augmented by the National Policy tariffs which gave the city preference as a wholesale centre for the region, at least until after World War I.... The whole urban, commercial, industrial and transportation structure of the region during the agricultural period was centred in Winnipeg.[3]

At the same time, we cannot ignore the traditions of protest and the various institutions, strategies, and discourses that were put in place by province-builders to offset Central Canada's domination of the public agenda. Furthermore, at the time of Confederation, "there were those people in the west, especially among the Red River Metis who were favourably disposed to a United States connection. Although not entirely happy about the Hudson's Bay Company trading monopoly, they would willingly have accepted a continuation of Company authority or annexation to the United States rather than any form of Union with the Canadian provinces, that is, the East."[4]

By Confederation, circumstances had changed very quickly with the influx of unsympathetic outsiders and the imposition of new institutions and an economy built around a national plan. Had local institutions and cultures been allowed to evolve, the pull of the north-south axis might have been stronger — but this was not to be.

New trends began to emerge in Manitoba as a result of the imposition of the First National Policy. The government intended to exploit railways, pioneer settlement, tariffs, and the North-West Mounted Police for the sole purpose of gaining control of the region from the Americans and the Metis. The need to change the economic and political system was apparent early on, and a number of steps were taken that facilitated the rise of a new regime controlled by a group of ex-Ontarians of British descent. This group of economic and political élites had a major impact on the institutional and cultural foundations of the province.

At a crucial time in Canadian history, when the agricultural economy was being established and new relationships were unfolding in line with the original national plan, economic and political élites in Manitoba came to appreciate the benefits of an integrated approach to economic development. The very fact that Manitoba's governments have been less radical and more open to centralization over the years is probably a reflection of these experiences. The national policy created and sustained a system in Manitoba that was quite different from those of the other western provinces.

These circumstances provide key insights for understanding the general willingness of Manitoban governments to accept and even endorse the need to reinforce the east-west axis. Adding further to this dynamic is the fact that Manitoba is a "have-not" province that is highly dependent on federal transfers and initiatives. Such interdependence has naturally reinforced the importance of a strong national government and the need for an integrated approach to economic and political development. Manitobans would not benefit much from increased decentralization and they have shown less interest than the other western provinces in endorsing radical political solutions.

Dyck suggested that "Even in the period of agrarian revolt in the 1920s, the province's leading figures, T.A. Crerar and John Bracken, did not stray far from Ontario rural liberalism."[5] It was no coincidence that the Manitoba members of the Progressive Party were more committed to winning concessions from Ottawa than defending principles in the 1920s; nor was it surprising that the Reform Party failed to mobilize much support in this province during the 1993 federal election. Over the decades, Manitoba has consistently been more open to national solutions and a more orthodox style of government than has either Alberta or British Columbia.

It is important to note that when Manitoba was first settled, there was an influx of new immigrants from Ontario; this point has significance in explaining why the province has been more supportive of national objectives and policies over the decades.[6] The stability of this system required that the party system and government be controlled by those who embraced more traditional ways of thinking. Ironically, the first premiers in Manitoban history played a critical role in defending traditional English-Canadian values. According to J. Arthur Lower,

> In 1888 the Liberals succeeded in electing Thomas Greenwood. His government opposed bilingualism and was responsible for the controversial Manitoba Schools question. Laurier convinced Greenwood to adopt a more moderate stance but lost the premier much of his support. The Conservatives had a vigorous leader in Hugh John Macdonald, the son of John A. Macdonald. By asserting the British character of the province and opposing the immigration of French and European's, he won the election of 1899.[7]

Western regional discontent comes in different forms. In the early part of the century, the direct model of democracy that had so much appeal in places such as Alberta did not have the same impact in Manitoba. This approach was rejected, and it eventually destroyed the Progressive Party. The Manitoba wing of the party was never really interested in fundamental change. Manitoba supported Ontario's push for provincial rights and increased local control over domains such as the railways and public lands, which did not threaten the benefits of east-west integration. Manitoba's dilemma was the same as Ontario's when it came to the integration question, and they had much in common.

In a political system that was dominated by a coalition of Anglo-Saxons in the south, Premier Rodmond Roblin, who served from 1900–1915, never showed much interest in the kinds of reforms put on the agenda by rebels in Alberta. T.A. Crerar (who led the Manitoba Progressives) was not an ideologue either. Nelson Wiseman suggested that Crerar was simply "a spokesman of the west but remained a product of the east."[8] Friesen echoed these sentiments: "The Manitoba Progressive government was cautious, reasonable, and pragmatic."[9] During his political career, Crerar had been offered "the premierships of both Ontario and Manitoba."[10] With leaders such as these, it was little wonder that Manitobans viewed Canadian politics from a unique perspective.

In its early years, Manitoba was influenced by the Progressive and labour-socialist movements. With the general ascendence of the more conservative Anglo-Saxon Protestants who dominated politics until the late 1960s (thanks in part to an electoral system that discriminated against non-British voters in urban areas), the system became known more for conservatism than for radicalism. The British group from Ontario that guided both the economic and political systems managed to stay in power by mobilizing the community on an ethnic rather than class basis.[11] Although immigration patterns eventually changed, the old élite-dominated political system and culture did not. As Lower noted in his description of Premier Norris (1915–22),

> In the antialien climate engendered by the war, Norris took steps to strengthen British influence and to force the assimilation of non-British groups by making English compulsory in public schools and by establishing a Civil Service Commission that hired on the results of competitive examinations which were a handicap to non-English-speaking applicants.[12]

Such an approach naturally intensified ethnocultural conflicts; however, it also guaranteed that established élites remained in power.

The Manitoba political tradition has normally been less radical when compared with that of some of the other provinces in the West. Despite the Winnipeg General Strike and the influence of labour, the political discourse in the province rarely focused on radical solutions. Rather, as Netherton suggested,

> Unlike most other provinces, farmers sought out the support of business in an alliance that promised to give Manitobans a "business-like" government. This alliance proved successful at the polls as the UFM won the 1922 election. Under different names this "Liberal-Progressive" political group held power until 1958. It is important to define the Liberal-Progressive's paradigm of state intervention because it is the benchmark for all subsequent changes.[13]

In the 1960s, Manitoban experiences with respect to the need for upgrading and industrial planning were similar to those of New Brunswick. With the declining influence of the rural vote and the rise of Duff Roblin's Conservative government, a new and more progressive approach to governing emerged. The premiership of Roblin (1958-1967) and the decisions to embrace rational planning, introduce popular social reforms, and establish new commissions and economic planning agencies represented an important watershed in the regional integration debate in the West.[14] Prior to Roblin's tenure, none of the premiers showed much interest in pushing for a more integrated approach to regional development; Roblin played a key role in forcing the issue on the agenda.

These were unusual times in Manitoba politics; during this period of province-building, there was a significant shift in paradigm thinking. As is typical of such shifts, there were incentives to build stable coalitions and change the political dynamic. According to Netherton,

> The 1958 election signalled the beginning of a twenty-year process of modernization. The dominant paradigm of state intervention was Keynesian in that the full weight of public power was used to foster economic growth and full employment and to establish provincial welfare services. Emphasis turned from agriculture and rural Manitoba to manufacturing, large scale resource industrialization because of the extensive institutional development of the public sector.[15]

Rational planning was no longer avoided. The provincial government devoted considerable energy to putting in place the policies and structures that were necessary for facilitating industrial growth. Seeking to mobilize support for a more rational and integrated approach to economic development, the Manitoba government attempted to convince others in the West, as well as in the nation's capital, of the need for fundamental change. In the drive for economic development that was influenced by the assumptions of Keynesian theory, Duff Roblin went to great lengths to promote the ideas of regional cooperation and integration. The Manitoban government played a critical role in initiating a high-stakes debate over the balance between provincial and regional powers, and it operated under the assumption that it had much to gain from the initiative. For its part, Manitoba was gaining little from the shift in power towards Alberta and British Columbia, and the government, logically, sought new ways for promoting western unity. Within Manitoba, the forces and ideas that began with the original national plan provided a valuable resource for those reformers in Ottawa who supported the integrated approach to community-building. From Ottawa's perspective, it made sense to exploit the interdependence issue to strengthen associational ties along the east-west axis.

Saskatchewan: The Determination to Experiment

Saskatchewan also has unique themes, institutions, ideas, and historical legacies. While the experiences and expectations of the people are similar to those of their neighbours, they differ in many ways; the people and governments of Saskatchewan have a distinct viewpoint of Canadian politics. These experiences were the result of isolation, dependence on the wheat economy and federal transfers, a unique party structure, and a separate institutional system.[16] Policy conflicts over boundaries occur naturally in Canada as a result of separate structures and processes operating at the provincial level. Such factors provide key insights for understanding the different perspectives that have been adopted by the western provinces to make sense of a constantly changing world.

Populist traditions on both the left and right have shaped state-building in Saskatchewan, as well as the identity of its people and their responses to external influences. As one would expect, the influence of British socialist thinking and a more positive view of the state (which facilitated the rise of the Co-operative Commonwealth Federation (CCF) in Saskatchewan and inspired the conception and development of the Second National Policy) has been more heartfelt in Saskatchewan than in Alberta. Influenced by the cooperative movement, the depression, a one-crop economy, and a more diverse ethnic population, the response in Saskatchewan to perceived injustices has been very different than in Manitoba or Alberta.[17] British-inspired social democratic models have had a more lasting influence than American forms of protest and populism. These dissimilarities in protest activity help to illustrate the various cultural divergences and political orientations that continue to divide the West.

As mentioned in Chapter One, there are different ways of defining marginalization and underdevelopment; the province of Saskatchewan did not employ the same assumptions as the others, or rely on the political parties and institutions that have dominated the politics of other provinces. This approach produced a very different dynamic and perspective on problem solving, as well as community-building. Saskatchewan has tended to be a more collective-oriented province, as exhibited in the tendency to endorse central planning at both levels of government.[18] Much has been written on the history of the CCF. Saskatchewan politics is most unique in its years of socialist rule and the struggle to solve local development problems according to the assumptions of social democratic thought.

Dyck indicated that, while the Progressives were committed to the principles of direct democracy, the Saskatchewan social democrats demonstrated "unbounded faith in planning."[19] He argues that such diversity in the West can be explained, in part, by differences in demography. According to his analysis, "unlike Manitoba, rural Saskatchewan was populated by many members of the British working-class and fewer Ontario liberals. There were also fewer Americans than in Alberta, and those who were attracted to Saskatchewan from the U.S. were more likely to be of Scandinavian than English background, and socialists rather than people only interested in monetary reform."[20]

The Saskatchewan experience also challenges the notion that all rural societies resist change. As Dunn and Laycock succinctly stated in their analysis of provincialism in Saskatchewan,

> Modernity and its pursuit mean different things to different people: technological advancement, an increased standard of living, heightened investment flows, and the desire to experiment with new governing instruments. The drive for modernity is not unique to Saskatchewan, of

course; but what is different is the province's willingness to experiment with different political institutions, public policies, and political parties in order to achieve it.[21]

A major factor in seeking to understand why people respond differently to common problems is the distinct historical experience of the communities involved. Saskatchewan society and politics have been fashioned by a diverse set of historical circumstances and forces, which have no doubt influenced the way governments have approached the issue of integration and the pressures of economic technological change. For the most part, people and governments in Saskatchewan have generally been more open to the call for central planning and the need for state-regulated forms of redistribution; this is openness reflected in their history of experimentation.

Another key point is that development can take various paths. With the variety of provincial histories, cultures, and institutions in the country (coupled with the various interpretations of underdevelopment that exist in the literature), one would not expect one theory or approach to be endorsed by all parties. The Saskatchewan–Prince Edward Island comparison is useful in this regard: unlike Prince Edward Island, Saskatchewan lacks a "garden myth." Rather, the province is better known for its "cult of modernity."[22] Because of their roots, the people of Saskatchewan have been much more concerned about achieving a higher standard of living than about defending old cultures, institutions, or ideas against outsiders.

As a consequence, there has been much less apprehension about the need for experimenting, bringing in outside experts, or relying on external ideas than in, for example, Prince Edward Island or Newfoundland in the 1970s. Indeed, a unifying thread in Saskatchewan history is the determination to experiment and to create the kind of intellectual capital and bureaucratic structure required to sustain economic growth. The government placed less emphasis on defending a unique culture against outside pressures and conforming to the dominant models established by outsiders. Indeed, it focused on borrowing and building upon the frameworks that had been successful in other societies and doing what was required to push ahead. The restructuring and streamlining of government programs under the auspices of Roy Romanow's NDP government clearly illustrates the capacity of Saskatchewan governments for introducing fundamental changes.

Alberta: Views from the New West

As will be discussed in Chapter Five, British Columbia has consistently demonstrated the most resistance to the idea of building regional economies and coordinating economic development policies on a regional as opposed to a provincial basis. For generations, governments and citizens of this province have tended to view themselves as a distinct society and to see Canada's evolution and identity from a five-region perspective. Regional divisions within British Columbia and a populist style of state-building have exerted a centrifugal pull on the integration movement.

The idea that the Prairies are a single socio-economic and political region has never received much support in Alberta. Next to British Columbia, Alberta has been the most resistant to the call for restructuring according to a regional formula. This resistance stems from perceptual factors and past experiences. Albertans, because of their experience with integrationist policies such as the National Energy, tend to be concerned about any changes that would impose a second-class status on the province. Especially in recent times, Albertan governments have been strong defenders of the principle that every province should be treated equally.

Another concern involves the costs associated with regional co-operation. If there was no economic advantage for the residents of the province, it would make little sense to give up the power to shape the processes of federalism and its effects on the local economy and society. Alberta, as one of the richest provinces in the country, could end up subsidizing other communities in the region even further. Another critical factor is that Alberta has less in common with Saskatchewan or Manitoba than is often thought by outside observers. Alberta has its own agenda and it would not be easy to integrate its history, ideas, processes, and institutions within a new economic and political system. Indeed, Albertans have generally preferred the option of integrating with British Columbia, despite the fact that the Pacific province has always resisted this idea.

As seen in the 1993 federal election and national unity debates, Alberta and British Columbia feel alienated by the national political process and its lack of accessibility, integrity, and accountability. Citizens in these two provinces appear to be committed to seeking new solutions. Such feelings of discontent are well ingrained within the political landscape, and they provide a valuable resource for the Reform Party under the leadership of Preston Manning.

The Albertan sense of exclusion and perception of Canadian political reality have been built upon a set of circumstances and experiences that differs from those underlying the perspectives of the other two provinces. After years of division and in light of their distinct institutional and party experiences, Albertans draw their own conclusions about the advantages and disadvantages of developing regional linkages along the east-west axis.

Since 1905, in the course of dealing with various political and economic problems, Albertans have experimented with protest parties with dissimilar ideological traditions,[23] and a brand of province-building that Pratt and Richards characterized as an executive-dominated, "managerial and quasi-corporatist style of government."[24] These models of democracy and state intervention are a reflection of a pluralistic society that is constantly changing in response to new forces and challenges.

Alberta's cultural, political, and ideological setting was different from that of either Manitoba or Saskatchewan. Even if we ignored the issue of funding for a regional approach to restructuring, other factors would make it difficult for the three Prairie provinces to work together in defining and solving common problems.

The forces and ideas underlying the Albertan perspective of Canadian federalism and economic development have helped to reinforce a unique approach for resolving inequalities within Canadian society. Because feelings of dependence and lack of control emerged under different circumstances, province-building traditions in Alberta were more a product of American populism than British-style socialism. Albertans have experienced depression, exploitation, and economic prosperity. To understand current realities we need to analyze these experiences and forces, which have contributed to the growth of a unique culture in Alberta.

For instance, the province was once a "quasi-colonial" resource hinterland where "one in five Alberta residents at one point was American-born while the national ratio was less than one in twenty-five."[25] From these beginnings grew a strong free-enterprise spirit and a negative attitude toward socialism or any other model that called for the centralization of power along the east-west axis. The message sent out by the 1993 election has a special poignancy for those in Ottawa, such as Lloyd Axworthy, who support the integration solution. The image of the West as one region has taken a beating in recent political events, but these fundamental differences in opinion can be traced back through history.

Federal policies on freight rates, tariffs, and natural resources created a sense of alienation early in the province's history, as illustrated by the rapid demise of the provincial Liberal party. Unlike Saskatchewan, which the Liberals dominated until 1944, Alberta, from early on was more unorthodox than her Prairie neighbours.

The Progressives, originally the United Farmers of Alberta, were first organized in 1909, but the opportunity to enter politics did not occur until 1919. Under the leadership of Henry Wise Wood, they presented a new radical democratic model with the hope of increasing local control over development. The United Farmers of Alberta were more radical than democratic populists in Manitoba or other provinces. Indeed, David Laycock, in his analysis, *Populism and Democratic Thought in the Canadian Prairies,* concluded that the "radical democratic populism" espoused by leaders of the Alberta wing of the Progressive movement provided a unique vision and discourse for the country.[26] These events gave momentum to a unique approach to problem solving and the tradition of "going it alone" in Alberta.

In his description of the "crypto-Liberal" populism, which had great impact on early reform movements in Ontario, Manitoba, and Saskatchewan, Laycock provides a critical insight for understanding why Alberta's brand of populism stood alone. According to Laycock,

> W.L. Morton coined the word "crypto-Liberalism" to refer to the politics of a small group of federal MPs from Saskatchewan and Manitoba from 1921 to 1926. The prefix "crypto" indicated the questionable dedication of men such as J. Johnston, Robert Forke, and of course T.A. Crerar, to a grain grower politics independent of the Liberal party…The prefix "crypto" is warranted because, of all modes of prairie populism we will examine, crypto-Liberalism broke least with contemporary Liberal party ideology and policy perspectives in Canada. Its populism was thus closest to being a "disguised" Liberalism. This appellation is most appropriate for the leaders of the National Progressive party from Saskatchewan and Manitoba, and of almost all provincial administrations in the prairie provinces from 1905 to 1944.[27]

The radical, progressive ideas of the theoreticians proved to be incompatible with the cabinet-parliamentary system of government.

The Alberta brand of radical populism, which was influenced by American democratic thinking and the direct democracy model, was a spent force by 1935. However, dissatisfaction in the province provided fertile ground for the emergence of a new movement that continued the tradition of opposing federal policies that hurt local rural interests. Albertans have spent decades trying to create their own political environment; they have expended much energy attempting to scale down the negative impact of national integrationist policies.

In 1935, it became evident that Albertans were more open to right-wing American-inspired populist solutions than were the people of Saskatchewan or Manitoba. Premier William Aberhart presented new theories to explain the depressed conditions in the province. Ironically, the poor performance of the United Farmers of Alberta helped to create a countermovement to the unorthodox direct democracy theory. The leader of the Social Credit protest movement advocated a government controlled directly by experts, not by the people. During this time, the direct democracy model was replaced by "plebiscitarian populism"[28] This period was also the dawning of an era of right-of-centre government problem solving and community-building.

Again, the radical vision put forward by the premier proved to be incompatible with the institutional structure. Once in power, the new administration attempted to pass legislation designed to undermine the influence of Central Canadian banks. However, these attempts were either disallowed by Ottawa or ruled *ultra vires* by the courts. Since the government had no incentive to hire experts to implement a new experiment in monetary policy, Aberhart dominated every aspect of government decision making thereafter.

The Social Credit government, while authoritarian and antidemocratic, managed to stay in power by attacking socialism and defending provincial rights and more conservative values against outsiders. Albertans did not endorse the centralist assumptions of the CCF and were naturally suspicious of anyone inspired by the social planning concept. As the idea of planning gained strength in Ottawa, Manitoba, and Saskatchewan, Alberta became increasingly isolated. This isolation made it more difficult to organize provincial governments within the region around common causes or models.

Laycock argued that "Although Aberhart and the Social Credit press attacked planners, centralizers, and the bureaucratic state in the early years of the movement, it was not until 1937 that this became a centre-piece of their appeal. 'Bureaucracy' representing planning, centralization, collectivism, and a whole host of related evils, was eventually presented as the people's principal antagonist."[29]

The Social Credit promise of decentralization (which was inherited by the Conservative government in 1971) helps to explain why the West is so divided. There are substantial differences between the three prairie provinces in terms of economic development, political preferences, demographics, ideology, and external linkages. These differences will make it very difficult for the provinces to find a common ground.

Since 1937, Alberta's agenda has been to decentralize power within the federation and meet the threat posed by planners and state socialism. Laycock noted that "Decentralization became more important to Social Credit political discourse following federal and Supreme Court rejection of Social Credit legislation regarding credit regulation in 1937. Aberhart justified his attack on centralized power by claiming he had no choice, given Albertans' suffering and will for self-improvement."[30]

This attitude has been reflected in the actions of governments in Alberta ever since. Alberta province-building has been greatly influenced by the free-enterprise spirit and the desire to defend provincial interests against outsiders. Even though a more modern bureaucracy eventually emerged under the premiership of Peter Lougheed, Albertan governments have differed in their attitude to state planning from Saskatchewan or Manitoban governments.

John Richards and Larry Pratt knew this well when they compared the ambitions and styles of province-builders in Alberta and Saskatchewan:

> In Saskatchewan a resurgence of Fabianism within the government bureaucracy and the leadership of the NDP in the 1970s has provided the requisite entrepreneurship, but it lacks a broad popular base and has antagonized local business elites. Its future is precarious. In Alberta, by contrast, local entrepreneurial energy is being generated by the province's upwardly mobile urban middle class — in effect, a rising urban bourgeoisie comprising leading indigenous entrepreneurs, managers and upper-income professionals — linking private and public sectors in a quasi-corporatist alliance of interests.[31]

With the expansion of the Alberta economy in a north-south direction, inequalities among the Prairie provinces naturally increased. The Prairies were beset by internal differences over the need for further effective integration. From the beginning, Alberta was less open than other provinces to outside calls for further integration according to an integrated plan.

In summary, we have investigated the differences between the western provinces in order to understand the challenges facing those committed to an integrated approach to regional development. Even though the western provinces have faced common problems, they have been shaped by different experiences and forces. The West is not a monolithic entity; in reality, it is comprised of four distinct entities. As a consequence, regional integration remains a challenge, in spite of common pressures and a federal government that has encouraged regional solutions.

Lack of a Common Regional Vision

Regional inequality and alienation have shaped political behaviour in the West, but in unpredictable ways. For some, the solution was left-wing populism and increased centralization; for others, right-wing populism and further decentralization. These major ideological divisions have created obstacles for those pushing for a common approach to problem solving. For Albertans, who oppose any Central Canadian–inspired industrial development plan that fails to take into account local preferences and that weakens market opportunities, the north-south axis provides an alternative solution. In the other two prairie provinces, governments have tended to be more open to east-west solutions. Each provinces has its own resources, traditions, priorities, institutions, and interests to worry about.

Interregional relationships are more complex in the West, due to the vast differences in economic power and transnational influences. In particular, state-building and the entrepreneurial development strategies of governments in British Columbia and Alberta are less constrained by economic considerations and federal powers than strategies in "have-not" provinces in either periphery. Both provinces have been able to follow development paths and break the constraints of Canadian policies for the purpose of entering the international stage and defending their own interests. Consequently, and in response to transnational influences and the activities of Quebec,[32] both provinces have been motivated to establish new international ties.[33]

Ironically, the questioning of existing boundaries and the challenge of globalization have provided an opportunity for some subnational communities to develop new ways to decentralize power.

One clear implication of globalization for North America is that external forces and the possibility of cross-border regional economies are pushing the most competitive provinces in a north-south direction. In the climate of Canadian politics in the 1990s, subnational territorial interests are aware of the advantages associated with establishing their own priorities and competing in the international sphere.[34]

An Integrated Approach to Regional Development

The traditional approach to economic development in Canada was rather haphazard, having depended on old assumptions about the marketplace and established federal institutions. For generations, provincial governments operated in a vacuum, and Ottawa did not target regional economic development as an area that required federal intervention. With the emergence of new forces and theories, and Ottawa's commitment to solving the regional disparity problem in 1957, the western provinces suddenly faced great pressure to recognize the benefits of cooperative action. In the remainder of the chapter, we retrace the history of struggle over regional integration to explain the differences in the stakeholders' responses to regional cooperation and the need to advance new forms of wealth in the West.

Many factors influence the provinces' responses and adaptation to new challenges: economic form, historical experience, the political formation of the provincial state and its solidarity, and cultural and intellectual traditions. As explained in the first two chapters, the provinces have faced numerous difficulties, operating in a context where there were separate and competing institutions, agendas, and even imagined regions. As one might expect, new theories or approaches are often pushed by outsiders and thus reflect their needs. This has certainly been true for the historical drama that has been played out in the debate over integration in Canada. These factors help to explain why some provinces resisted a more integrated approach to economic development. To understand this resistance and the provinces' differing responses, we have discussed the history of development of each provincial economy and society. We can now turn to the history of regional cooperation and conflict in the West.

The creation of models for development has involved a great power struggle. Ottawa's prime concern has been to retain the capacity to intervene in the turf wars over integration: this power would ensure that the federal government's economic and political interests were well defended against the threat posed by continentalism and provincialism. A more integrated approach to managing the affairs of the western periphery had strong appeal to those in Ottawa who saw the benefits of achieving stronger regional economies, but along the east-west axis. Further, Ottawa has had to deal with the threat posed by underdevelopment, without tilting the power balances in the direction of continentalism or provincialism.

With legitimizing support provided by experts and faith that state intervention and rebuilding were both desirable and feasible, Ottawa addressed regional integration a number of times over the decades. Behind the frequent territorial and ideological conflicts over the integration question were the orthodox planners who gave respectability to the campaign, but who were never in control of the process. The experts helped to reinforce the myth that underdevelopment was solvable if rational principles were applied and capable people were recruited to fix the problem. They also helped to reinforce the idea that decentralization was less efficient for peripheral regions. Their principal contributions to the discourse were legitimizing the call for integration and challenging old provincial institutions, ideas, and cultures. These planners helped to promote the idea that economic planning could aid in overcoming internal obstacles to development.

As discussed in Chapter Two, the Rowell-Sirois Commission was a catalyst for introducing the concept of regional integration onto the national agenda;[35] but, like other controversial issues raised by the experts hired for this study, the issue lay dormant for years. Remarkably, the debate did not surface for at least two decades. By 1957, the regional disparity problem and the rise of a new federal commitment to dealing with these problems (based on a more integrated, rational economic approach) had changed the political dynamic. Another contributing factor was the rise of the Conservative Roblin government in Manitoba, and the premier's commitment to building a new coalition in support of a more integrated approach to economic and political development in the West.

Manitoba's Agenda and Subsequent Regional Initiatives

The premier took on this crusade for a number of reasons. At the end of the 1950s, Manitoba was not benefiting much from the status quo. By the time of the Second National Policy, industrialization was spreading to other western provinces, such as Alberta and British Columbia. These provinces had both the resources and organization necessary for taking full advantage of changing circumstances, new technologies, and a more integrated North American marketplace. The dynamic of provincialism, the pull of continentalism, and the natural inclination towards free-market economies in a north-south direction did little to advance the interests of Manitoba. Behind the call for a new approach to regional development was the obvious desire to re-establish Manitoba as the industrial centre of the region. Surpassing New Brunswick, Manitoba became the strongest proponent of change, no doubt influenced by Premier Roblin's central assumption that such a policy would "benefit his province the most."[36]

To understand the history of the struggle, we need to consider the desire of the Manitoban government to reassert control over the pattern of association in the West. In this struggle, Ottawa and Manitoba had much in common, since both were concerned about the continentalization of production. There was a natural fear that the country was losing control over the regional economies and that the growth of an increasingly transnational economy would add further to the unity problem, as well as to the problem of maintaining national programs.

In 1958, fully aware of Ottawa's interest in regional cooperation and the activities of the Atlantic Provinces Economic Council, Premier Roblin proclaimed his commitment to establishing a Prairie version of the experiment being conducted in the eastern peripheral region.[37] Manitoba decided that regional integration offered the best possibility for improving economic conditions.

In 1959, the Manitoba government provided the leadership and initiative required to put regional integration on the agenda. Under the direction of Premier Roblin, a number of officials produced a document that questioned the benefits of fragmentation, addressed common regional development problems, and offered a blueprint for cooperative action. The authors were highly critical of the lack of economic planning on a regional basis, and they concluded that the

Prairies were suffering and would probably continue to suffer unless there was a new commitment to cooperation.[38] In particular, the report cast doubt on the benefits of division and called for the establishment of a Prairie economic council.

The premier was a strong advocate of new attitudes and the need to reverse the trend towards further fragmentation into different provincial government centres. Presumably aware of the fact that wealthier provinces such as Alberta had their own distinctive bureaucratic, ideological, and institutional traditions to consider, the Manitoba government formulated a model that did not in any way threaten the territorial or jurisdictional interests of the provinces involved.

Despite these assurances, from the beginning, the province of Alberta was less than enthusiastic about the need to build a professional, regionally based technostructure. Ernest Manning, who served as Social Credit premier in Alberta between the years 1943 and 1963, promptly decided that it would be far more productive to have national discussions on key regional development issues instead of adopting a regional approach to planning. With fewer reasons to challenge the status quo and with the reputation for being "disinclined toward elaborate involvement in things of a regional nature,"[39] the Alberta government turned down the offer to participate in any new experiment. Even then, Alberta tended to view itself as an equal province within the federation, rather than as a member of a region. Saskatchewan Premier Tommy Douglas (1944–61) felt that the premiers should at least meet to consider the project; however, without Alberta's support the idea lay dormant for a few years.

The debate over the need to establish a regional economic council began again in 1964 as a result of Premier Manning's initiative. Little had actually changed, since the Albertan government saw such a body as performing only an advisory function. The shift towards the establishment of planning structures for federal-provincial bargaining had created a new kind of political dynamic in the country, and Alberta and the other provinces saw an advantage in working together to fight turf wars with Ottawa. The Albertan government came to recognize the need to explore new ways for defending its interests at intergovernmental conferences.

Ian McAllister places the debate in context: "1966 is an arbitrary dividing date. It lies mid-point of a decade that was a period of experimentation by industrialized countries in their effort to tackle regional problems associated with underdevelopment (e.g., the Canadian Atlantic Provinces, the Italian South, Northern Scotland, and Central and South Western France)."[40] In addition, despite the fact that nothing seemed to work, no modern "country would really dare refrain from using virtually any regional development instrument, not because they had confidence in its efficacy, but because they did not wish to admit they were not using it when their neighbours were."[41]

Between 1965 and 1972, the Prairie provinces began their experimentation with regional cooperation. Faced with a number of challenges and calls for structural change, the provinces decided to establish the Prairie Provinces Economic Council.[42] There was never any intent to limit or challenge provincial powers or institutions. Unlike the Maritimes, the Prairies did not establish a regional bureaucracy or permanent secretariat to assist the premiers. Rather, the new initiative provided an opportunity for the premiers to meet and discuss common problems. The lack of resources and the infrequency of meetings in the first three years and none in 1971, clearly restricted the opportunity to gain a better understanding of common problems in the region. However, these meetings facilitated useful exchanges of information between governments and provided an opportunity to initiate a few joint ventures.[43]

Ironically, the demand for coordination of common interests came at a time when the provinces were beginning to flex their muscles and had even more opportunities to control the process of development. Even poor provinces were never put in a position where they were forced to abandon old ways. During this time, the provinces did not feel pressured to change direction.

In 1970, five years after the first experiment in regional cooperation, the discourse over integration and the boundary issue in Western Canada was highlighted at the One Prairie Conference? at the University of Lethbridge, which was organized with the assistance of the Canada West Foundation and the *Lethbridge Herald.*[44] The conference acted as a conduit for those interested in debating the merits of the project. The campaign to undermine the threat posed by provincialism was no doubt strengthened by this conference, which brought together ordinary citizens, as well as a number of prominent academics, community leaders, and provincial and national state élites, who were there to broaden the discussion and examine new approaches.[45]

With the lack of regional institutions and the diversity of interests of the territorial competitors, the conceptions of the region put forward by the participants were very different. Alberta premier Harry Strom focused on the topic of a British Columbia–Alberta union. British Columbia premier W.A.C. Bennett took the opportunity to lay the basis for a discussion on the merits of dividing the country into five economic zones.[46] Bennett emphasized the uniqueness of British Columbia and the extent to which British Columbians see themselves as a separate entity. Much of his presentation, which was no doubt influenced by earlier conflicts with Ottawa and Alberta over the north, drew attention to the need for extending provincial boundaries in a north-south direction. He made a clear attempt to shift the agenda away from a Prairie union, as both premiers flexed their political muscles and tried to promote their own separate visions. As one might expect, the conference reflected the divisions within the region.

In the early 1970s, a federal initiative resulted in the decision to dismantle the Prairie Provinces Economic Council and establish the Western Premiers Conference. The national agenda embraced the need to reconsider traditional approaches to development in the West and Prime Minister Trudeau put forward the idea in the 1972 throne speech that the four premiers should meet with him to discuss common problems and develop a greater degree of cooperation on a regional basis. The intention was to "consider concrete programs for stimulating and broadening the economic and industrial base of Western Canada."[47] Given the lack of western representatives in his government, his commitment to rational planning, and concerns about the linkages between province-building and continentalism, Trudeau was looking for a new vehicle for initiating a program of cooperative action in the region. Again, Trudeau was clearly attempting to influence the evolution of the debate over regional integration, but from a national perspective.

The decision to hold another conference to discuss common problems and facilitate regional cooperation was clearly influenced by the federal government. In addition, the efforts of reformers and experts to push the concept of regional integration onto the public agenda were a contributing factor. Writers of public policy analysis in the liberal-pluralist camps have presented convincing evidence that a major determinant of new policy initiatives is often the campaigns of such individuals.[48] There is little question that the activities of experts influenced the integration debate in both peripheries. In addition, the prime minister, a former academic himself, was committed to challenging old ideas and institutions guided by a rational philosophy.

In an attempt to force the provincial governments to be more open, accountable, and less inward looking, Ottawa put forward the idea of holding yet another public forum on regional cooperation. This suggestion represented an obvious attack on the traditional federal discourse, which was insular and dominated by provincial governments. Ottawa wanted to see the rise of a new approach that was more open, democratic, rational, and regional. Likely influenced by the Maritime Union Study and the One Prairie Conference, which was attended by Jean Marchand (the minister responsible for regional development), Ottawa tried to create the conditions necessary for the rise of a regional discourse.[49] The federally inspired Western Economic Opportunities Conference that was held in Calgary in 1973 was a deliberate attempt to mobilize new regional forces and attack the power of the provinces.

Considering the approach and priorities of the Trudeau government at the time, the premiers took little comfort in the fact that Ottawa embraced the call for change. In their defence, the dilemmas they faced as political leaders in a highly fragmented and competitive federal system were numerous, and they played to very different audiences. Within such a context, the premiers had little option but to resist the federal government's pledge to restructure the system according to a more integrated approach. Ironically, any hint of a suggestion that Ottawa supported a regional approach to economic development elicited a defensive response from the premiers. In Canadian federalism, the path of provincial resistance to outside pressures for integration has been well travelled, and such a knee-jerk reaction was more a product of old patterns than a response to the merits of any debate.

Under these circumstances, it was a foregone conclusion that the forum would not accomplish very much, and Trudeau did not achieve his goal of establishing a new national policy.[50] The survival of provincial government autonomy was at stake and, with the legacy of distrust and competition in the field of federal-provincial relations, the premiers took the opportunity to place their items on the agenda for public consumption. Starting with issues such as transportation, economic development, agriculture, and the need to increase local control over financial institutions, the premiers worked together to defend their common interests.

There is little question that the premiers benefited from the historic meeting with Ottawa. The decision to prepare common position papers on key policy issues changed relations between the governments in Western Canada in significant ways — albeit not in the way anticipated by Ottawa. These papers were prepared by bureaucrats who specialized in intergovernmental relations and who were responsible for defending the territorial interests of their respective provinces against outsiders; this fact most likely influenced the outcome.[51] Although the federal government was the catalyst for the emergence of a new system of interprovincial relations in the region, Trudeau found few opportunities to gain support for Ottawa's list of priorities. The premiers refused to endorse Trudeau's vision of the country.

The premiers were clearly committed to building on the principles and policies agreed upon at the conference. They were united in their efforts to fight against what they perceived as a pattern of systematic discrimination against the region. In particular, they focused on challenging federal policies in a way that would create more opportunities for people living in the region without sacrificing provincial interests or powers. The western premiers felt that a united front would probably increase the West's influence in national politics, while not threatening existing provincial government institutions or powers.

Trudeau's attempt to develop a more integrated approach to regional concerns ultimately provided the provincial governments with a vehicle for taking on the federal government. The premiers had their own considerable demands at the intergovernmental table, and there was no evidence that Ottawa's goal of establishing a new national policy was ever on their agenda. Well-entrenched, the premiers seized control of the regional experiment for their own advantage.[52] Instead of responding to Trudeau's challenge, the premiers turned the situation around in their favour. The most significant by-product of these proceedings was the decision to establish the Western Premiers' Conference as the basic mechanism for discussing and coordinating regional policies.

With the premiers firmly in control and no permanent regional structures in place to challenge the province-based power-sharing system, the four provincial governments moved resolutely away from the radical changes intended by Ottawa. Over the years, these rather informal meetings have produced few agreements dealing with intra-regional, internal, or functional issues. Indeed, the premiers have never shown much interest in establishing a more institutional-ized system of intergovernmental cooperation.

Elton commented that "the most important function performed by the Western Premiers Conferences has been that of providing a mechanism and forum for coordinating the western provinces' inter-actions with the federal government."[53] The system of interprovincial consultation was designed to deal more with "external" than "inter-nal" challenges such as the territorial and jurisdictional interests of the provinces. Although Ottawa had hoped the regional forum would be the catalyst for setting intergovernmental relations on a more conciliatory path in the West, the premiers turned the tables. Under-lying the discussion of common problems and regional solutions was the desire to assert provincial sovereignty, especially as far as the wealthier provinces were concerned.

The premiers have fully exploited the regional experiment as an instrument of provincialism over the years. Without organizational ligatures between the possible supporters of a more regional ap-proach, proponents of effective integration were in no position to gain control over the agenda. As one might expect, the premiers took full advantage of the opportunity to defend their turf against Ottawa. A prime example is the 1976 joint initiative, which dealt with the premiers' view that Ottawa was interfering in more and more areas of provincial jurisdiction. Rather than protesting on an individual basis, the premiers pooled their resources and established the re-gional Task Force on Constitutional Trends. Headed by the ministers responsible for intergovernmental relations, the task force set out to document federal intrusions into provincial matters in a clear attempt to defend provincialism against outside attack.

There have been other benefits associated with such an informal system of interprovincial cooperation. For example, in spite of the highly competitive federal structure, these subnational political units have been involved in a number of worthy cooperative ventures.[54] In addition, the particiating governments have undoubtedly established better working relationships. If nothing else, these discussions have highlighted issues important to Western Canada, while establishing regular lines of communication between the governments in the western periphery.

In consideration of the interdependent relationships between near-border populations in Western Canada (coupled with the call for the elimination of international borders)[55] more and more governments are also embracing the need to establish new kinds of relationships with their American neighbours. The rise of more formal interactions between the western premiers and the western governors, as well as new bilateral relations between individual provinces and their state counterparts,[56] has clearly aggravated the national unity problem. With the questioning of the logic of boundaries, borderland regions have gained momentum and power.

New Realities

Ironically, the questioning of boundaries by Ottawa has helped to reinforce the pull of continentalism in the west and these intergovernmental forums have been pivotal for developing common policies in a north-south direction. In the 1990s, calls for the restructuring of Prairie/Western Canada have resurfaced. As in the past, this campaign has been influenced by external actors and the forces of globalization, transnationalism, and interdependence. Yet, solutions have been difficult to find within the confines of a territorially segmented, pluralistic structure, in which different actors play to different audiences. Harmony among territorial competitors has always been rare in Canadian politics. These days, federal spending powers have declined, major divisions exist between "have" and "have-not" provinces, and national borders are becoming more porous (with provinces like British Columbia, Alberta, Quebec, and Ontario forming new alliances with their subnational counterparts south of the border). In such a context, reaching a consensus on the integration question is an even greater challenge.

With the impact of the changing international economy on ideas, culture, policy, and local economic circumstances, Canadian nationalists (and anyone else committed to the goal of defending the east-west axis) are naturally concerned about losing control over future patterns of development in the country. Lloyd Axworthy and the federal Liberals have attempted to add a new twist to the regional integration option and force the issue back onto the agenda. On the other hand, as evidenced in Paul Martin's recent budget, the trend towards decentralization is on the increase as Ottawa's spending power declines. Moreover, Lloyd Axworthy's batting average has not been very good in recent years. Regional integration may suffer the same fate as Axworthy's social policy initiatives.

The Liberal's Red Book (produced for the 1993 federal election)[57] and Axworthy's leadership have certainly influenced the debate over the need to redraw boundaries and build upon the concepts of "Alsaskatoba" and even "British Alsaskatoba."[58] The extent of such influence on the debate over the integration question is difficult to estimate, and as in the past, there are a number of obstacles standing in the way of resolution.

One important milestone in the struggle to build a new consensus on the regional integration question was the holding of a conference on Prairie integration. Lloyd Axworthy relied on the old strategy of assembling representatives of government, business and labour with experts to discuss the desirability and feasibility of regional integration and organized a conference that produced a "blueprint of economic renewal for the Prairie region."[59] In an attempt to address globalization, the threat of Quebec nationalism, and province-building, Axworthy played a pivotal role in bringing together people who were interested in the regional option. These actions were understandable for a left-leaning federal politician who grew up in Manitoba.

Conclusion

The debate over the merits of regional integration, corresponding in form to new forces and ideas in the environment, will no doubt be influenced by the institutional structure and those who operate within such a context. As in the past, there will be an interplay between ideas, structures, and process, where competing interests will respond to new challenges on the basis of their own particular needs. As the perceived limits of the state are influenced by globalization and economic and technological changes, new ideas, cultures, institutions, and patterns of economic and political development will emerge. Just as previous generations could not imagine the political changes that would occur in the country in response to constantly changing circumstances, we find it almost impossible to forecast future trends in state-building or patterns of development in Western Canada. Yet, unless steps are taken to bridge the differences between the provinces in terms of issues such as institutional experience, culture, and economic structure, the goal of harmonious integration will never be achieved.

Five

British Columbia: A Distinct Economic Zone?

There are obvious links between the regional/national integration question in British Columbia and the threat of Quebec nationalism to the Canadian political order. We need to take stock of the contending forces that underlie an old feud between the defenders of a five-region vision of Canada and the supporters of other normative frameworks.

It might be useful to begin our analysis of British Columbia by highlighting Hershel Hardin's thought-provoking interpretations of Canadian economic history. His assessment of the Canadian economic culture (which he contends has been influenced by a shared commitment to interregional redistribution and Canadian public enterprise) seems to have had less of an impact on British Columbia than on other provinces.[1] Within British Columbia, the forces and ideas that envisaged a different perspective of Canadian federalism began with the premierships of Richard McBride (1903–15), Dufferin Pattullo (1933–41), and W.A.C. Bennett (1952–72). If we look at previous struggles over territorial integrity involving these premiers, we shall not be tempted (as Hardin was) to underestimate the historical force of a defensive strategy that was born out of the reaction against planners, Ottawa, and the threat posed by integration.

Hershel Hardin stresses the importance of confronting the fundamental contradictions and paradoxes that have contributed to the emergence of a unique economic culture in Canada. Rather than lamenting the threat posed by continentalism and Quebec nationalism, and the challenge presented by the regions to national unity, he tries to illuminate the contributions of these contending forces to the growth of a vibrant Canadian culture. As Hardin observed,

> We discover a Canadian economic civilization based on
> powerful indigenous roots: first of all on the contradiction
> between Canada and the United States, or more precisely
> the contradiction between the small Canadian domestic
> market next to the large American one; and secondly on
> the contradictions between French and English Canadas
> and between the regions and the centre. Out of the first
> has grown a unique entrepreneurial style which might best
> be described as "Canadian public enterprise." Out of the
> internal contradictions has come the adoption, and the
> elaboration as a fundamental principle, of the unAmerican
> transactional mode of redistribution, as opposed to the
> American transactional mode of market exchange.[2]

In addition, Hardin espouses the view that the frontier experience
was different in Canada, and, as a consequence, a distinct method for
sharing wealth and power emerged. He tries to convince the reader
that the combination of these external and internal contradictions
reinforced a unique approach for dealing with inequalities in Canadian society.

From his perspective, such cultural traditions and Canada's redistributive culture, in particular, are closely linked to the need to
accommodate Quebec. According to Hardin, "Quebec being a region
not like the others, its existence in Canada gives to the redistribution
culture an unambiguously unAmerican schema all its own, totally
unimaginable anywhere but in the Canadian context."[3]

In the judgement of Hardin: "What is most revealing in all this is
not that there is so much grumbling and querulousness on the part of
the richer provinces — Ontario, Alberta and British Columbia at the
moment — but there is so remarkably little."[4] Indeed, he argues that
Canadians have been prepared to accept the interregional redistribution principle "because to question it is to question the existence of
Canada itself."[5]

Conditions have changed since Hershel Hardin presented his discussion of Canadian economic history nearly two decades ago. In the
1990s, it is acceptable even in Ontario to question the costs associated with interregional redistribution. Furthermore, with issues such
as globalization, a massive debt problem, and high levels of unemployment in the forefront, few people in the country are calling for
the establishment of new megaprojects or crown corporations. Ques-

tions are also being raised regarding the implications of redistributing wealth by means of the welfare state on a territorial basis. It is an era when few people are promoting the need to rely upon the state to redistribute wealth.

Especially in British Columbia and Alberta, the attitude that the country can no longer afford to placate Quebec has emerged. This attitude was reflected in both the 1993 election, which saw the rise of the Reform Party, and the national referendum on the Charlotte-town Accord. Hardin's thesis provides little insight for interpreting the weakening national economic logic and bitter regional tensions that have been generated by Quebec's "cheque-book" approach to federalism and restructuring.

It is perhaps time to revisit Hardin's interpretation of Canadian economic history. This turn of events offers compelling reasons for questioning old assumptions and theories. At the very least, such changes suggest that Hardin may have exaggerated the level of support for interregional redistribution in provinces such as British Columbia, especially as far as W.A.C. Bennett was concerned. To understand current realities, we will analyze the experiences of British Columbia over the past few decades. Along the way, we should gain a better appreciation of the province's contemporary condition.

The primary purpose of this chapter is to explore the history of province-building in the Pacific province and the historical struggle to resist an east-west axis approach to economic and political development in the country. British Columbia warrants special attention because, for decades, political leaders in that province have deliberately resisted the call for interregional redistribution of wealth. They also worked against outside attempts to build a transportation infrastructure along the east-west axis that aimed to control the spatial pattern of economic development in British Columbia according to the needs of external political competitors. Ottawa and British Columbia had different ideas about regional development policy and whether north-south or east-west patterns of association should be promoted and even encouraged by common policies. A better appreciation of past events might help us to make more sense of current realities.

A critical issue is the lack of attention focused on cross-border relations and the history of struggle over the British Columbia border. Despite a long history of conflict over the provincial boundary, a large body of research to inform public opinion does not exist. Part of the problem might be the absence of a Provincial Hansard until the early 1970s. The task of gathering hard data on province-building has not been easy, especially during the W.A.C. Bennett years. Adding further to the problem is that "Compared to the outpouring of economic, and economic-history, studies of the prairie provinces or even of the Maritime provinces, British Columbia has had remarkably little attention."[6]

Another factor may be the myths, negative images, and stereotypes about British Columbian politics that recur in Canadian historiography and the media. This pattern has been consistent for generations and helps to explain the lack of research on the British Columbia agenda. Often portrayed as a lotus-land or fantasy-land, the company province, the spoiled child of confederation, or the province with a split personality, British Columbia has received little respect.[7]

Nor have her politicians remained unscathed: they are often characterized as incompetent, amateur, wacky, unprincipled, without vision and shortsighted, and have been called pawns of special interests and Canada's *Poujadists*.[8] Not surprisingly, few people pay close attention to their ambitions for or visions of the country. Although such images may be soothing for supporters of interregional sharing of wealth, these negative attitudes have most likely inhibited critical thinking and research. It is time for a change in attitude and a marked redirection of research from the centralist paradigms that have dominated the Canadian literature.

As A.D. Scott argued, the call for "eastern economic nationalism"[9] that has been championed by "Ontario-based writers [has] simply equated Canada's national interests with the continuing dominance of 'metropolitan centres.'"[10] In an attempt to understand frontier development in North America, scholars such as "Lower, Creighton, Saywell, McNaught, [and] Morton, write mostly about the success of Ontario, plus or minus Quebec, in not relaxing its hold on the west or the north, in spite of foreign temptations."[11] Within British Columbia, these theories about Canadian nationalism, and the kind of integration they seek, represent a direct attack on local resources and development priorities. Scott is correct in his assessment that British Columbians have good reason to feel threatened by those who advocate east-west integration.

British Columbian premiers have faced many difficulties in pushing their agendas within a political system that discouraged and even denied the benefits of building communication and transportation linkages in a north-south direction in every province.[12] Over the years, they have encountered resistance to their attempts to ensure that the province was allowed to operate in its own political environment.

In British Columbia, conflicts over the integration question strike at the heart of a division within the federation that originated generations ago. Yet, few Canadians outside the province are even aware of the issue. It is clear that we need to examine the ideas of political community in British Columbia that are relevant to the defensive expansionist theme.

Lack of Common Interests and the Struggle over Territory

British Columbia is unique; its separateness and alienation is a product of geography and different economic and social conditions.[13] The unique way British Columbians define the problems of underdevelopment is also a reflection of underlying institutional inclinations and tensions. Because traditional parties and established national institutions failed to address local concerns, new forms of political stewardship and new approaches to the problem of underdevelopment emerged. The unwavering commitment demonstrated by populist premiers in trying to gain greater control over the process of development suggests that we have either underestimated or neglected the forces that have contributed to the politics of dissociation in British Columbia.

As Morley argued, "B.C. politics are inherently paradoxical and this has been the case since the time of Union with Canada."[14] David Elkins further suggests that, "If ambiguity and contradictions are the hallmarks of Canadian identity, as many argue, then B.C. is the most Canadian of all provinces."[15] These conflicts help to explain not only the history of protest in the province, but also why various governments' preoccupation with the provincial unity problem. Just as Canadian nationalists have often used the threat of American imperialism to reinforce a sense of alienation and community, British Columbian leaders have focused much attention on the threat to the provincial state created by Canadian integrationist policies.

One theme has dominated British Columbian politics and isolated the province from the Prairie provinces: the desire to integrate the community along a Pacific axis. British Columbia does not feel akin to her Prairie neighbours, and their concerns and ambitions are, to a great extent, irrelevant to local considerations. British Columbia's physical geography and internal divisions are important factors in understanding the strength of the populist streak and the determination to develop and maintain a viable identity in the face of outside pressures to assimilate and share wealth with other communities in Canada.

British Columbia is both blessed and cursed by her diverse and rugged terrain. In such a setting a number of premiers have wrestled with the problem of creating and maintaining a sense of identity by building a more integrated transportation system. Each premier has understood that defending the territorial and jurisdictional interests of the province would be much simpler if there emerged a unique, vital provincial culture and common vision. Any attempt to understand British Columbia must take into account the physical setting and its reinforcement of a weak sense of provincial identity. British Columbian premiers have tended to downplay issues and conflicts that cut across the provincial boundary. Instead, they have focused on the provincial unity and the inequality of power and wealth within rather than outside the province. Since McBride's leadership, various leaders have attempted to deal with the regional disparity problem by building an infrastructure to address the issue of spatial inequality.

In reality, there are at least ten regions within the provincial boundary; this diversity is clearly reflected in the social and political geography of British Columbia.[16] Jean Barman states that "the differing topography, geological formation, and human habitation of the ten regions comprising British Columbia point up the complexity of the larger whole. The regions' distinctive attributes begin to explain why impressions of British Columbia are so diverse and, just as important, why the province's development has differed from that of other parts of Canada."[17] Secluded populations have always created special problems for the provincial level of government. Within such a context, which is compounded by a constantly changing population base, the premiers have to establish an integrated transportation and communication system and reinforce a sense of identity, while fostering economic development. Providing both the infrastructure and vision required to integrate the province is challenging, especially when outside critics question the costs involved.

To complicate matters, British Columbia began with few established political traditions. It was a place without a set of myths, political institutions, or a set of assumptions for interpreting and responding to the outside world. Party lines were introduced as late as 1903,[18] and there were few opportunities for uniting such diverse elements within a disciplined party system. Rural British Columbians shared only a pioneering spirit and the desire to defend their interests against established élites. As Black indicated, "An extreme orientation towards action is typical of frontier communities — as is a lack of respect for traditional political procedures."[19] Thus, British Columbian governments have been preoccupied with creating a sense of solidarity, and the mobilization of the population against outsiders has proved to be an effective means for accomplishing this goal.

With respect to the threat to British Columbia's independence by outside forces, various administrations over the decades have tried to unite the province through the building of a physical infrastructure in a north-south direction. Perceiving the development of an east-west communication and transportation system as a threat to the territorial and jurisdictional interests of the province, various leaders since McBride's premiership set out to develop an alternate north-south infrastructure. Indeed, the McBride administration had introduced an ambitious rail-building policy after the British-American Commission established the Alaskan boundary in the north and restricted British Columbia's access to the northern frontier. McBride's "personal dream of developing the northland" originated in his childhood and remained with him throughout his political career.[20] As Roy indicated, "Above all, he never forgot British Columbia was composed of a number of regions and localities. Thus his railway programs were designed to appeal to most of the settled parts of the province."[21]

Premier McBride was best-known for solidification of party lines, his ambitious railway plans, and his reputation as an Ottawa-basher: he was a leader who thrived in a frontier environment.[22] He also provided a role model for future leaders of the province. The Conservative premier survived an unprecedented twelve years in public office because of his forthrightness, his confidence in the development possibilities of British Columbia, and his willingness to go to great lengths to maintain the territorial integrity and political autonomy of the province.

His unorthodox style and determination to open up frontier areas of the province were popular with voters, and, by focusing much attention on the need for "better terms" from Ottawa and on frontier development, he provided a convenient way to pull the disjointed regions of the province together.[23] Although McBride's Pacific Great Eastern (PGE) Railway did not unite North Vancouver with Fort

George, the Peace River area, or Alaska, as he had intended, the northern dream was handed down to future administrations. Roy argued that the PGE was "McBride's partial answer to increasing interest, especially in Vancouver, in a direct connection from that city to the GTP's (Great Trunk Pacific) main line and beyond to the Peace River, which was then falling into Edmonton's commercial orbit."[24]

Province-Building under Dufferin Pattullo

The next great figure in British Columbian politics to take on McBride's project was Dufferin Pattullo. Unfortunately, he had fewer opportunities to realize his ambitions for remaking the province, since he operated in a time of economic collapse, within a traditional party structure dominated by élites. Nevertheless, his optimism about the development prospects of the province (especially in the north), his reputation as an anti-establishment figure, and his five-region conception of Canada all had a major impact on the thinking of W.A.C. Bennett, who inherited the job of implementing these ideas when economic conditions later improved.[25] Implementation was easier once a protest party system was established.

The influence of Pattullo's leadership on the rise of a new normative model for restructuring the province and country was a significant factor in the contemporary discourse over the territorial ambitions of British Columbia. The new model addressed the struggle to open up the north and focused on ensuring that British Columbia was not inhibited from developing her own empire and resolving her own development problems. The policy was defensive in an east-west direction and expansionary along the north-south axis. This concept had an indelible impact on future premiers, and it reflected the conditions within a political system organized around competing interests. It was a curious paradox; yet, it made sense in a province often characterized by nineteenth-century Canadians as "the West beyond the West."[26] Pattullo's preoccupation with a five-region model for Canada's reconstruction was greatly influenced by these underlying cultural and economic realities.

Pattullo was greatly influenced by Ontario premier Oliver Mowat's model for province-building and the struggle between Ontario, Ottawa, and Manitoba over the location of the provincial boundary. The issue gained momentum in 1878 when Sir John A. Macdonald disallowed a provincial statute that gave Ontario control over the territory. In 1884, the British Privy Council, who had heard from Premier Mowat, ruled in Ontario's favour. Pattullo had strong views about the need to exploit the power of the provincial state to open up new frontiers and control the process of development.[27] When Patullo was growing up, Oliver Mowat was a regular visitor at his home. In fact, Pattullo's father was even a commissioner for the province of Ontario in the struggle with Manitoba over the boundary issue.[28] From such a background, Premier Pattullo became the next champion of provincial rights and northern development in British Columbia.

As far as Pattullo was concerned, the provincial state in British Columbia had a positive role to play in resolving the provincial unity puzzle and development problems. He went to great lengths to fight Ottawa and anyone else who opposed his expansion plans. As Mitchell noted, "Entwined with this vision was his imperialistic desire to annex the Yukon territory and thus increase even more the scope and richness of B.C.'s northern prospects."[29] Premier Pattullo was determined to make British Columbia (with an extended northern border) a separate economic empire. As far as he was concerned, "opening up the north depended on establishing lines of communication and transportation,"[30] and any outside attempt to undermine such a plan was indefensible. He argued that it made sense for everyone involved to implement a more realistic approach to development.

Long before W.A.C. Bennett began his crusade, Duff Pattullo had been convinced of the merits of following the example of state-directed province-building first established in Ontario. He was vigilant in his attempts to persuade others that the problems of underdevelopment in British Columbia were caused by outsiders manipulating the development process. As a consequence, he vehemently opposed the claims in the Rowell-Sirois Commission report that British Columbia's problems were internal. In rejecting the centralist, orthodox assumptions made by Ottawa and the authors of the study, he planned on "going it alone," and was even contemplating establishing a "semi-autonomous provincial economy."[31] Such resistance was shaped by his strong faith in the development potential of the province and by his suspicion of outsiders. Furious at what he considered to be a betrayal, he was determined that the report should never be implemented.

The decision to oppose the Rowell-Sirois report was a watershed, not only because it eventually destroyed Pattullo's political career, but also because it contributed to the eventual collapse of the traditional party system in the province. At the time, Pattulo's decision to walk away from the table and form an alliance with the premiers of Alberta and Ontario was highly controversial. The three provinces worked together to obstruct the implementation of the study, which focused on solving national problems through the implementation of a new integrated model at the expense of provincial concerns and priorities.

Pattulo's decision was significant for another reason: even though W.A.C. Bennett would later model his populist style and northern vision on Pattulo's example, Bennett originally decided to enter public life because he also opposed the centralist thrust of the Rowell-Sirois study.[32] However, unlike Pattullo, he felt the province should have stayed at the conference and defended its interests. Young Bennett, who later became a passionate defender of the five-region concept of Canada and the northern vision, spent twenty years in office, controlling patterns of spatial interaction within the province through the construction of physical infrastructures in the frontier regions. Many of his policies were patterned on Pattullo's grandiose conception of a semi-autonomous empire, but he operated under different circumstances.

Pattullo's model for reconstruction helped to legitimize Bennett's populist and controversial approach to governing. These circumstances provide the context for Bennett's persistence in opposing encroachments on provincial territory. Pattullo's experience loomed large in Bennett's thinking because it reinforced his strong distrust of local élites, experts, and the Ottawa establishment. A new era in British Columbian politics was beginning. With the rise of a distinct protest party system under Bennett's leadership, the five-region model was now a permanent fixture on the Canadian agenda. This potent combination heightened tensions with Ottawa and reinforced an isolationist stance in joint problem-solving ventures.

In politics, timing is everything. Perhaps Pattulo's biggest mistake was walking away from the negotiation table at a time when Canadian patriotism ran high and everyone was pulling together to fight a common cause. Given the impact of the war on national pride, most commentators were highly critical of the premier's actions. As Burns argued,

> There is no doubt at all that his stand at Ottawa was almost universally unpopular with most of his colleagues, and

with the public. The loss of his majority in 1941, in an
election that he should have won and expected to win
easily, cost him the premiership and the leadership of the
Liberal Party and led to the coalition government under
his finance minister John Hart, which assumed office in
December 1941.[33]

The decision to form a coalition government was predicated on the
need to facilitate a more integrated approach to planning and problem
solving within the larger federal system; however, in the end, it very
likely contributed to the rise of the protest party structure and the
complete separation of the provincial and federal party systems. The
politics of exclusion, which was naturally reinforced by the collapse
of traditional party support and the rise of a confederal, protest party
system, provided a new outlet for mobilizing territorial interests. The
no-nonsense populist approach to government established by W.A.C.
Bennett may not have emerged without the unusual combination of
events that began with the decision by traditional party élites to oust
Pattullo.

W.A.C. Bennett's Rise to Power

Any account of the history of the Social Credit's style of populism
should include a review of the events that led to the rise of W.A.C.
Bennett as premier. A critical factor behind Bennett's unorthodox
approach to implementing Pattullo's ideas was the way various élites
(both inside and outside the province) had treated the former Liberal
premier. Early in his political career, Bennett set out to ensure that
he dominated the public agenda.

Initially, the Liberal-Conservative coalition government under
John Hart was successful, even though the decision to oust Pattullo
and combine the two parties weakened party identities and loyalties.
In 1941, conditions were ideal for the new experiment in power
sharing. It was only later, when the government was under fire, that
these changes created problems for the Liberals and Conservatives.

As is often the case in politics, the calm and tranquil times did not
last very long. In 1946, cracks within the foundations reached the
surface with the sudden death of Conservative leader, R. L. Maitland.
Suddenly, the leadership question and disputes over cabinet representation were central issues, which contributed to problems of fac-
tionalism. The honeymoon had come to an abrupt end.

Incidentally, W.A.C. Bennett, who was first elected as a Conservative MLA (Member of the Legislative Assembly), was a member of the coalition. At one point, he had even been offered a position in the cabinet, but he declined.

During these years, Bennett travelled the frontier regions of the province, learning first-hand about the development problems that confronted isolated communities on a daily basis. As an active player on the twelve-member Post-War Rehabilitation Council, Bennett "derived most of the ideas he was to put into effect later."[34] Young Bennett came to understand and appreciate the problems of underdevelopment in the periphery, and, like Pattullo and McBride before him, he became a supporter of the need to use the provincial state as an instrument of defence.

By 1947, Bennett was critical of many aspects of government policy, and, by 1952, he had contributed in a significant way to the collapse of the coalition arrangement. Originally working within the traditional party alliance, W.A.C. Bennett led a group of renegade Conservative back-benchers who had concerns about Herbert Anscomb's leadership and approach to social and economic management. By March 1951, the abrasive and independent-minded Bennett had had enough, and he crossed the floor to sit as an independent.

The election of 1952 was full of surprises. The original intention was to sever the coalition arrangement without providing an opportunity for the socialists to form a government; however, in the end, the traditional party system was replaced by a protest party structure with the CCF as the opposition to the new Social Credit government.

Then, in a deliberate attempt to undermine the threat posed by the CCF, the Liberals and Conservatives changed the electoral system. By introducing an "alternative voting system," they intended to enhance traditional party support at the expense of the left.[35] The goal was to retain the benefits of the alliance while the parties remained separate, but the plan backfired.

Ironically, the confusion created by the new electoral system provided ideal conditions for the emergence of an entirely different party system and a new style of leadership. Although the CCF mobilized a higher percentage of the popular vote, the leaderless and scattered Social Credit Party ended up in the winner's circle. Many of the voters picked the Social Credit Party as their second choice, and this support paved the way for a regime shift and the creation of a confederal, protest party system in British Columbia.

W.A.C. Bennett became the leader of the party, as well as premier. He sold himself as the only alternative to socialism and since he was not supported by major economic and political interests inside or outside the province, Bennett had few debts to pay. The new premier inherited a protest party system that provided much more autonomy than was possible during the Pattullo administration. Thus, Bennett was in a much better position to defend the five-region model against Ottawa, experts, and other competitors. The combination of an insular party structure and financial independence provided the means for Bennett to give relevance to Pattullo's vision.

The Politics of Territoriality and its Institutional Roots

W.A.C. Bennett made a point of criticizing the traditional academic, economic, and political élites, who were seen as contributing to the development problems of British Columbia. By his definition, these outsiders, who had little appreciation of local development prospects, were part of the problem, not the solution.

The primary change with regard to Bennett's management of economic and political development was his determination to maintain control over every aspect of policy formulation and implementation within the province. He paid little respect to experts or any other élites who were critical of the British Columbia agenda. The populist politician preferred to manage the economy without experts who were critical of the hopes and aspirations of frontier societies.

As Noel argued, "Provincial Premiers occupy roles of unique significance in Canadian politics. Each in his own province has a standing and a public visibility unmatched by any federal politician, except perhaps the Prime Minister himself."[36] With his domination of the party and its cabinet, legislature, crown corporations, and financial reporting system, Bennett was well placed to challenge old images and impose his own definition of the problems and policy challenges facing British Columbia. By challenging old definitions and blaming Ottawa, the experts, and the bureaucrats who had always dominated the parties on the right and left (as he himself had), the premier was able to justify a "plebiscitarian" approach to government.[37] Ironically, as more state structures were expanded and an infrastructure was built to open up the frontier, the province became more isolated within the federation, and there were fewer opportunities for popular participation.

The key to the new regime's dedication to opening up the hinterland and finally solving the enigma of underdevelopment was shifting British Columbia's geohistorical position within the context of the federation. Hence, the initial intent was to defy the pull of the east-west axis and defend the provincial boundary against outside penetration. By erecting a physical infrastructure, Bennett was determined to reinforce transportation and communication lines in a north-south direction. The primary objective was to gain greater power to control the spatial pattern of economic development within the province.

At the report of the Royal Commission on the British Columbia Railway in 1977, Bennett and former members of his cabinet presented evidence that the Social Credit administration had deliberately gone to great lengths to resist attempts by the Alberta and federal governments to impose their development priorities on the province.[38] From the beginning, the Bennett government was concerned about the threat posed by outsiders in frontier regions of British Columbia, and the need for an aggressive response. There are obvious links between these concerns and subsequent events.

Guided by the premier's ambitions and natural suspicion of planners and other élites, the government designed and implemented a new development strategy without relying on a large bureaucratic structure or team of experts. This initiative provided an important opportunity for Bennett to control the agenda and put in place his vision. Implicit in the defensive expansionist approach to development was the assumption that the government itself played a key role in controlling patterns of associational activity within the province. His policies and conclusions echoed Pattullo's five-region idea of Canada.

It was highly significant (especially given current realities) that, in 1960, Bennett opened the first Alaska–Yukon–British Columbia Conference (which he organized) by discussing the need to establish new linkages in the Pacific sphere and the importance of involving California, Oregon, and Washington State in future discussions.[39] The notion that the Canadian federal system consisted of five economic zones had a major impact on his ideas for development, and it provided the incentive for challenging other visions of the country.[40] As Mitchell argued, "Bennett was completely serious in his advocacy of a five-region Canada,"[41] and the need to reinforce new linkages along the north-south axis. It was a clear endorsement of the need to annex the north and strengthen ties within this borderland region of North America.

According to Lauren McKinsey and Victor Konrad,

> Borderlands is a region jointly shared by two nations that houses people with common social characteristics in spite of the political boundary between them. In a more narrow sense, borderlands can be said to exist when shared characteristics within the region set it apart from the country that contains it: residents share properties of the region, and this gives them more in common with each other than with members of their respective cultures. More broadly, the borderlands is an area in which interaction has a tempering effect on the central tendencies of each society.[42]

Even though Bennett's questioning of the benefits of national economic integration generated tensions with Ottawa and other provinces, these events attracted little attention at the time because the premier adopted an isolationist policy and "discouraged regular intergovernmental contacts."[43] Besides, few people held respect for British Columbia's agenda. Bennett felt that such an approach to restructuring made perfect sense, although his musings about Canada as five distinct economic zones (which had great appeal to many British Columbian voters) were seen by critics as a fantasy or a joke. Especially since the time of Pattullo, this definition of region has had much appeal for those seeking a rallying point for British Columbians of all stripes. This is a major reason why Bennett took such a strong position when it came to outside attacks on his vision. His popularity was closely linked to this issue and the extent to which development was controlled by the province.

Bennett saw good reasons for transforming the country according to the changing economic realities of North America[44] and he announced these ideas at the 1969 constitutional conference. Recognizing that there had been twelve boundary changes since 1867, Bennett, in a passionate exchange with Premier Robarts of Ontario, defended the five-regions concept and the need to extend the British Columbia boundary into the north. Despite considerable economic prosperity, an "underdog" attitude prevailed among British Columbians; in combination with self-confidence, this attitude made for an unusual style of entrepreneurial leadership that was not well understood in other parts of the country. As Bennett stated at the time,

> I am going to tell you at one time Ontario was a very small Province. You got all your northern territories. Why not British Columbia? Why not the Prairies, my friend? Fair treatment to one; fair treatment to all.[45]

Bennett's model for restructuring the system rested on the assumption that proper boundary maintenance was imperative for the growth of a more stable and prosperous country. Imbued with a British Columbian ideology that stressed a value system different from that described by Hardin, the premier was critical of any plans calling for sharing wealth "between" provinces through centrally administered programs. At the time, the premier was highly critical of the concept of equalization, believing that money should not be wasted on regions with less economic hope. He argued that it made little sense to exploit national spending power to prop up arbitrary regions within the country when there were distinct economic zones with much more potential for generating new forms of wealth. His arguments against the merits of equalization directly challenged the principle of interregional redistribution.

Indeed, Bennett believed it made little sense to provide "fiscal support to an economically weak and natural resource-poor Atlantic region." His solution was to provide assistance to needy individuals through a "nationally administered guaranteed annual" income program and to meet the challenges of regional disparity guided by his five-region vision of Canada.[46]

In the 1960s, Bennett's model for development and restructuring was often criticized because it directly attacked old ideas, institutions, and established élites. The premier simply did not have the power to change the national agenda at the time. Remarkably, in the 1990s, others have come to see the advantages of embracing a borderland region concept as both an empirical and normative model for restructuring the federation.[47] We have also seen more questions raised about the merits of redistribution and regional development programs.

Throughout his political career, Bennett was critical of federal regional development initiatives and, in particular, the practice of exploiting national spending power "to encourage unsound development in some areas which for various reasons will never be self-supporting."[48] He hypothesized that Ottawa's encroachment on regional development matters posed a major threat to the prosperity of the nation. To Bennett, it made no sense to exploit the federal spending power and divert funds away from rich provinces such as British Columbia, when these funds would be wasted on projects with little chance of economic return. His primary concern was keeping Canada competitive in a global market.

The premier was convinced that the original intent of the British North America Act (as indicated in the regional system of representation for the Senate) was to create five distinct economic zones.[49] He thus suggested that his plans for northern expansion were justified by the history of Canada, as well as changing economic realities. Bennett argued that "if Canada [was] going to be able to compete in world markets, it must have efficient and large economic regions and be able to cut down some of the overhead of the government."[50] As mentioned, he opposed unconditional equalization payments to "have-not" provinces and called for "communication links and trade patterns running north and south rather than east and west."[51] In a major clash with Premier Smallwood of Newfoundland over the principle of interregional sharing, Bennett stated his belief that such a policy made no economic sense.[52] He also defended his vision for economic development in British Columbia. In response, Smallwood argued that these resources belonged to all Canadians. The facts show that Bennett, in his quest to restructure the Canadian economy to changing conditions, had already tried to exploit provincial state initiatives and autonomy for such a purpose.

Defending the British Columbia Agenda

British Columbia's development problems were always a top priority for Bennett, and he faced an awesome task of opposing Ottawa and the élites in the province who were opposed to his leadership. The struggle to realize many of his ideas was made easier by a political structure that offered the premier a great deal of autonomy. These powers provided him with an opportunity to reinforce the north-south axis and neutralize the impact of the east-west axis. His personalized, hands-on approach to politics and sheer dominance over every aspect of the political process allowed him to focus on issues that were important to his government. By limiting public debate, and controlling the financial records that were presented to the legislature, Bennett effectively undermined the influence of those critics who did not support his vision.

Throughout his years in power, the actual costs associated with his development scheme were never made public. Confronted with so many critics and forced to operate under conditions inherited from the past, Bennett focused on making dramatic structural changes that took priority over effective legislative control or the need to establish a more rational and expert-dominated system of planning.[53] Langford and Swainson indicated that the problem of non-accountability of public institutions, which was the product of the premier's refusal to implement reforms that had become popular elsewhere, no doubt enhanced executive control over the development scheme.[54] It also ensured that the government's priorities did not have to be balanced with the views of planners and interest groups, who found few opportunities to scrutinize the government's plans for developing the province. Although Ottawa and other governments were more internally divided and vulnerable to outside pressure, Bennett was consistent in pushing for increased provincial control over the development process and emphasizing the need for a new approach. Such a style of politics provided the premier with much autonomy when dealing with the question of integration.

At the conference that Ottawa organized for the purpose of discussing the Rowell-Sirois report, Bennett had condemned Pattullo for failing to defend the development needs of the interior and north. However, the premier himself did not play a prominent role at federal-provincial conferences. As Simeon indicated, Premier Bennett was not very effective in defending or promoting the provincial interest during intergovernmental negotiations.[55] Instead, the premier preferred to operate outside the established federal-provincial lines of communication.

By remaining outside the loop, Bennett most likely had fewer constraints inhibiting his actions. Under such conditions, the premier dealt with a different kind of dynamic, insulated from outside pressures. He preferred operating on his own. Yet, by restricting public debate and refusing to initiate complex bureaucratic reforms, he was in a much better position to implement his priorities for development.

Premier Bennett's Territorial Goals and Ambitions

The Bennett government became involved in a major struggle with Ottawa and Alberta over competing development priorities and the best way to balance the forces of continentalism, provincialism, regionalism, and nationalism, within the context of a constantly changing policy environment. For Bennett, the dynamics of federal-provincial relations and the need to gain control over the develop-ment process required that he play a key role in counterbalancing the threat posed by these outsiders. His intention was to increase provin-cial control and remold internal dependencies within the province, but not on the basis of the old east-west axis that had been designed and imposed by Ottawa and other traditional thinkers.

When Bennett took over the reins of power in the 1950s, he inherited a province with a number of transportation and communi-cation problems. Frontier communities were isolated, and, despite the economic potential of primary resources, high transportation costs and the lack of a well-planned intra-provincial transportation system meant that much of the province remained undeveloped. Bennett understood the disappointments, problems, and fears of fron-tier communities.

By 1952, Alberta was well positioned to become the main bene-ficiary of northern development. With assistance from Ottawa, the province was becoming the gateway between the north and markets in the United States. According to one submission at the presentation of the Royal Commission on the British Columbia Railway, "Alberta had made considerable progress to date in advancing and upgrading its transportation links with the Northwest Territories, knowing that trading and transportation patterns, once established, would be diffi-cult to change. Similar efforts are long overdue by British Columbia to create a trading corridor from the Arctic to the Pacific, opening up the Yukon and the Northwest Territories."[56] The premier could not have said it better himself. With his commitment to a five-region vision of the country, he designed infrastructural policies, as the Vancouver *Province* reported in 1954, "to ensure that the trade chan-nels do not develop in other directions."[57]

In 1954, the Bennett administration presented Ottawa with a plan that outlined the development priorities of the province. Within the policy statement, Bennett noted that,

The cost inherent in the geographical character of British Columbia is high and rigid. Compact settlement of population throughout the province is impossible. Its rich natural resources, which are the basis of provincial wealth and income, are separated by large, barren areas. The opening up and development of new resources in the central and northern interior, essential to the further expansion of the economy require costly transportation facilities.[58]

The record shows that Bennett saw himself as pursuing the same policies initiated by Ottawa under the First National Plan, but along the north-south axis.[59] Initially, he tried to convince Ottawa of the merits of building an infrastructure and reversing the dependency on Alberta's markets and transportation centres. Once Ottawa had rejected such claims and British Columbia's pleas for special consideration, the premier felt compelled to defend his periphery against outsiders. Thus, he opposed the principle of interregional sharing between provincial communities.

Bennett's fortress mentality was reinforced by his experiences with federal government officials and their refusal to deal with the development problems of British Columbia. The premier came to recognize that pre-emptive action was necessary, and he indicated in his statement to the Royal Commission on the British Columbia Railway that,

In the course of these great undertakings I met repeatedly with four different Prime Ministers of Canada, Canadian National Railway president, Donald Gordon, and many other federal representatives, in efforts to illustrate the negligence of national railway policy. These efforts were met with vacillation and procrastination. The pattern was clear. British Columbia had to pioneer on its own. The national railway, content with the conventional operation and cash flow of the Edmonton to Prince Rupert corridor, ignoring both north and south, shied away from virgin and pioneer territory. Only when the risks were taken by this Province, and the hard work completed, did the CNR and federal Ottawa express interest in the open frontier.[60]

Ray Williston, a member of Bennett's cabinet, noted that there was a long-term development plan that intentionally exploited rail transportation, oil and gas policy, hydro development, and other policy initiatives for the purpose of advancing the government's development preferences against Ottawa, Alberta, and established élites.[61] Such a commitment was not based strictly on economic considerations, nor was it the result of outside business pressure. Rather, many of these decisions were influenced more by the government's territorial ambitions than by the attempt to provide the most efficient transportation system.[62] Bennett hoped that the push toward provincial integration would eventually pay dividends. It was a gamble that Bennett felt was necessary, in the same way that Ottawa supported the building of a railway along the east-west axis to keep the Americans out during the First National policy.

K. Rupenthal and T. Keast argued that since these initiatives made no sense from a strictly economic perspective, such actions were essential for "a redrawing of the political map of Canada to provide for the incorporation of the Yukon into British Columbia."[63] Bennett fully comprehended the need to promote and defend the territorial integrity of the province through the building of an integrated transportation system. Although the plan would involve high costs and not everything was achieved, Pattullo's vision was finally permanently embedded within the culture and institutional system.[64] Since the premier controlled the flow of information to the public, the true costs were never known. As a result, there was ample opportunity to duplicate Ottawa's initiatives, which ultimately resulted in the building of a more expensive and inefficient transportation system.[65] These changes help to explain the province's response to outside pressures for reinforcing the east-west model of development.

In the 1970s, new forces emerged that had to be recognized by any government who inherited the political institutions and socioeconomic patterns that were augmented by Bennett's policy initiatives. Frontier communities had come to depend on the physical infrastructure that was built to reinforce the north-south axis. With the sunk costs and popularity of Bennett's policies, successive governments had good reason to continue building a more autonomous and prosperous community along the Pacific axis. The natural friction between regional integration in Western Canada and Bennett's five-region conception of Canada was fully institutionalized.

If we take into account these old battles over competing visions of the country, we gain new critical insights on the integration question. British Columbia's attack on the need for interregional redistribution is no doubt deeply rooted in the peculiar brand of populist politics that was established by W.A.C. Bennett between the years 1952 and 1972. With new developments and the threat of Quebec separatism, British Columbians feel that they have a major stake in the debate over restructuring. In addition, as British Columbia became more self-confident and isolated, more people have focused on the costs associated with national policies. As a strategy, the premier's move to reinforce the provincial boundary won the hearts and minds of provincial citizens.

The NDP Era

The new New Democratic Party (NDP) government that came to power under Dave Barrett in 1972 was far more flexible when it came to redistributive priorities and intergovernmental affairs. The necessities of cooperation between administrations and joint problem-solving approaches that emerged in Canada during the 1970s and 1980s meant that future premiers in British Columbia could no longer isolate themselves and dominate every aspect of policy making as Bennett had.[66] This development created problems for the premiers because being a player in the game meant that they had to give up certain things in the process. As Ruff indicated, "Not only did Premier Barrett recognize equalization payments as an expression of the economic integration of Canada but, without sacrificing provincial demands, he also argued for a strong federal role in the safeguarding to national levels of public service."[67] Nevertheless, the degree of support in British Columbia for what Bill Bennett described at the time as "national socialism" was open to question.[68]

When Barrett became premier, he made some definite changes with regard to approaches to political interventionism and public policy. Yet, his changes had more to do with reforming and updating than anything else. The public was ready for change in an election that "pitted a tired populist of the right against a more energetic populist of the left. Each based his appeal on being an anti-establishment outsider, essentially a loner."[69] How could it be otherwise in a province that defined itself as a peripheral society and completely institutionalized an ideology of protest?

The aging Social Credit leadership was losing momentum. However, in the wake of a massive wave of community mobilization as a result Bennett's province-building initiatives, no government could afford to simply ignore these new political forces and old agendas. It is astonishing that ideology has a greater impact on parties than on governments in British Columbia.

Indeed, ideological differences between the right and left have had only a marginal impact on the politicians who have been responsible for promoting and defending the territorial and jurisdictional interests of the province.[70] Faced with a population with little respect for élite rule and few shared traditions, premiers have had few opportunities to mobilize voter support for complex ideological arguments or policy frameworks. Rather, the pattern of politics, since the regime change in 1952, has revolved around the best way to stimulate economic development and promote integration, while reinforcing communication and transportation in a north-south direction. Historical claims of British Columbia (which have deep cultural and institutional roots) have created built-in tensions between national state-sponsored regionalism and province-building along the north-south axis.

The degree of federal-provincial conflict over key development questions is influenced by the surrounding culture and institutions. We should not lose sight of the influence of these peripheral aspirations on the actions of the government. When we consider the salient features of the culture, it is hardly surprising that a left-wing populist leader adopted the confrontational approach to federal-provincial relations and economic development that had worked for Bennett and other premiers.[71] For example, the NDP administration, in a determined bid to gain greater control over the development process, purchased a number of mills in the north that were in danger of closing down.[72] The government also feuded with Ottawa over whether Peace River coal should be transported through the Canadian National Railway terminal in Prince Rupert, or the British Columbia rail infrastructure at Squamish.[73] Barrett naturally preferred the second option. In another clear attempt to defend the jurisdictional powers of British Columbia against an outside competitor, Barrett established the British Columbia Petroleum Corporation for the purpose of avoiding federal regulations.[74] Although there were policy differences between the NDP and Social Credit governments, they approached key economic issues from a common territorial perspective.

As Elkins noted, in his description of the similarities between the Social Credit and NDP parties, rancorous legislative debates, extravagant campaign rhetoric, and partisan acrimony have often masked the underlying consensus about what is good for B.C. As Edwin R. Black has phrased it, B.C. politics revolves around "exploitation": how to harness a bountiful nature, achieve economic progress, and spread the benefits around. The means to these ends are debateable, although not always contested; and that sort of dispute or even disagreement over some goals should not blind us to the apparent consensus on many political goals.[75]

Premier Barrett clearly advocated a more populist and decentralized approach to problem solving than NDP leaders elsewhere. Only in the context of British Columbia politics would it have made sense for a socialist leader to request, for example, that jurisdictional powers over unemployment insurance and family allowances be handed over to the provinces.[76] The political discourse, which had been permanently transformed by W.A.C. Bennett's policy initiatives, naturally restricted the choices that were available to Dave Barrett when he inherited these ideas and institutions.

Revival of the Social Credit Party

Not surprisingly, the William R. Bennett government, which took power in 1975, continued to press for greater provincial control over economic development while modernizing the provincial state that began under the short-lived NDP government. The push for power stemmed partly from the problems of governing in a complex society that was divided along many lines and from the great distance between the periphery and the centre of policy making. The young premier inherited old structures and political definitions from his father, as well as the NDP. Once the consensus was established on the need to exploit the provincial state for the defence of territorial and jurisdictional interests against Ottawa and outside élites, there was little reason for changing direction. Centre-periphery conflicts and the sense of alienation that ran through the British Columbia political discourse had a great impact on the government's actions. As well, Bill Bennett attempted to synchronize his father's vision with the goal of modernizing the party and the government. In the end, these two initiatives intensified the contradictions within both the party and the government.

As Barman stated,

> Bill Bennett headed a more austere administration than had his father. In the view of some he lacked an overall plan for the future. "Slick advertising types and many non-elected people from outside the province have more say than MLAs and many ministers." David Mitchell argued that "W.A.C. Bennett was the last B.C. government to have a clear idea of where it was going and how to get there."[77]

One of the greatest dilemmas facing governments in British Columbia since the time of W.A.C. Bennett has been the struggle to blend together the traditions of populism with modern structures and processes. As a consequence, governments have had difficulty dealing with the interplay between these two forces. Yet, the populist streak has complicated the drive for integration on an east-west basis.

Bill Bennett remained suspicious of the outsiders and continued to push for the development needs of the province in spite of the high risks involved. He proved this dedication by attacking the National Energy Policy; preventing the sale of MacMillan Bloedel to Canadian Pacific Investments; creating the British Columbia Resources Investment Corporation to take over the mills acquired by the NDP; investing in new dams in the Peace River and Revelstoke areas; and pledging support for the controversial Northeast Coal project. Like his father before him, Bennett was committed to building expensive rail connections, highways, a new townsite, and other infrastructures in the north, and this commitment was based more on faith than on anything else. Even though the new northern project had a very high price tag and was controversial for a government committed to restraint, it clearly demonstrated the importance of the north-south axis for the young premier.

On the other hand, Bill Bennett was the first to push political reforms in other jurisdictions and restructure governmental relations according to the principles of centralized control and enlightened management.[78] He had more in common with other governments at intergovernmental meetings, and he eventually established a reputation for being less confrontational and more of a team player than either his father or Dave Barrett, especially during his early years in power.[79]

His approach and reputation created divisions within the party and contributed in a significant way to the rise of Bill Vander Zalm as party leader in 1986. Vander Zalm was successful, in part, because he presented himself as a proponent of the old style of leadership, established by W.A.C. Bennett. He promoted his populist reputation by pledging to reclaim the party from established élites and professional public relations experts who, at least in his mind, were setting policy and dominating the public agenda. Despite this rhetoric, Bennett himself always dominated the public agenda.

Even though Bill Bennett relied more on planners and the bureaucracy than his father did, he remained in power in the early 1980s by developing a "tough guy" image. He pledged to reduce the size of the bureaucracy, increase the power of the cabinet in a number of policy fields, deregulate the economy, directly challenge the power of public sector unions, and open up the north.[80] The premier remained the most dominant political figure in the province, and his determination to defend the northern vision never wavered.

The tradition of an executive-dominated political process continues to be a fact of life in British Columbian politics even today. As Howlett and Brownsey pointed out, the reforms introduced in the 1970s did not threaten the premier's dominance over the public policy decision-making process, and the restraint program introduced in 1983 "represented a new manifestation of the long-term trend in provincial government administration towards personal control by the cabinet over a wide range of provincial affairs."[81]

In addition, during the constitutional negotiations in the early 1980s, the premier, like his father, was not a major player on the federal-provincial stage. As Dyck argued, "Bennett had the opportunity to develop a national reputation, but he was not particularly successful, and it was left to others to engineer the final constitutional accord."[82] Again, while things change, they also stay the same.

There were several reasons why Bennett was out of step with the other premiers. Most importantly, he was determined to create a new political definition of Canadian federalism based on five distinct economic regions. Like Pattullo and his father, Bennett strongly endorsed the view that Canada was and should be organized on the basis of five distinct zones. The other premiers had their own agendas, and the British Columbia proposal failed to generate much enthusiasm outside the provincial boundary. The British Columbia vision of the country directly threatened the territorial and jurisdictional interests of the other players involved in constitutional reform. Quite simply, the British Columbian government did not have the power to generate support for its proposals for change on a national scale.

The British Columbian government, in its constitutional proposal, focused on convincing others that the province was a separate region that should receive equal representation in national political institutions. Rejecting the principles of provincial equality and a two-nation model, the government argued that the federal system should be restructured based on five regions. The premier presented a British Columbia perspective of Canadian federalism that was based on early history, socio-economic trends, geography, trade patterns, and many other factors.[83]

At the time, even Bennett's call to strengthen the "provincial bargaining power within the central government in the case of British Columbia" had little impact on the other provinces.[84] The reform of central institutions would not become a major issue until the next round of constitutional negotiations. In Alberta, the call for Senate reform had little appeal in the early 1980s. A few years later, the idea of Senate reform caught on in Alberta, but the model was based on the principle of provincial equality, not on a five-regions perspective. With the tensions inherent to these competing definitions of Canadian citizenship and boundary setting, the British Columbian government became further isolated during these negotiations.

The importance of adopting a comparative approach to the regional integration question is obvious. The province of British Columbia, in its search for solutions to the problem of underdevelopment, has tended to look more in a north-south direction than has been true for Ottawa and Central Canadian experts. The British Columbian agenda has been greatly influenced by the assumption that underdevelopment has been caused by outside influences. As a consequence, the government has focused a great deal of attention on promoting a more integrated provincial economy and society along the north-south axis and increasing the power and autonomy of the provincial state. According to this hypothesis, certain local powers and institutions are required to ensure that the frontier community has the capacity to control its own destiny. Undoubtedly, the government has not found it easy to achieve these objectives within a competitive federation. Without the foregoing analysis of British Columbia's history, we would have difficulty understanding why a consensus on the regional integration question has been so difficult to achieve.

The Five-Region Concept and the Emergence of "Cascadia"

Over the decades, premiers in British Columbia have responded unfailingly to economic and political changes by offering a model of Canadian federalism that reflected local concerns about economic development. They pushed a reform agenda that would have required Ottawa to stop subsidizing the east-west economy and transportation system, which they perceived as inefficient and expensive. The other members of the federal family have always reacted by defending their own imperialistic visions of the country. In the past, the British Columbian agenda and blueprint for restructuring has not been taken seriously by other governments or academics because it questioned basic assumptions that were considered sacred. The well-known inclination of academics and other élites to support old ideas and approaches further reinforced feelings of alienation on the West Coast.

Today, Canadians see the British Columbian agenda in a different light. This shift in attitude has as much to do with changes taking place in the surrounding milieu as it does with new forces within the provincial boundary. Nevertheless, to place the contemporary discourse over restructuring in its proper context, we have attempted to draw a parallel between the current issues and the agendas and experiences of previous provincial administrations. Our main purpose was to highlight the various contexts that have fostered a defensive expansionist strategy, which aimed to shift patterns of economic and political development geographically. The British Columbian agenda and local feelings of alienation are rooted in the fact that for decades the people of this province have felt exploited and ignored. Consequently, the principle of interregional redistribution and other calls for integration have become the targets of those influenced by the leadership of Pattullo and W.A.C. Bennett.

Examples help to illustrate the influence of the five-region vision on policy discussions. If we examine the history of the government's tendency to rely on such a conception of community, we see the striking dominance of this paradigm over time. Economic, social, and political problems have often been defined according to the logic of

a long-standing territorial imperative. Since the interregional redistribution principle and the east-west integration drive were perceived
as obstacles to the development needs of British Columbia, the defenders of the province proposed a new kind of federal system.

In recent discussions on economic and political change, the British
Columbian government has presented various documents, political
evaluations, and strategies in highlighting the theme of renewal
guided by the five-region prototype. For example, a technical background document produced by intergovernmental relations officials
during the Vander Zalm years outlined the challenges of change in
an age of globalization and the increasing irrelevance of trade with
the "Rest of Canada."[85] The paper provided several solutions for
resolving issues such as the national unity problem. One popular
option was the "confederalism of five-regions model," which had
been defended by governments in the past.

Such an approach to restructuring has been pushed repeatedly onto
the public agenda by various governments and commentators over
the years. As outlined by Rafe Mair, a former Social Credit cabinet
minister in the Bill Bennett government and well-known radio personality who gained national prominence as a critic of the Charlottetown Accord, British Columbia is regarded by most residents as a
distinct region, and even a nation. According to Mair, in his reading
of British Columbia history,

> There was, as there is today, a strong north-south pull —
> in the early days, for example, mail from the colony went
> out via San Francisco. The importance of history — as
> well as geographical realities which have always been of
> prime concern — to B.C./Canada relations is profound.
> We are not and never have been part of "The West" but
> are the Pacific Region which has always looked west and
> south as much if not more than east. This, if it has been
> understood at all by Ottawa (for which there is no evi-
> dence), has never been officially recognized. What has
> been seen by the Ottawa power clique as simply B.C.
> bitching again had really been frustration at the inability
> of the federal power structure to comprehend that British
> Columbia, like all political, social, and economic units
> had historical, economic, geographical and demographic
> features which set it apart, and which must be taken into
> account.[86]

The framework selected by the government of British Columbia for renewing the federation has often focused on challenges such as globalization, changing trade patterns and demographics, and competing loyalties, but it was organized around the principle of five regional economies and the natural pull of the north-south axis. New patterns of economic activity, a more integrated north-south transportation system, a strong sense of self-reliance, and a unique culture (with well-embedded populist roots) have all contributed to the call for building on the realities of the power blocs emerging within North America. As British Columbia faces the uncertain future, the existing boundaries are still seen as insignificant and as a source of frustration. Any future attempt to group British Columbia with the Prairie provinces will have to deal with these realities.

Melvin Smith, a key advisor to various British Columbian governments over the years, argued that the lack of consensus on the centralization-decentralization dilemma stems mainly from the significant differences between provinces in terms of economic strength. Uniform solutions simply do not work, because "have-not" provinces are naturally less inclined to support decentralization and the need to embrace the north-south axis. As a result, the search for the most appropriate formula for pooling sovereignties has been endless and futile. As Smith noted,

> In his own way, Premier W.A.C. Bennett was among the first to propose a solution to the problem. He recognized that, given the structure of federal institutions, it was virtually impossible for provinces of disparate strength to be effectively and evenly treated in their dealings with Ottawa. He held the view that federal-provincial relations would not work well as long as the federal government could play the wealthy provinces off against the weaker ones.[87]

Even the recent rise of an NDP government has not dampened the enthusiasm for such an approach to restructuring in the Pacific region of the country. For instance, during the recent 1992 constitutional debate, when old ideas and arrangements were being questioned and new solutions were pushed onto the agenda, the five-region model was defended at various times by the Harcourt government. As Alberta, Newfoundland, Saskatchewan, and others were defending the principle of provincial equality, and Quebec kept referring to the other provinces as the "Rest of Canada," British Columbia pushed the five-region model.

For example, Premier Harcourt indicated at various times that any new Senate should be representative of the five regions because the province is "economically and geographically different than Alberta" and its citizens "feel more similarities exist in a north-south direction."[88] In light of the past commitments to such an approach for restructuring and its popularity among citizens of the province, the Harcourt administration's defence of such an approach was only logical.

In the end, Premier Harcourt compromised on the Senate issue in the name of national unity and accepted a constitutional deal that would have given the province a greater number of seats in the House of Commons.[89] The consensus achieved in Charlottetown dictated that Quebec, Ontario, British Columbia, and Alberta would all receive extra seats in return for allowing the smaller provinces equal representation in the second chamber. Although a number of factors influenced the final negative vote, a major reason for the general response of British Columbians to the accord was the feeling that Premier Harcourt had failed to defend the territorial and jurisdictional interests of the province. Often characterized as an incompetent or weak leader, the premier faced much criticism for not being more forceful in defending British Columbia's interests.[90] It was a lesson he would never forget. Whether he deserved this reputation or not, Premier Harcourt has found it difficult to change the impression that he lacked some of the entrepreneurial skills that afforded W.A.C. Bennett the opportunity to permanently structure the political landscape based on a common vision.

British Columbians' deepening committment to the Pacific regional economy and to the strengthening of linkages in a north-south direction is indicated by the increasing popularity of the concept of "Cascadia," and the ideas associated with the Georgia Basin initiative, which emerged after the British Columbia Round Table on the Environment and the Economy.[91] The primary purpose for establishing these new alliances and coordinating development strategies within the Georgia Basin–Puget Sound area was to officially recognize the natural interdependence that exists between British Columbia and the Pacific Northwest border region.[92] Worldwide globalization, the threat of Quebec nationalism, and other forces of change have all reinforced new linkages and strengthened old ties across boundaries. Now, more than ever, the British Columbia govenment continues to focus in a north-south direction.

Such a regional political-economic system will enable those involved to respond to new forces and establish new forms of cooperation. In an era of globalization, state élites may not be able to control the process of development as they did in the past. On the other hand, coalitions and institutions can be created to gain advantages in a new political game.

Premier Harcourt, who was a strong advocate of regional cooperation within the Pacific Corridor when he was the mayor of Vancouver, has generally supported the call to establish new linkages within a distinct borderland region of North America. Yet, he has some ideological concerns about establishing a Pacific Northwest economic zone. Harcourt has the support of various business interests for a more integrated approach to planning and economic development, but he must deal with the concerns raised by Ken Georgetti of the British Columbia Federation of Labour and Bob White of the Canadian Labour Congress; naturally, the premier is ambivalent about a project that could hurt workers in his province. However, other labour leaders support the call for more open borders. Harcourt has indicated that even though he supports the building of new trade alliances, he would prefer to deal solely with Washington State, rather than a power bloc that also includes Alberta, Montana, Alaska, Oregon, and California. Like other premiers before him, he has resisted the idea of including Alberta in the regional integration experiment.[93]

The concept of such a regional bloc can be traced back to the days of W.A.C. Bennett, Pattullo, and McBride. As people increasingly recognize the advantages of a cross-border rather than a national approach to communication, urban planning, education, transportation, the environment, banking, and research and development, they must also make note of the new alliances and forces that are challenging old ideas, institutions, and policy processes in Canada. Political discourses no longer revolve solely around national or provincial issues.

Several problems will need to be resolved if Cascadia is to be fully realized. Divided loyalties, ideological conflicts between the left and right, and territorial and jurisdictional disputes will create complications. In particular, old rivalries between Ottawa, Alberta, and British Columbia will require special attention. Alberta wants be included in any new relationship involving the other members of the regional bloc, but British Columbia is again preventing her old territorial rival from joining the new club.[94] At the same time, the reassertion of subnational political forces and economic logic will inspire common strategies.

The concept of Cascadia is gaining momentum: plans for a commission and the Georgia Basin–Puget Sound Urbanization Project Steering Committee are in place, several studies on the advantages of strengthening north-south linkages are now complete, and a magazine to facilitate communication on a regional basis is being published.[95] Given the high degree of alienation towards Ottawa and past commitments to defending and promoting the north-south axis against outside political competitors, these events are hardly surprising. The extent of the experiment and the identities of future participants are open to question. In the end, the answers will depend on the interplay between ideas, institutions, and the political leaders involved in the decision-making process.

Conclusion

Approaching the struggle over regional integration from a historical and comparative standpoint gives us a window of opportunity for understanding the complexity of the issue and the diversity of competing perspectives on the topic. In British Columbia, any form of integration based on an east-west development plan must be approached with caution. Over the decades, governments have resisted any call for a more integrated approach to economic and political development in Western Canada. Despite the tendency in Canadian historical and political studies to either ignore or treat lightly the actions of British Columbian governments, various leaders have been committed to defending the territorial interests of the province against outsiders.

Several factors help to explain the persistence and relative strength of such a vision in the context of British Columbian politics. The frontier province lacks established political traditions and is geographically isolated, internally divided and alienated by élites across the country. Various political leaders, beginning with Pattullo, McBride, and W.A.C. Bennett, have seen the benefit of exploiting the power of the provincial state to mobilize competing and diverse forces against Ottawa and outside economic and political competitors. Once these policies were in place, and structures built, few politicians resisted the pull of the north-south axis and the power of the five-region vision of the country.

From a national perspective, the rationale behind redrawing boundaries and promoting integration on a regional basis was to reinforce common policies and a common approach to development. The intent has always been to simplify the process of decision making and to create a more effective way of managing the affairs of the federation, as well as the national economy. Indeed, the intent was also to make sure that the future was not jeopardized by parochialism and short-sighted territorial competitors, who were more concerned with defending their turf than meeting the challenges associated with change.

For British Columbia, the five-region model has provided a convenient way to decentralize power. For the most part, the model offered suggestions for overcoming the threat posed by small provinces and Ottawa to the regional economies in North America. The plan was influenced by British Columbia's desire to solve its development problems by changing the dynamic of federal-provincial relations and exploiting national spending power. Due to the diversity of these perspectives and agendas, not much has been achieved in terms of regional cooperation in the West.

The nation state in Canada will continue to be challenged by the economic interests of borderland regions in North America, as well as by the strength of wealthier provincial states. In the 1990s, interests, values, and ideologies in Canadian politics are very much linked to old political cleavages and experiences. Thus, the influence of state-building traditions in Canada on the centralization-decentralization questions warrants much attention.

Six

Future Patterns of Cooperation

Our main objective has been to provide a deeper understanding of
the institutional and cultural forces underlying the struggle over
integration in the Atlantic and the West. By situating the Liberal
government's call for regional integration in a historical context, we
have provided new insights on the likely influences of fragmented
intergovernmental decision making, as well as the emergence of new
environmental forces, on the movement. When viewed in the institutional context of Canadian federalism, politics in either periphery
is marked by divisions of interest between territorial competitors.

Understanding Atlantic and Western politics requires that we take
into account not only the major social and political cleavages, but
also the influence of political factors and institutions.

On the basis of historical and comparative evidence, we have
pointed out the difficulties of effecting fundamental change within a
confederal structure of intergovernmental relations that have consistently constrained the negotiation of solutions to economic problems
on a regional basis.

Obstacles to effective integration in the West and the Atlantic
include an institutional structure that reinforces an ambiguous and
competitive political game. Indeed, it is structurally easier for premiers to work together in defending their territorial interests against
Ottawa than in solving common economic problems. This mode of
action has been institutionalized, as well as internalized, within the
provincial cultures that were highlighted in our comparative analysis.

In addition, we argue that the declining capacity of the national
state to defend the east-west axis will likely push the regions in
opposite directions. As in the past, the way we define future problems
will depend on the management of public discourse and our interpretations of changing circumstances.

In other words, Canadians need to prepare themselves both psychologically and intellectually for major changes, especially in the

Atlantic. Our analysis has ventured beyond stereotypical images of the two peripheries to encourage readers to make their own judgements about the processes of external control and the internalization of control that occur as a result of competitive state-building. The dynamics of political competition and the role of the state as the promoter and defender of eleven distinct political cultures have not helped us perform the functions of integration and adaptation; isolation impedes the achievement of a consensus. We hope that the arguments we have provided will contribute to this discussion and enhance understanding of a complex issue.

Our federation has always faced concurrent pressures for integration and disintegration. In spite of modernization theory, increasing interdependence, and changes in the policy process, the two peripheries have been far more diverse and pluralistic than predicted. In the interplay between ideas, interests, and institutions, especially in the post-war era, Ottawa has been seduced by the benefits of the north-south trade, which has made it difficult, if not impossible, to reinforce common values and unite regional socio-economic and political forces along the east-west axis. Despite three national policies that aimed to further the cause of integration, the territorial pluralism of Canadian federalism has not faded, nor have the threats of continentalism diminished.

In the 1990s, the only certainty about the future of intergovernmental relations is that the status quo is no longer an option. Let us hope that we can remain within the same political structure and prosper. Canada must redefine itself, accept new realities, and determine new ways to manage common problems while accentuating the positive aspects that are inherent to such diversity. We have no choice but to redefine the country, and the public should be well informed of this process.

A realistic transformation of the political spectrum is necessary, but this transformation must not rely on the old negative images and theories that have forced some provinces to turn inward to preserve themselves. Now, more than ever, we need to understand the differences in interpretations of earlier experiments across provinces and determine positive ways to change the political dynamic. Perhaps we can learn from the experiences of members of the European community, since they have dealt with comparable redistribution issues within the context of intergovernmental structures.

The conventional view of Canadian politics has always been based on the assumption that the centralizing influences of modernization would eventually create a new form of politics in the peripheral provinces. For planners, the federal government, and provinces such as New Brunswick and Manitoba, promoting cooperation on a regional basis made sense. Concerned about a sprawling federation with competing visions, these interests had much in common. They also, at one time, could exploit Ottawa's spending power to entice or threaten compliance. On the other hand, since negotiations in intergovernmental forums have always been constrained by the principle of unanimity, the rules have favoured those interests that supported the status quo.

Intergovernmental arenas have always been obstacles to those wanting to challenge provincial ideas, interests, and institutions. Furthermore, the political game involves different socio-economic and institutional circumstances that condition the responses of both the premiers and the federal government.

Two issues must be addressed before any changes can be made to the existing intergovernmental alignments. First, past events must be analyzed. In order to fully understand the prospects for reform, we must learn from yesterday's experiences. Even though Canada has to reinvent itself, previous institutional arrangements and inherited traditions will likely affect the actions of the political actors and the way they respond to any new initiatives.

As mentioned in Chapter One, Simeon's model provides a convenient framework for analyzing decision making and policy making in intergovernmental settings.[1] We have attempted to describe the influences of the perceptions of the participants, competing visions and identities, resources, and the gaps created by previous competing state-building policies on the politics of intergovernmental bargaining in Atlantic and Western Canada. The lack of institutional change and the dominance of the premiers have guaranteed that cooperative efforts would not interfere with provincial powers. As a result, the movement has remained leaderless, with few opportunities for community-building on any basis other than a provincial one. For a variety of reasons, some provinces disliked the loss of autonomy and found the regional idea repulsive.

Another complicating factor is that conceptions of the state and perspectives on the causes of underdevelopment vary from province to province. These historical experiences and cultures, which have been fully institutionalized on a provincial basis, have worked against the movement. The rise of borderland regions has also created conflict. For example, the popularity of the "Cascadia" movement in British Columbia and Alberta has complicated efforts to link the Western provinces. The direction of political change has not been uniform across provincial boundaries, in spite of national integrative policies and Ottawa's imperial overspending in areas that interfered with provincial economic priorities and powers.

The second issue that must be considered before changes can be made is that the likely impact of both new forces and old inherited visions, objectives, and political resources on future outcomes should be taken into account. Predictably, Ottawa and other supporters of the movement are concerned about the challenge of transnationalism and the continued failure of political institutions, such as political parties or interest groups, to resolve regional economic problems. As a result, they have looked again to intergovernmental structures for solutions and approaches to dealing with new circumstances. The extent of consensus achieved will depend on a number of factors, but, in the end, power will ultimately determine the final outcome, as it always does.

Confronted with declining powers and the loss of state instruments necessary for controlling the actions of the provinces, Ottawa faces a period of intense political horsetrading, as supporters of the recent movement prepare themselves for a rigorous debate on the merits of the project. Although most people support the call for greater cooperation, this support involves some self-deception. The fact remains that both the lack of regional institutions and the self-interests of the bigger provinces will push Atlantic Canada further along the integration continuum. In Western Canada, the prospects for achieving a higher degree of integration are weaker. Indeed, the most direct challenge to the goal of regional cooperation along the east-west axis is the considerable autonomy, political resources, and ambitions of the richer subnational units in the far West. The decline of the federal government will help to forge new north-south associational ties, especially in the West.

To be sure, Preston Manning's call for future economic development based on north-south trade initiatives, rather than east-west transfers, is not new; nor is his lack of faith in experts or special interests who identify with integrationist policies.[2] Past concerns about ineffective redistribution policies found expression in the Social Credit movements in both Alberta and British Columbia; today, they have a new vehicle for expression. The fact that these assumptions and ideas became permanently embedded in the political culture and institutions has no doubt complicated the campaign for effective integration along the east-west axis. The campaign will also create added pressure to reduce the cost of government in Atlantic Canada. The accelerating withdrawal of federal authority will create the conditions necessary for changing the premiers' attitudes about restructuring and cooperation.

In my view, no matter how desirable the goals of regional cooperation might be, any development strategy that ignores the British Columbian and Albertan agendas will fail. The reason seems obvious: widespread cynicism about experts, negative experiences with previous integrationist policies, changing demographics, and expanding north-south trade opportunities have made it difficult, if not impossible, to mobilize support for the movement in these two provinces. Unless the political and institutional context for negotiation changes significantly, government self-interest and concerns over the regional distribution of cost and benefits will likely continue to frustrate coordinated, cooperative efforts along the east-west axis in the West.

In the contemporary world, the tentacles of Central Canadian imperialism are losing their power as the forces of continentalist liberalism replace national state interventionism. The challenge of change is occurring at a time when these new forces and our intergovernmental arrangements will play a major role in determining future behaviour and debate.

Our analysis has been based on the assumption that wealthier provinces such as Alberta and British Columbia have little incentive to cooperate to any great extent. In the beginning, official boundaries were political creations, but Ottawa no longer has the same power to defend or promote her territorial interests in the context of a changing North America. The rise of powerful provincial states in the West, the fiscal imperative, and an economy where provinces trade more with neighbouring states than with each other have complicated the task of integrating the country.

As Ottawa tries to reinvent itself, certain realities will have to be faced. A major hindrance to collective effort is the fact that policy issues and problems are often subordinated to the territorial and jurisdictional interests of the governments. As a consequence, the federal-provincial context will make it more difficult to involve the general public, especially given the tendency of premiers to maintain control of the process. Finally, questions regarding costs and benefits will have to be addressed.

What are the ramifications of these circumstances? Can the federal Liberal government's pledge to promote cooperation among the provinces, especially in the West and the Atlantic, have positive results?

All of the provinces have grievances against previous national policies; they also share common problems. Since governments are also interdependent, they have an incentive to adopt a coordinated approach to restructuring. Despite these factors, obstacles to this policy imperative still remain, and the tendency of the far West to focus on jurisdictional and redistribution questions will make it more difficult to achieve much progress. Whereas the Atlantic provinces have extra incentive, with the reduction of transfers, to embrace the regional cooperative model, the political dynamic has not changed very much in the West.

Since Ottawa lacks the capacity to control interprovincial policies, an alternative approach is to consider ways to minimize intergovernmental conflicts and maximize performance. Different models for each region also make sense since conditions are very different in the Atlantic and West. From my perspective, new patterns of social cooperation based on tolerance, trust, and respect must be promoted on a regional basis in Atlantic Canada. In the face of external pressures and changing conditions, the premiers seem to be moving away from a strictly provincial community model to a more regional, policy-oriented approach.

It is essential that this trend continues, but citizen groups should be more involved in the process. Greater participation could be achieved by holding public forums or even a constituent assembly to study new ways for revitalizing the process of integration in the future. Any new regional framework should include a deeper level of commitment to a program of democratization.

We should also focus on learning from the European Community experience and ensuring that integration has a positive impact on all the provinces involved. Shared social and environmental policies might help to create trust between rural and urban communities. Such a regional discourse might result in new patterns of cooperation and widespread norms of active citizen participation. It should also facilitate the process of legitimation.

The federal government has already shown great determination to open up the process. Under intense media glare and with rising expectations, federal ministers, premiers, community leaders, and academics assembled in Moncton in December 1994 to participate in a conference entitled, "The Atlantic Challenge: Shaping the Future of Regional Development." It was sponsored by the Atlantic Canada Opportunities Agency (ACOA) and organized by the Atlantic Provinces Economic Council. The main thrust of the effort was to inform the public, while reinforcing trust and ties between the governments and citizens involved.

As seen in the case studies, few premiers or provincial civil servants, accustomed to old patron-client relations and to working independently, relish the prospect of increased public accountability. Yet the right mix of public forums and innovative policies may go a long way in convincing Atlantic citizens that they are well on the way to building the kind of regime necessary for dealing with new challenges. If we can expose the darker recesses of old quasi-traditional political practices to public scrutiny, the region's capacity for economic growth and democratic self-government may increase. And if the premiers continue to change the public discourse in a way that reduces the pull of old cleavages, which have always undermined restructuring efforts in the past, the returns could be higher.

Restructuring economic and social policy in the region will not be painless. However, fear and outside pressure demand that consideration be given to overhauling the current system of interprovincial relations. The citizens of Canada will be very poorly served if the Atlantic premiers approach intergovernmental structuring as an opportunity to defend their competitive brand of provincial politics against outsiders. These governments and the people they represent cannot afford the status quo.

The risks involved in such a political game are enormous. The premiers face the task of breaking old cycles of dependence and eliminating norms of favour-seeking that operated on a provincial basis. They will encounter difficulties in their assault on the operation, ethos, and provincial control of the social and economic landscape, especially given the fact that each premier operates in a provincial context. By relying on old ideas and institutions, the premiers could derail the entire reform process and end up with nothing. Even though their visions of regional cooperation differ, all of the premiers recognize that little can be achieved without collective action. The choice is theirs. Fortunately, the premiers are not alone in dealing with some of their dilemmas. The territorial restructuring of European countries has focused much attention on the development of new intergovernmental models based on globalization and interdependence. In addition, there has been a spate of commissioned studies on Maritime union since 1970.

The fiscal realities described in the 1970 Maritime Union Report never fully materialized because Ottawa continued to rely on foreign borrowing to enhance her power to control public policy issues. The fiscal imperative will now change the practical face of Canadian federalism, and the trend towards decentralization will continue.

The Atlantic premiers have begun the adjustment to a new style of problem solving that is coordinated, cooperative, and functional. However, they must consider the next step: making the institutional changes necessary to facilitate the management of new problems. Each provincial agenda must now be considered in establishing a more affordable and functional government.

The crucial element is not political union, but rather a more co-operative attitude. In the end, any changes must reflect local priorities, but everyone could save considerably if new forms of partnering, aimed at reducing government cost and duplication are adopted. Emphasis must also be placed on eliminating zero sum conflicts among the provinces wherever possible.

Even though its use is justified in certain policy fields, it is time to consider replacing provincial unilateralism with a more functional approach to intergovernmental relations in Atlantic Canada. Improved institutions for intergovernmental coordination could play a vital role in resolving issues that created paralysis within the old confederal system. The national unity/fiscal agenda is changing the face of federalism, and the current intergovernmental structure is unsustainable, at least for Atlantic Canada. In spite of ideological, cultural, and territorial challenges, it is time for fundamental reform.

The premiers can provide the basis for a new political game by striking a balance between provincial interests and functional logic. The system could, like the European unity experiment, be based on a looser intergovernmental arrangement that does not rely on mutual vetoes. The role of the secretariat should be expanded but there seems to be little need to establish a commission, regional parliament, or regional courts. Rather, new policies should continue to be designed and implemented on an intergovernmental basis, through cooperation, not competition.

Given the growing communication capacity within the region, the four provincial parliaments could be linked together whenever necessary to discuss common problems or to help legitimize joint policies. Regional cooperation would also be enhanced by reducing the number of representatives within these parliaments. Stable public finances and effective government will require rethinking of the functions of political and state institutions.

Greater emphasis should also be placed on regional administration of joint undertakings. Permanent arrangements should be made for joint administration and the building of new policy communities on a regional basis. New relationships, including interchange with experts, would help to create closer ties and a web of common experiences. Common policy frameworks and networks among municipal officials, public servants, different sectors of industry, and other actors would make it easier for the Atlantic premiers to mobilize support for common causes. Habits of consultation and cooperation would not be encouraged until the fragmented, pluralistic, and competitive system of associations is more integrated. It is time for the creation of the consultative mechanisms that are necessary for changing the political dynamic: once these are in place, we can focus on increasing the level of cooperation within the region. Both the private and public sectors must be restructured to meet new challenges and to encourage cooperation within the regional economic zone.

Any new intergovernmental system should be subject to established voting procedures that will allow the premiers to transcend provincial divisions and deal with regional interests and problems. Within such a framework, the use of the principle of unanimity at Atlantic premiers' conferences should be greatly restricted. We need to recognize the wide range of institutional arrangements possible under federalism and the variety of options for the organization of power sharing that exist around the world. For example, the premiers could create new regional institutions and voting procedures through the negotiation of treaties that would be approved by each provincial legislature. Such an initiative would complement the actions of the premiers in building a more consensual approach to problem solving, without threatening their powers.[3] Until conditions of unanimous decision making are reconsidered, the political dynamic will probably change very little.

Whenever possible, the premiers should adopt a common approach to economic restructuring, the welfare state, and federal-provincial relations. In this regard, for example, the Atlantic Provinces Economic Council could be restructured to include advisors representing a broad range of academic perspectives and interests. Such an organization would have joint objectives and responsibilities and would function as an ongoing royal commission, responsible for inciting discussions, keeping the public informed, and generating new ideas. It would likely have a major impact on the push for a more consensual, integrated approach to problem solving. Yet, in the end, the executives of the subnational units within the federation would still play a key role in the decision-making process.

Essentially, the Atlantic premiers have no choice but to respond to external pressures for change with a new approach. It is time for action and profound political changes. A pan-Atlantic Canadian vision must take root within the society, economy, and political structure. However, we should not underestimate the force of territorial politics in the region. In spite of increasing economic interdependence and modernization, Atlantic politics will still have a powerful territorial dimension. As a consequence, any new system of intergovernmentalism must recognize territorial considerations.

The situation is very different in the West. Over the years, the interprovincial economy of Western Canada has expanded and become more integrated, but the economic and institutional priorities of the two most powerful provinces have led to greater decentralization — not to centralization, as predicted by modernization theory. Unfortunately, the Liberal government's regional integration policy will encounter more obstacles in the West than in the Atlantic provinces. Westward shifts in economic power and populations will hamper efforts to mobilize support for regional integration. Since future negotiations will probably take place in forums controlled by the premiers on the basis of unanimity, as our case studies suggest, Alberta and British Columbia will have the power to block any regional initiative.

As a consequence, proposing the same cooperative model for reorganizing intergovernmental relations in the West makes little sense. Rather, the vision for Western Canada requires a more decentralized and less structured arrangement, which allows for varying degrees of cooperation. Certain regional policies will benefit the building of a stronger interdependent society and economy in the West, but it would be pointless and counterproductive to push the cause to a breaking point.

If we have learned anything from the Meech Lake and Charlottetown constitutional accords, it is that British Columbia and Alberta are prone to populist uprisings. We can achieve much more by accepting the differing levels of commitment to the regional integration initiative and the fact that Alberta and British Columbia tend to view east-west political initiatives as more of a problem than a solution to perceived future economic challenges.

Considering the strength of populism on both the left and right in British Columbia, the tendency to defend the provincial boundary cannot be simply wished away or transformed by some federal campaign promise. This attitude has become fully institutionalized. Any effort by Ottawa or planners to sell the theory that decentralization undermines economic modernization and interdependence will not succeed, especially given the West's desire to enhance north-south trade opportunities and its high level of economic growth. Integration or modernization theories have been out of touch with the forces of change. Unilinear and deterministic approaches to development have never been supported in places like Alberta or British Columbia.

Alberta has a less polarized political culture but shares many of British Columbia's concerns over regional integration and the need to give up provincial power. Factors such as the weakening of federal government power, concerns about sharing wealth, and shifting populations have helped to strengthen provincial forces in the West. The economic, social, and political context in the West is markedly different from that of the Atlantic provinces; it would be pointless to recommend the same cooperative model.

Given this history of federal-provincial tensions over the integration question in the West, revitalization of the intergovernmental process should be organized around a more competitive model. Despite the benefits of a more integrated, coordinated approach, the strong capabilities and significant policy differences that have always worked against the campaign have not changed. As a result, continuing to waste resources and working at cross-purposes would be foolhardy.

The system for problem solving in the West should be based on the old system, which allows for some experimentation and policy innovation. The Western provinces have proven that there are different manifestations of federal unilateralism. Ultimately, better results might be obtained if Ottawa encouraged a more fiscally responsible approach to problem solving, instead of seeking to constantly control the fragile processes of intergovernmental relations in the West. Each time Ottawa has made this attempt, the strategy has backfired. As history has clearly demonstrated, whenever Ottawa set out to reinforce the east-west axis, provinces such as British Columbia went out of their way to work at cross-purposes. In the 1990s, it is clear that we cannot afford this duplication of effort.

It must be stressed that such an approach has never worked in the past, and much of this failure is related to the underlying political economy, as well as the competing interests of the national and provincial state élites. Unless Ottawa can justify the expenditure of new resources in either solving economic problems or enhancing the national identity, it seems pointless to provoke further conflicts with the Western premiers. The premiers are more likely to see the concrete benefits of working together if that cooperation is not secondary to the defence of their interests against an outside competitor. A more cooperative approach to solving common "internal" problems has greater chances for success if Ottawa does not participate.

In conclusion, there is a need for new arrangements in managing interdependence in Canada, but external pressures will create more changes in the Atlantic than in the West; Atlantic Canada needs a more integrated approach to problem solving. We know from past experience that reforming provincial institutions will be much more difficult if outsiders rely upon old negative images and are seen as imposing a regional agenda. Reconciling different visions and agendas will not come easily, but the Atlantic premiers must persist in overhauling intergovernmental structures. In particular, they must address the thorny question of replacing the unanimity rule with a system of majority voting. Much of this can be accomplished with administrative agreements and the coordination of objectives in interdependent policy areas.

Such an approach to restructuring provincial government activities would bring many benefits to the West, as well. However, it seems unlikely that the same level of integration can be achieved in the West. For this reason, we should concentrate our energies on finding practical solutions that have a chance of being implemented. The supporters of regional integration for the West must be flexible because they do not have the power or resources necessary for carrying out the policy.

Notes

Chapter One

1. Liberal Party of Canada, *Creating Opportunity: The Liberal Plan for Canada* (Ottawa: Liberal Party, 1993), p. 59.
2. See Nova Scotia, New Brunswick and Prince Edward Island, *Report on Maritime Union* (Fredericton: Maritime Union Study, 1970), pp. 53-63 and Appendix A.
3. For more information, see Edwin Black, *Divided Loyalties: Canadian Concepts of Federalism* (Kingston and Montreal: McGill-Queen's University Press, 1975).
4. It is worth noting that Roger Gibbins, in his comparative study of the concept of regionalism, discovered in the American literature that "Regionalism, although sometimes employed as a synonym for sectionalism, more commonly refers to amalgamations of states into geographical, cultural, economic, or administrative regions, and to resemblances in politics and policies among such states." His detailed discussion of regionalism calls attention to the possible connection between the search to facilitate further homogenization of provinces within the regions of Canada and the development experiences of the United States. See Roger Gibbins, *Regionalism: Territorial Politics in Canada and the United States* (Toronto: Butterworths, 1982), p. 4.
5. Richard Simeon, "Regionalism and Canadian Political Institutions," in J. Peter Meekison, *Canadian Federalism: Myth or Reality* (Toronto: Methuen Press, 1977), pp. 292-3.
6. For details, see Gerald Friesen, "The Prairies as a Region: The Contemporary Meaning of an Old Idea," in James McCrorie and Martha Macdonald, eds., *The Constitutional Future of the Prairie and Atlantic Regions of Canada* (Regina: Canadian Plains Research Centre, University of Regina, 1992), pp. 1-17.
7. Janine Brodie, *The Political Economy of Canadian Regionalism* (Toronto: Harcourt Brace Jovanovich, 1990), p. 17.
8. For further discussion, see Alan Cairns, "Constitutional Change and the Three Equalities," in Ronald Watts and Douglas Brown, eds., *Options for a New Canada* (Toronto: University of Toronto Press, 1991), pp. 77-102; and Janine Brodie, *Canadian Regionalism*, pp. 6-18.

9. Richard Simeon argues that "institutions are not simply the outgrowth or products of the environment and that they are not just dependent variables in the political system. They can also be seen as independent forces, which have some effects of their own: once established they themselves come to shape and influence the environment." See Richard Simeon, "Regionalism and Canadian Political Institutions," p. 297.

10. Ralph Winters, "Federal-Provincial Fiscal Relations and Maritime Union," in Donald Savoie and Ralph Winters, *The Maritime Provinces: Looking to the Future* (Moncton: The Canadian Institute for Research on Regional Development, 1993), p. 216.

11. According to Jackson and Jackson, "Ideology refers to an explicit doctrinal structure, providing a particular diagnosis of the ills of society, plus an accompanying 'action plan' for implementing prescribed solutions." See Robert Jackson and Doreen Jackson, *Politics in Canada: Culture, Institutions, and Public Policy*, 2d. ed., (Scarborough: Prentice-Hall, 1990), p. 82.

12. For further discussion, see Richard Simeon and David Elkins, eds., *Small Worlds: Provinces and Parties in Canadian Political Life* (Toronto: Methuen Press, 1980); Robert J. Brym, ed., *Regionalism in Canada* (Richmond Hill: Irwin, 1986); and David Bell, *The Roots of Disunity: A Study of Canadian Political Culture*, rev. ed., (Toronto: Oxford University Press, 1992).

13. The term *executive federalism* was first coined by Donald Smiley. See D.V. Smiley, *Canada in Question: Federalism in the Seventies* (Toronto: McGraw-Hill Ryerson, 1976), chap. 3.

14. See Richard Simeon, *Federal-Provincial Diplomacy: The Making of Recent Policy in Canada* (Toronto: University of Toronto Press, 1972), Introduction.

15. It has never been easy promoting cooperative and effective decision making in a system of intergovernmental relations organized around competing principles. For details on how the blending of federalism and parliamentary government has created intense pressures for increased diversity, pluralism and decentralization in Canada, see Alan Cairns, *Constitution, Government, and Society in Canada* (Toronto: McClelland and Stewart, 1988); and Alan Cairns, *Disruptions: Constitutional Struggles from the Charter to Meech Lake* (Toronto: McClelland and Stewart, 1991).

16. D.V. Smiley, *Canada in Question: Federalism in the Seventies* (Toronto: McGraw-Hill Ryerson, 1976), p. 184.

17. For details on the concept of province-building, see E. Black and A. Cairns, "A different Perspective on Canadian Federalism," *Canadian Public Administration*, IX, 1 (March 1966), pp. 27-45.

18. Alan Cairns, *Constitution, Government and Society*, p. 144.

19. See G. Horowitz, *Canadian Labour in Politics* (Toronto: University of Toronto Press, 1968); and J. Porter, *The Vertical Mosaic* (Toronto: University of Toronto Press, 1965).

20. See A.V. Dicey, *Introduction to the Study of the Law of the Constitution* (London: Macmillan Canada, 1964); A. Schonfeld, *Modern Capitalism: The Changing Balance of Public and Private Power* (London: Oxford University Press, 1965); and S. Tarrow, "Introduction" in S.Tarrow *et al.*, eds., *Territorial Politics in Industrial Nations* (New York: Praeger, 1978), pp. 1-27.

21. Alan Cairns, "The Embedded State: State-Society Relations in Canada," in Keith Banting, comp. *State and Society: Canada in Comparative Perspective* (Toronto: University of Toronto Press, 1986), p. 55.

22. This quote appeared in Gabriel A. Almond, "The Development of Political Development," in Myron Weiner and Samuel Huntington, eds., *Understanding Political Development* (Boston: Little, Brown and Company, 1987), p. 446.

23. Roger Gibbins, *Regionalism* (Toronto: Butterworths, 1982), p. 4.

24. See Gabriel Almond and G. Brigham Powell, Jr., *Comparative Politics: A Developmental Approach* (Boston: Little, Brown and Company, 1966); and Gabriel Almond and Sidney Verba, eds., *The Civic Culture Revisited* (Boston: Little, Brown and Company, 1980).

25. Janine Brodie, *Canadian Regionalism*, p. 17.

26. See *Ibid.*, pp. 17-18.

27. Donald Savoie, "The Atlantic Region: The Politics of Dependency," in R.D. Olling and M.W. Westmacott, *Perspectives on Canadian Federalism* (Scarborough: Prentice-Hall, 1988), p. 293.

28. For details, see Norman L. Nicholson, *The Boundaries of the Canadian Confederation* (Macmillan Canada, 1979).

29. For examples, see J. Murray Beck, "An Atlantic Region Political Culture," in David Jay Bercuson and Philip A. Buckner, eds., *Eastern and Western Perspectives* (Toronto: University of Toronto Press, 1981), pp. 147-68; David Bellamy, "The Atlantic Provinces," in David Bellamy, Jon H. Pammett and Donald C. Rowat, eds., *The Provincial Political Systems* (Toronto: Methuen Press, 1976), pp. 3-18; and David Elkins and Richard Simeon, "Provincial Political Cultures in Canada," in *Small Worlds* (Toronto: Methuen Press, 1980), pp. 31-76.

30. R.A. Young, "Teaching and Research on Maritime Politics: Old Stereotypes and New Directions," in P.A. Buckner, ed., *Teaching Maritime Studies* (Fredericton: Acadiensis Press, 1986), p. 153.

31. For examples, see E.R. Forbes, *Challenging Regional Stereotypes* (Fredericton: Acadiensis Press, 1989); Ian Stewart, "Studying Maritime Politics," in P.A. Buckner, ed., *Teaching Maritime Studies*, pp. 136-45; and Peter Boswell, "The Atlantic Provinces," in Michael Whittington and Glen Williams, eds., *Canadian Politics in the 1990s* (Scarborough: Nelson Canada, 1990), pp. 119-36.

32. For example, Robin Fisher in his book on Premier Patullo's approach to province-building begins by stating, "I began to look at the life of Duff Patullo because a provincial premier who was unanimously condemned by the historians of central Canadian politics was bound to be extremely interesting." See Robin Fisher, *Duff Patullo of British Columbia* (Toronto: University of Toronto Press, 1991), p. x. I have also argued that one of the great myths of the study of British Columbia politics is the dominant view that the rise of the W.A.C. Bennett administration in 1952 introduced an era of incompetent and short-sighted leadership. See Stephen Tomblin, "W.A.C. Bennett and Province-Building in British Columbia," *BC Studies*, 85, (Spring 1990), p. 45. For other examples, see R. Douglas Francis, "Changing Images of the West," in Eli Mandel and David Taras, *A Passion for Identity* (Toronto:

Methuen Press, 1987), pp. 342-59; Doug Owram, "Reluctant Hinterland," in R.S. Blair and J.T. Mcleod, eds., *The Canadian Political Tradition* (Scarborough: Nelson Canada, 1989), pp. 104-19; and Roger Gibbins, *Prairie Politics and Society: Regionalism in Decline* (Toronto: Butterworths, 1980).

33. *Toronto Globe and Mail*, 2 December 1993.

34. Richard Simeon, *Federal-Provincial Diplomacy: The Making of Recent Policy in Canada* (Toronto: University of Toronto Press, 1974), pp. 11-12.

Chapter Two

1. Edwin R. Black, *Divided Loyalties: Canadian Concepts of Federalism* (Kingston and Montreal: McGill-Queen's University Press, 1975), p. 1.

2. Bruce W. Hodgins, John J. Eddy, Shelagh D. Grant, and John Atchison, "Dynamic Federalism in Canada and Australia: Continuity and Change," in Bruce W. Hodgins, John J. Eddy, Shelagh D. Grant, and James Struthers, eds., *Federalism in Canada and Australia: Historical Perspectives 1920-1988* (Peterborough: Broadview Press, 1989), p. 20.

3. There have been three National Policies or attempts to carve regions out of the geographic landscape. The First National state economic growth model started in 1869 and ended decades later with the settling of the West. The Second National Policy began in the 1940s and ended in the 1970s. The 1970s witnessed the rapid rise and decline of our Third National Plan within one decade. For details see Janine Brodie, *The Political Economy of Canadian Regionalism.*

4. The supporters of a Triple-E Senate have been fighting for a second chamber based on the principle of provincial equality. For many westerners and Atlantic Canadians, the current second chamber is seen as a symbol of their second-class status since it is based on a regional rather than a provincial formula. For further discussion on the Senate issue, see Roger Gibbins, "Alberta and the National Community," in Allen Tupper and Roger Gibbins, eds., *Government and Politics in Alberta* (Edmonton: University of Alberta Press, 1992), pp. 75-77; Peter McCormick, Ernest Manning, and Gordon Gibson, *Regional Representation: The Canadian Partnership* (Calgary: Canada West Foundation, 1981); Roger Gibbins, *Regionalism: Territorial Politics in Canada and the United States* (Toronto: Butterworths, 1982); and Donald Smiley and Ron Watts, *Intrastate Federalism in Canada* (Toronto: University of Toronto Press, 1985).

5. Larry Pratt and John Richards, *Prairie Capitalism* (Toronto: McClelland and Stewart, 1979), p.15.

6. For futher details on the First National Policy, see D.G. Creighton, *Canada's First Century: 1867–1967* (Toronto: Macmillan Canada, 1970); D.V. Smiley, "Canada and the Quest for a National Policy," *Canadian Journal of Political Science* 8(1975) pp.40-62; Vernon Fowke, *The National Policy and the Wheat Economy* (Toronto: University of Toronto Press, 1957); C.B. Macpherson, *Democracy in Alberta* (Toronto: University of Toronto Press, 1953); Peter Leslie, *Federal State, National Economy* (Toronto: University

of Toronto Press, 1987); and Janine Brodie, *The Political Economy of Canadian Regionalism* (Toronto: Harcourt Brace Jovanovich, 1990).

7. For further details on the emergence of a "quasi-colonial" economy in the West, see C.B. Macpherson, *Democracy in Alberta*, pp.5-10.

8. B. Kaye and D.W. Moodie, "Geographic Perspectives on the Canadian Plains," in Richard Allen, ed., *A Region of the Mind* (Regina: Canadian Plains Study Centre, 1973), p. 17.

9. *Ibid.*, p. 17.

10. For details, see Joel S. Migdal, "Strong States, Weak States: Power and Accommodation," in Myron Weiner and Samuel Huntington, eds., *Understanding Political Development* (Boston: Little, Brown and Company, 1987).

11. V. Fowke, *The National Policy* (Toronto: University of Toronto Press, 1957), p. 282.

12. Jean Barman, *The West beyond the West: A History of British Columbia* (Toronto: University of Toronto Press, 1991), p. 346. For details on the debate over Confederation, see British Columbia Legislative Council, *Debate on the Subject of Confederation with Canada* (Victoria: Queen's Printer, 1870).

13. For futher details on the many obstacles that were imposed on British Columbia, see Margaret Ormsby, *British Columbia: A History* (Toronto: Macmillan Canada, 1958); Robin Martin, *Pillars of Profit* (Toronto: McClelland and Stewart, 1973); James Aylsworth, "From Ruin to Rule: The Conservative Party of British Columbia, 1928–54" (Ph.D. Thesis, University of British Columbia, 1975); Patricia Roy, "Progress, Prosperity, and Politics: The Railway Policies of Richard Mcbride," *B.C. Studies* 47(1980), pp. 3-28; David Mitchell, *W.A.C. Bennett and the Rise of British Columbia* (Vancouver: Douglas and McIntyre, 1983); Jean Barman, *The West beyond the West*; and Robin Fisher, *Duff Pattullo of British Columbia* (Toronto: University of Toronto Press, 1991).

14. See A.D. Scott, "Introduction: Notes on a Western Viewpoint," in Dickson M. Falconer, ed., *British Columbia: Patterns in Economic Political and Cultural Development* (Victoria: Camosun College, 1982), p. 172.

15. It is worth noting that Ottawa's management or mismanagement of the Peace River Block was seen by W.A.C. Bennett as a major cause of underdevelopment in his province. For details, see *B.C. Government News*, February 1958, p. 3. It was an odd situation in which a national government controlled a region within a province that had great economic potential. Control over the territory was returned to British Columbia at the same time that the prairie provinces gained control over their natural resources.

16. For W.A.C. Bennett's views on the Peace River Block and the high costs imposed by Ottawa on the province, see "Presentation to Royal Commission on the B.C. Railway from W.A.C. Bennett," 6 September 1977, University of British Columbia, Main Library, Special Collections, exhibit 173A; and *B.C. Government News*, February 1958, p. 3.

17. Quoted in Jean Barman, *The West beyond the West*, p. 346.

18. Donald Creighton, *Canada's First Century* (Toronto: Macmillan Canada, 1970), p. 21.

19. For more information on this debate, see T.W. Acheson, David Frank, and James Frost, *Industrialization and Underdevelopment in the Maritimes, 1880-*

1930 (Toronto: Garamond Press, 1985); F.W.P. Bolger, *Prince Edward Island and Confederation, 1863–1873* (Charlottetown: St Dunstan's University Press, 1964); Frank MacKinnon, *The Government of Prince Edward Island* (Toronto: University of Toronto Press, 1951); J. Murray Beck, *The Government of Nova Scotia* (Toronto: University of Toronto Press, 1957); G.A. Rawlyk, ed., *The Atlantic Provinces and the Problems of Confederation* (Halifax: Breakwater Press, 1979); and H.G. Thorburn, *Politics in New Brunswick* (Toronto: University of Toronto Press, 1969).

20. Ernest Forbes, *Maritime Rights Movement, 1919–1927* (Kingston and Montreal: McGill-Queen's University Press, 1979), p. 4.

21. For an excellent overview of Maritime history, see Eric Sager and Lewis R. Fischer, "Atlantic Canada and the Age of Sail Revisited," in Douglas McCalla, ed., *Perspectives on Canadian Economic History* (Toronto: Copp Clark Pitman, 1987), pp. 97-117.

22. For details, see G.A. Rawlyk and Doug Brown, "The Historical Framework of the Maritimes and Confederation," in G.A. Rawlyk, ed., *The Atlantic Provinces and the Problems of Confederation* (Halifax: Breakwater Press, 1978), p. 22.

23. For futher details, see Philip J. Wood, "Nova Scotia: Social Structure and Politics," in Keith Brownsey and Michael Howlett, eds., *The Provincial State* (Mississauga: Copp Clark Pitman, 1992), pp. 57-80.

24. See James P. Bickerton, *Nova Scotia, Ottawa and the Politics of Regional Development* (Toronto: University of Toronto Press, 1990); and Ernest Forbes, *Maritime Rights Movement* (Kingston and Montreal: McGill-Queen's University Press, 1979).

25. Ernest Forbes, *Maritime Rights*, p. 22.

26. Ernest Forbes, *Challenging the Regional Stereotype* (Fredericton: Acadiensis Press, 1989).

27. For more information on the history of the Progressive Party, see David Laycock, *Populism and Democratic Thought in the Canadian Prairies, 1910 to 1945* (Toronto: University of Toronto Press, 1990); and C.B. Macpherson, *Democracy in Alberta*.

28. Anthony Careless, *Initiative and Response* (Kingston and Montreal: McGill-Queen's University Press, 1977), p. 19.

29. The evidence clearly indicates that the Maritimes and Prairies suffered more than B.C., Ontario, or Quebec during the depression years. For details, see Richard Simeon and Ian Robinson, *State, Society, and the Development of Canadian Federalism* (Toronto: University of Toronto Press, 1990), p. 63.

30. For further discussion, see Roger Gibbins, *Regionalism* (Toronto: Butterworths, 1982), chap. 2.

31. For a discussion of Keynesian economic theory and the impact on state planning in Canada, see Robert Campbell, *Grand Illusions: The Politics of the Keynesian Experience in Canada, 1945-1975* (Toronto: Broadview Press, 1987).

32. See Canada, *Report of the Royal Commission on Dominion-Provincial Relations* (Ottawa: King's Printer, 1940), often referred to as the Rowell-Sirois Commission study.

33. Alan Cairns, *Disruptions* (Toronto: McClelland and Stewart, 1991), p. 182.

34. For details on how experts acquire power and on the problems that are created for politicians, see Eva Etzioni-Halevy, *Bureaucracy and Democracy* (London: Routledge and Kegan Paul, 1983); and Guy Benveniste, *The Politics of Expertise* (San Francisco: Boyd and Fraser, 1977).

35. For details, see Doug Owram, *The Government Generation: Canadian Intellectuals and the State* (Toronto: University of Toronto Press, 1986), pp. 52-55, 77-78, 163.

36. Richard Simeon and Ian Robinson, *State, Society, and the Development of Canadian Federalism* (Toronto: University of Toronto Press, 1990), p. 122.

37. Doug Owram, *Government Generation*, pp. 131, 192-220.

38. See *ibid*, pp. 63-64, 77-78, 121, 139, 144, 147, 152, 220.

39. See *ibid*, pp. 221-41.

40. Richard Simeon and Ian Robinson, *Development of Canadian Federalism*, p. 84.

41. For further information, see D.V. Smiley, *Canada in Question: Federalism in the Eighties* (Toronto: McGraw-Hill Ryerson, 1980), p. 166.

42. For further discussion, see Richard Simeon and Ian Robinson, *Development of Canadian Federalism*, pp. 84-86; and Anthony Careless, *Initiative and Response*, p. 24.

43. James Bickerton, *Politics of Regional Development*, p. 91.

44. D. Smiley, ed., *The Rowell-Sirois Report, Book I* (Toronto: McClelland and Stewart, 1963), p. 138. This quote appeared in Janine Brodie, *Canadian Regionalism*, p. 140.

45. For details, see *Rowell-Sirois, Book II*, pp. 165-71.

46. For details, see Donald Creighton, *Canada's First Century*, p. 231

47. *Rowell-Sirois, Book II*, pp. 105-107.

48. See J.K. Galbraith, *The New Industrial State* (Boston: Houghton Mifflin, 1967).

49. Harold Laski, "The Obsolescence of Federalism," *New Republic*, 3 May 1939, p. 367.

50. See P. Resnick, *The Land of Cain* (Vancouver: New Star Books, 1977); Wallace Clement, *The Canadian Corporate Elite* (Toronto: McClelland and Stewart, 1975); James Laxer and Robert Laxer, *The Liberal Idea of Canada* (Toronto: James Lorimer and Company, 1977); Wallace Clement, *Class, Power and Property* (Toronto: Methuen Press, 1983); and Melissa Clark-Jones, *A Staple State* (Toronto: University of Toronto Press, 1987).

51. See Robert Campbell, *Grand Illusions* (Toronto: Broadview Press, 1987).

52. As indicated by Keohane and Nye, transnational is defined as "contacts, coalitions, and interactions across state boundaries that are not controlled by the central foreign policy organs of governments." See Robert O. Keohane and Joseph S. Nye, Jr., "Transnational Relations and World Politics: An Introduction," in Robert O. Keohane and Joseph S. Nye, Jr., eds., *Transnational Relations and World Politics* (Cambridge: Harvard University Press, 1972), p. xi. This information was first discovered by the author in Roger Gibbins' article on borderland regions. See Roger Gibbins, *Canada as a Borderlands Society*, Borderlands Monograph Series, no.2, (Orono, Me.: Borderlands Project, 1989), p. 3.

53. Richard Simeon and Ian Robinson, *Development of Canadian Federalism*, p. 120.

54. See Joel Garreau, *The Nine Nations of North America* (New York: Avon Books, 1982).

55. See Department of Reconstruction, *White Paper on Employment and Income* (Ottawa: King's Printer, 1945).

56. Dominion-Provincial Conference on Reconstruction, *Proposals of the Government of Canada* (Ottawa: King's Printer, 1945).

57. See Craig Heron, *The Canadian Labour Movement* (Toronto: James Lorimer and Company, 1989), p. 80.

58. Keith Banting, *The Welfare State and Canadian Federalism*, 2d ed. (Kingston and Montreal: McGill-Queen's University Press, 1987), p. 31.

59. Richard Simeon and Ian Robinson, *Development of Canadian Federalism*, p. 120.

60. See Government of Newfoundland, "Proposal for the New Income Supplementation Program and Other Reforms to the Income Security System," December 1993, issued by the Economic Recovery Commission.

61. For further details, see *ibid.*, pp. 85-88.

62. For further discussion of these many problems, see Newfoundland, *Royal Commission on Employment and Unemployment, Final Report: Building on Our Strengths* (St John's: Queen's Printer, 1986), pp. 406-9.

63. See Newfoundland and Labrador, *Change and Challenge: A Strategic Economic Plan for Newfoundland and Labrador* (St John's: Queen's Printer, 1992); and Dr. Charles J. McMillan, *Standing Up to the Future: The Maritimes in the 1990s* (Halifax: Council of Maritime Premiers, 1989).

64. Keith Banting, *Canadian Federalism*, p. 119.

65. *Ibid.*, p. 88.

66. Much of this paragraph was influenced by interviews conducted by the author.

67. See Liberal Party of Canada, *Creating Opportunity: The Liberal Plan for Canada* (Ottawa: The Liberal Party, 1993), p. 59.

68. See *Toronto Globe and Mail*, 27 January 1994.

69. For details, see T.N. Brewis, *Regional Economic Policies in Canada* (Toronto: Macmillan Canada, 1969), chaps. 6,7,8.

70. Anthony Careless, *Initiative and Response*, p. 38.

71. *Ibid.*, p. 187.

72. For details on the Department of Regional Economic Development, see Peter Aucoin and Herman Bakvis, *Centralization-Decentralization Conundrum: Organization and Management in the Canadian Government* (Halifax: The Institute for Research on Public Policy, 1988); and Donald Savoie, *Regional Economic Development* (Toronto: University of Toronto Press, 1986).

73. For an assessment of Trudeau's approach to federalism, see Alan Cairns, *Charter versus Federalism* (Montreal and Kingston: McGill-Queen's University Press, 1992); and Alan Cairns, *Disruptions* (Toronto: McClelland and Stewart, 1991).

74. Donald Savoie, *The Politics of Public Spending in Canada* (Toronto: University of Toronto Press, 1990), p. 271.

75. For details on General Development Agreements, see Donald Savoie, *Federal-Provincial Collaboration* (Kingston and Montreal: McGill-Queen's University Press, 1981).

76. For further discussion on the breakdown in the Keynesian consensus and the rise of monetarism, see Stephen Brooks, *Public Policy in Canada* (Toronto: McClelland and Stewart, 1989), pp. 166-172.

77. For further discussion, see G. Bruce Doern and Richard W. Phidd, *Canadian Public Policy* (Toronto: Methuen Press, 1983), chap. 14.

78. David Milne, *Tug of War* (Toronto: James Lorimer and Company, 1986), p. 70-71.

79. For further details, see Pierre Elliot Trudeau, *The Constitution and the People of Canada* (Ottawa: Queen's Printer, 1969); Pierre Elliot Trudeau, *Federalism and the French Canadians* (Toronto: Macmillan, 1968); Canada, *A Time For Action* (Ottawa: Queen's Printer, 1978); Pierre Elliot Trudeau, "Who Speaks for Canada?: Defining and Sustaining a National Vision," in Michael D. Behiels, ed., *The Meech Lake Primer* (Ottawa: Ottawa University Press, 1989), pp. 60-99; David E. Smith, "Party Government, Representation and National Integration in Canada," in Peter Aucoin, research coordinator, *Party Government and Regional Representation in Canada* (Toronto: University of Toronto Press, 1985), pp. 1-68; Alan Cairns, *Charter versus Federalism*; and Alan Cairns, *Disruptions*.

80. For further details on consociationalism and Canadian federalism, see various articles in Kenneth McRae, ed., *Consociational Democracy* (Ottawa: McClelland and Stewart, 1974).

81. For further details on the role played by experts in the struggle to redesign the federal system based on a rational plan, see Colin Campbell and George Szablowski, *The Super-Bureaucrats* (Toronto: Macmillan Canada, 1979).

82. Peter Leslie, *Federal State, National Economy* (Toronto: University of Toronto Press, 1987), p. 8.

83. For further details on the third national development strategy, see *ibid.*, pp. 8-9.

84. For further details, see G. Bruce Doern and Glen Toner, *The NEP and the Politics of Energy* (Toronto: Methuen Press, 1985); Carlo Caldarola, ed., *Society and Politics in Alberta* (Toronto: Methuen Press, 1979); Roger Gibbins, Keith Archer, and Stan Drabek, eds., *Canadian Political Life: An Alberta Perspective* (Dubuque, Iowa: Kendall/Hunt, 1990); and J.D. House, *The Challenge of Oil* (St John's: Institute of Social Economic Research, 1985).

85. See Peter Leslie, *Federal State, National Economy*, p. 10.

86. For more information on the Foreign Investment Review Agency, see G. Bruce Doern and Richard W. Phidd, *Canadian Public Policy*, p. 427; and Stephen Brooks, *Public Policy in Canada*, pp. 29, 206, 231.

87. Peter Leslie, *Federal State, National Economy*, p. 18.

88. See G. Bruce Doern and Richard W. Phidd, *Canadian Public Policy*, pp. 432-47..Peter Leslie, *Federal State, National Economy*, p. 18.

89. Richard Simeon and Ian Robinson, *Development of Canadian Federalism*, p. 231.

90. For details, see Stephen Randall, Herman Konrad, and Sheldon Silverman, *North America without Borders?* (Calgary: University of Calgary Press, 1992).

91. Peter Leslie, *Federal State, National Economy*, p. 23.

92. Canada, *Report of the Royal Commission on Economic Union and Development Prospects for Canada* vol.1, (Ottawa: Queen's Printer, 1985), p. xi.

93. There are many examples of recent academic attempts to come to grips with the realities of shifting boundaries. The Canadian-American Center at the University of Maine has played a pivotal role in facilitating a discourse on the meaning of shifting boundaries in North America. Lauren McKinsey and Victor Konrad in *Borderland Reflections: The United States and Canada* (Borderlands Monograph Series no. 1, Orono, Me: Borderlands Project, 1989) provide a new framework for organizing a new discourse based on the realities of borderless economies and societies. Other important materials produced by the Canadian-American Center include: Roger Gibbins, *Canada as a Borderlands Society* (Borderlands Monograph Series no. 2, Orono, Me: Borderlands Project, 1989); and Martin Lipset, *North America Cultures: Values and Institutions in Canada and the United States* (Borderlands Monograph no. 3, Orono, Me: Borderlands Project, 1990). Other examples include: Stephen J. Hornsby, Victor A. Konrad, and James J. Herlans, eds., *The Northeastern Borderlands: Four Centuries of Interaction* (Fredericton: Acadiensis Press, 1989); Stephen Randall, Herman Konrad, and Sheldon Silverman, *North America without Borders?*; James McCrorie and Martha MacDonald, eds., *The Constitutional Future of the Prairie and Atlantic Regions of Canada* (Regina: Canadian Plains Institute, University of Regina, 1992).

94. For a review of the socio-economic and political changes that took place in Canada during the 1980s and the impact of Mulroney's leadership, see Daniel Drache and Meric Gertler, eds., *The New Era of Global Competition: State Policy and Market Power* (Kingston and Montreal: McGill-Queens University Press, 1991); Michael Atkinson, "On the Prospects for Industrial Policy in Canada," *Canadian Public Administration*, 27, (1984), pp. 454-67; David Bercuson, J.L. Granatstein, and W.R. Young, *Sacred Trust? Brian Mulroney and the Conservative Party in Power* (Toronto: Doubleday Canada, 1986); and Peter Aucoin, "The Machinery of Government: From Trudeau's Rational Management to Mulroney's Brokerage Politics," in Leslie Pal and David Taras, eds., *Prime Ministers and Premiers: Political Leadership and Public Policy in Canada* (Scarborough: Prentice-Hall, 1988), pp. 50-68.

95. For information on funding cuts for regional development programs, see Janine Brodie, *Canadian Regionalism*, pp. 215-16.

96. For details, see Earl H. Fry, "Subnational Federal Units in an Age of Complex Independence," and James D. McNiven and Dianna Cann, "Canadian Provincial Trade Offices in the United States." Both appeared in Douglas Brown and Earl Fry, eds., *States and Provinces in the International Economy* (Boston: University Press of America, 1988), pp. 75-90, and pp. 167-184, respectively.

97. For an account of these changes in Ottawa's approach to constitutional reform, see Canada, *A Guide to the Constitutional Accord* (Ottawa: Queen's

Printer, 1987); Ronald Watts and Douglas Brown, eds., *Options For Canada* (Toronto: University of Toronto Press, 1991); David Smith, Peter MacKinnon, and John Courtney, eds., *After Meech Lake: Lessons For the Future* (Saskatoon: Fifth House Publishers, 1991); and Michael D. Behiels, ed., *The Meech Lake Primer* (Ottawa: University of Ottawa Press, 1989).

98.   Alan Cairns, *Disruptions*, p. 156-57.

Chapter Three

1.   Canada, *Report of the Royal Commission on Dominion-Provincial Relations* Book II (Ottawa: King's Printer, 1940), p. 167.

2.   For further details, see David Easton, "The Analysis of Political Systems," in Roy C. Mcridis and Bernard E. Brown, eds., *Comparative Politics: Notes and Readings* (Homewood, Ill.: Dorsey Press, 1968).

3.   See Gabriel Almond and Sidney Verba, *The Civic Culture* (Princeton: Princeton University Press, 1963), pp. 13-14.

4.   Malcolm Macleod, *Kindred Countries: Canada and Newfoundland before Confederation,* The Canadian Historical Association, Booklet No. 52 (Ottawa: 1994), p. 26.

5.   Valerie Summers, *Regime Change in a Resource Economy* (St John's: Breakwater Press, 1994), p. 17.

6.   *Report of Newfoundland Royal Commission, 1933* (London: His Majesty's Stationary Office, 1934), commission was chaired by Lord Amulree.

7.   See Valerie Summers, *Regime Change,* p. 90.

8.   Valerie Summers, *Regime Change,* p. 17.

9.   For further information, see F.L. Jackson, *Newfoundland in Canada: A People in Search of a Polity* (St John's: Harry Cuff, 1984); A. Brian Peckford, *The Past in The Present* (St John's: Creative Printers, 1983); J.D. House, "The Mouse That Roars: New Directions in Political Economy-The Case of Newfoundland" in Robert Brymn, ed., *Regionalism in Canada* (Toronto: Irwin Publishing, 1986), pp. 161-97.

10.   See Richard Gwyn, *Smallwood: The Unlikely Revolutionary* (Toronto: McClelland and Stewart, 1968); Terry Campbell and G. A. Rawlyk, "The Historical Framework of Newfoundland and Confederation" in G.A. Rawlyk, ed., *The Atlantic Provinces and the Problems of Confederation* (St John's: Breakwater Press, 1979), pp. 1-47; David Alexander, *Atlantic Canada and Confederation* (Toronto: University of Toronto Press, 1983); Frederick Rowe, *A History of Newfoundland and Labrador* (McGraw-Hill Ryerson, 1980); Philip Smith, *Brinco: The Story of Churchill Falls* (Toronto: McClelland and Stewart, 1975); and Valerie Summers, "Newfoundland: Resource Politics and Regime Change in the Federal Era, 1949–1991," in Keith Brownsley and Michael Howlett, eds., *The Provincial State* (Mississauga: Copp Clark Pitman, 1992), pp. 9-30.

11.   See James Hiller and Peter Neary, eds., *Newfoundland in the Nineteenth and Twentieth Centuries* (Toronto: University of Toronto Press, 1980); S.J.R. Noel, *Politics in Newfoundland* (Toronto: University of Toronto Press, 1971); Gertrude E. Gunn, *The Political History Of Newfoundland 1832–1864*

(Toronto: University of Toronto Press, 1966); and Ian D.H. McDonald *To Each His Own: William Coaker and the Fishermen's Protective Union in Newfoundland Politics, 1908–1925*, J.K. Hiller, ed., (St John's: Institute of Social and Economic Research, 1987).

12. For further details, see Rosemary E. Ommer, "What's Wrong with Canadian Fish?" in Peter Sinclair, ed., *A Question of Survival* (St John's: Institute of Social Economic Research, 1988), pp. 23–44; and David Alexander, *Atlantic Canada and Confederation* (Toronto: University of Toronto, 1983), Chap. 1.

13. For a review of staples theory see Mel Watkins, "A Staple Theory of Economic Growth," in G. Laxer, ed., *Perspectives on Canadian Economic Development* (Toronto: University of Oxford Press, 1991), pp. 80–100; and Michael Howlett and M. Ramesh, *The Political Economy of Canada* (Toronto: McClelland and Stewart, 1992).

14. See Government of Newfoundland and Labrador, *Royal Commission on Employment and Unemployment, Final Report: Building on Our Strengths* (St John's: Queen's Printer, 1986), pp. 406–409.

15. *Ibid.*, p. 40.

16. For further details, see Gordon Inglis, *More Than Just a Union: The Story of the NFFAWU* (St John's: Jesperson Press, 1985); James Overton, "Small is Beautiful and the Crisis in Newfoundland," in Bryant Fairley, Colin Leys, and James Sacouman, eds., *Restructuring and Resistance: Perspectives from Atlantic Canada* (Toronto: Garamond Press, 1990), pp. 43–78; and A. Paul Pross and Susan McCorquodale, *Economic Resurgence and the Constitutional Agenda: The Case of the East Coast Fisheries* (Kingston: Institute of Intergovernmental Relations, Queen's University, 1987), Chap. 3.

17. See David Milne, "Politics in a Beleaguered Garden," in Verner Smitheram, David Milne, and Satadal Dasgupta, eds., *The Garden Transformed, 1945–1980* (Charlottetown: Ragweed Press, 1982).

18. David Milne, "Prince Edward Island: Politics in a Beleaguered Island," in Keith Brownsley and Michael Howlett, eds., *The Provincial State*, p. 32.

19. For further details on Prince Edward Island politics, see Frank MacKinnon, *The Government of Prince Edward Island* (Toronto: University of Toronto Press, 1951); Frank MacKinnon, "Prince Edward Island: Big Engine, Little Body," in M. Robin, ed., *Canadian Provincial Politics*, 2d ed. (Scarborough: Prentice-Hall, 1978); F.W.P. Bolger, ed., *Canada's Smallest Province* (Charlottetown: P.E.I. Centennial Commission, 1973); Ian Stewart, "Friends at Court: An Analysis of Prince Edward Island Provincial Elections," *Canadian Journal of Political Science,* (March, 1986); and Rand Dyck, *Provincial Politics in Canada*, 2d ed., (Scarborough: Prentice-Hall, 1991).

20. See Canada, Department of Regional Economic Expansion, *Development Plan for Prince Edward Island* (Ottawa: Queen's Printer, 1969).

21. See Rand Dyck, *Provincial Politics in Canada*, p. 106.

22. For details, see Della Stanley, *Louis Robichaud: A Decade of Power* (Halifax: Nimbus Publishing, 1984); Louis Robichaud, interview by Janet Toole, 7 June 1988, University of New Brunswick, Province Archives; and Robert Young, "Development, Planning and Participation in New Brunswick: 1945–1975" (Ph.D. Thesis, Linacre College, 1979).

23. For futher details on Ottawa's disregard for the constitution when it came to regional development policy, see Anthony Careless, *Initiative and Response: The Adaptation of Canadian Federalism to Regional Economic Development* (Kingston and Montreal: McGill-Queen's University Press, 1977).

24. See Robert Young, "Remembering Equal Opportunity: Clearing the Undergrowth in New Brunswick," *Canadian Public Administration* 30, 1 (Spring 1987); and Stephen Tomblin, "The Council of Maritime Permiers and the Battle for Territorial Integrity," *Journal of Canadian Studies* 26, 1 (Spring 1991).

25. Based on interviews.

26. For examples of stage theory, see John Wilson, "The Canadian Political Cultures," *Canadian Journal of Political Science* 7 (1974) pp. 438-83; and S.J.R. Noel, "Leadership and Clientelism," in David Bellamy *et al.*, eds., *The Provincial Political Systems* (Toronto: Methuen Press, 1976). For details on the orthodox perspective, see Robert Brym, ed., *Regionalism in Canada* (Toronto: Irwin Press, 1986). For details on the civic culture approach, see Gabriel and Sidney Verba, *The Civic Culture* (Boston: Little, Brown and Company, 1965); and David Elkins and Richard Simeon, "Regional Political Cultures," in David Elkins and Richard Simeon, eds., *Small Worlds* (Toronto: Methuen Press, 1980).

27. Much of the information presented in this paragraph was based on interviews conducted by the author.

28. As indicated by one scholar, "Nova Scotia has usually regarded itself, and has been seen by outsiders, as the most prosperous and progressive of the Atlantic provinces." See Rand Dyck, *Provincial Politics in Canada*, p. 103.

29. *Ibid.*, p. 110.

30. For details, see Fred Drummie, interview by Janet Toole, February 1987, University of New Brunswick, Province Archives.

31. See Margaret Conrad, "The Atlantic Revolution of the 1950s," in Berkely Flemming, ed., *Beyond Anger and Longing: Community and Development in Atlantic Canada* (Fredericton: Acadiensis Press, 1988).

32. Based on interviews.

33. See Fred Drummie, interview.

34. For further details on the struggle over municipal reform, see J.M. Beck, *The Evolution of Municipal Government in Nova Scotia, 1749–1973* (Halifax: A Study Prepared for the Graham Commission, 1974); Nova Scotia, *Royal Commission on Education, Public Services and Provincial-Municipal Relations* (Halifax: Queen's Printer, 1974); Donald Higgins, *Urban Canada* (Toronto: Macmillan Canada, 1976); and Harley d'Entremont, "Prospects for Provincial-Municipal Restructuring" (Ph.D. Thesis, University of Western Ontario, 1985).

35. A number of senior government officials interviewed in New Brunswick and Nova Scotia felt that the tendency of Nova Scotia élites to look down on people in New Brunswick probably influenced the way the issue of regional integration was interpreted in that province

36. See Paul Brown, "The Political Culture of Nova Scotia: An Historical-Cultural Analysis" (paper presented at the annual meetings of the Canadian Political Science Association, Halifax, May 1981).

37. For a fascinating look at the traditions of patronage in Nova Scotia politics, see Ian Stewart, "Despoiling the Public Sector? The Case of Nova Scotia," in John W. Langford and Allan Tupper, eds., *Corruption Character and Conduct: Essays on Canadian Government Ethnics* (Toronto: Oxford University Press, 1993), pp. 90-112.

38. Based on interviews.

39. For further details, see Council of Maritime Premiers, *Twenty Years of Partnership* (Halifax: The Council of Maritime Premiers, November, 1989); University of New Brunswick Archives, Records of the Office of Premier Hugh Flemming; Public Archives of Nova Scotia, Premier Henry Hick's papers (MG2 box 545, folder 1); and *The Atlantic Advocate*, June, 1957.

40. For further information on APEC, see Anthony Careless, *Initiative and Response* (Kingston and Montreal: McGill-Queen's University Press, 1977), pp. 30-31, 37, 111, 117-18; *The Atlantic Advocate*, November 1956; *The Atlantic Advocate*, September 1956; and Atlantic Provinces Economic Council, "APEC: Notes on the Proposed Agenda," Directors' meeting, 16 May 1955, Public Archives of Nova Scotia, box 550, F1/30.

41. See *The Atlantic Advocate,* September 1956, p. 15.

42. The New England Council, which began in 1925, provided a model for designing APEC. For further details, see "Speech to the Halifax Rotary Club by the President of APEC", Public Archives of Nova Scotia, 24 May 1955, box 550, F1/31.

43. For further details and discussion see Roger Gibbins, *Regionalism* (Toronto: Butterworths, 1982), chap. 4.

44. Much of the paragraph was informed by interviews conducted by the author.

45. See *The Atlantic Advocate*, September 1958.

46. *The Atlantic Advocate*, November 1959, p. 14.

47. *The Atlantic Advocate*, September 1958, p. 15-17.

48. See *The Atlantic Advocate*, September 1958; and "Records of the Office of Premier Hugh Flemming," University of New Brunswick Archives, RS 415 C9c, correspondence between Premier Flemming and the New England governors.

49. *The Atlantic Advocate*, September 1956, p. 38.

50. See Council of Maritime Premiers, *Twenty Years of Partnership*, p. 9; *The Atlantic Advocate*, September 1956, pp. 28-50; "Premier Henry Hick's Papers," telegram from Premier Hugh Flemming sent April 1956, Public Archives of Nova Scotia, MG2, box 545, folder 1.

51. For details on the Prime Minister's invitation and meetings with APEC officials in Ottawa, see *The Atlantic Advocate*, May 1957, p. 57; and *The Atlantic Advocate*, November 1956, p.9.

52. See *The Atlantic Advocate*, June 1957, pp. 11-13; and *The Atlantic Advocate*, September 1956, pp. 28-50.

53. See *The Atlantic Advocate*, June 1957.

54. See *The Atlantic Advocate*, September 1956.

55. For details, see Frederick Rowe, *History of Newfoundland and Labrador*, (Toronto: McGraw-Hill Ryerson, 1980), p. 520.

56. Parizival Copes, *The Resettlement of Fishing Communities in Newfoundland* (Ottawa: Canadian Council on Rural Development, 1972), p. 25.

57.   Raymond Blake, *Canadians at Last: Canada Integrates Newfoundland as a Province* (Toronto: University of Toronto Press, 1994), p. 6.
58.   For details, see Richard Gwyn, *The Unlikely Revolutionary*, pp. 184-198.
59.   *Ibid.*, p. 186.
60.   *The Atlantic Advocate*, November 1960, p. 82.
61.   Much of this paragraph was informed by interviews.
62.   See Louis Robichaud, interview, 7 June 1988.
63.   Della Stanley, *Louis Robichaud*, p. 59.
64.   For details on the Byrne Commission and the Equal Opportunity Program, see New Brunswick, *Report of the Royal Commission on Finance and Municipal Taxation* (Fredericton: Queen's Printer, 1963); Harley L. d'Entremont, "Prospects for Provincial-Municipal Restructuring" (Ph.D. Thesis, University of Western Ontario, 1985); R.A. Young, "Remembering Equal Opportunity: Clearing the Undergrowth of New Brunswick," *Canadian Public Administration*, 30, 1 (Spring 1987).
65.   These experts included A. Milton Moore, an economist from the University of British Columbia, Dr. Boudreau, Dr. John Graham, an economist from Dalhousie University, and Dr. H. White, a British economist. For details, see New Brunswick, *Royal Commission on Finance.*
66.   Many of the details provided in this paragraph came from interviews conducted by the author.
67.   See New Brunswick, *Royal Commission on Finance*, p. ix.
68.   *Ibid*, p. x.
69.   Louis Robichaud, interview, May 1987, p. 9.
70.   R.A. Young, "Remembering Equal Opportunity," p. 90.
71.   *Ibid.* p. 91.
72.   These planners included Donald Tansley, Desmond Fogg, Donald Junk, Robert Mclarty, and Graham Clarkson, among other outside experts who were attracted to New Brunswick because the Equal Opportunity Program provided an opportunity to apply theory. These experts were granted much autonomy in implementing the Byrne plan. See Della Stanley, *Louis Robichaud*, p. 92.
73.   Louis Robichaud, interview, 26 March 1987, p.4.
74.   *Ibid.* p. 3.
75.   See Council of Maritime Premiers, *Twenty Years of Partnership.*
76.   See Newfoundland and Labrador, *Royal Commission on Municipal Government in Newfoundland and Labrador* (St John's: Queen's Printer, 1974) p. 2.
77.   See *ibid.* p. 138.
78.   Economic Council of Canada, *Newfoundland: From Dependency to Self-Reliance* (Ottawa: Supply and Services Canada, 1980), p. 20.
79.   Based on interviews.
80.   Nova Scotia, New Brunswick and Prince Edward Island, *The Report on Maritime Union*, (Fredericton: Maritime Union Study, 1970), p. 25.
81.   *The Report on Maritime Union*, pp. 68-70.
82.   See *The Report on Maritime Union*, pp. 60-65.
83.   For further discussion on the impact of European integration and growth pole theory on regional development policies in Atlantic/Maritime Canada, see

William J. Coffey, W. Stephen Macdonald, and Andrew Harvey, "Intra-regional Disparities in Canada's Maritime Provinces," in A. Hecht, ed., *Regional Developments in the Peripheries of Canada and Europe* (Winnipeg: Department of Geography, University of Manitoba, 1983); Ian McAllister, *Regional Development and the European Community* (Ottawa: The Institute for Research on Public Policy, 1982); and Annual Report, Atlantic Provinces Economic Council, (1969–1970).

84.   For details, see Donald J. Savoie, *Regional Economic Development: Canada's Search for Solutions* (Toronto: University of Toronto Press, 1986), pp. 5-6.

85.   W.A.Jenkins, "Comments on the Paper on the Council of Maritime Premiers by A.A. Lomas," (paper presented at the 28th annual meeting of the Institute of Public Administration of Canada, Halifax, September 1976).

86.   For details, see Robert Stanfield, interview by Janet Toole, January 1988, University of New Brunswick, Province Archives.

87.   David Cameron, "The Report on Maritime Union," *Canadian Public Administration* 15, no. 1 (Spring 1972), p. 172.

88.   The premiers were naturally concerned about giving up power based on faith alone. For further details, see Alexander B. Campbell, Gerald A. Regan, and Richard B. Hatfield, "The Move toward Maritime Integration and the Role of the Council of Maritime Premiers," *Canadian Public Administration* 15, 4 (Winter 1972).

89.   These agencies included The Maritime Province Higher Education Commission, The Maritime Resource Management Service, The Maritime Municipal Training and Development Board; The Land Registration and Information Service. See *Fourth Annual Report*, Council of Maritime Premiers, (1975–76).

90.   Based on interviews.

91.   For a discussion of Nova Scotia's defensive approach to regional cooperation, see Andy Wells, interview by Janet Toole, 8 July 1987.

92.   Based on interviews.

93.   See Fred Drummie, interview.

94.   For more details, see Stephen Tomblin, "The Council of Maritime Premiers and the Battle for Territorial Integrity," *Journal of Canadian Studies* 26, 1 (Spring 1991), pp. 100-119.

95.   *The 22nd Session of the Council of Maritime Premiers* [press release], Charlottetown, P.E.I., 25-26 May 1976.

96.   See Fred Drummie, interview.

97.   For details, see J.D. House, "The Mouse That Roars".

98.   See J.D. House, "The Mouse That Roars," p. 170.

99.   *Ibid.*, p. 170.

100. For further discussion, see William E. Shrank, Noel Roy, Rosemary Ommer, and Blanca Skoda, "The Future of the Newfoundland Fishery," in James N. McCrorie and Martha MacDonald, eds., *The Constitutional Future of the Prairie and Atlantic Regions of Canada* (Regina: Canadian Plains Research Centre, 1992), pp. 122-51.

101. Based on interviews. Also see *St John's Evening Telegram*, 18 January 1985; and *Sunday Express*, 17 February 1991.

102. Based on interviews conducted by the author.
103. Donald Savoie, *Regional Economic Development* (Toronto: University of Toronto, 1986), p. 55.
104. For example, listen to the interview with Bob Rae conducted by The House, CBC Radio, 31 July 1993.
105. For further discussion, see The Morning Show, CBC Radio, 14 June 1991; Harry Bruce, Jennifer Henderson, and John Mason, "Hunt for Economic Union," *Commercial News* April 1991; *Toronto Globe and Mail*, 27 May 1991; *St John's Evening Telegram*, 26 May 1991, 27 September 1989, and 18 October 1989.
106. For examples, see Atlantic Provinces Economic Council, "Atlantic Economic Cooperation: An Exploration of the Concept, Its Benefits, and Costs," Background Paper, 1991, Dartmouth; Council of Maritime Premiers, "Challenge and Opportunity," 1991, Halifax, a discussion paper on Maritime economic integration; and *Toronto Globe and Mail*, 27 May 1991.
107. For a more radical interpretation of the integration question in Atlantic/Maritime Canada see Bryant Fairley, Colin Leys, and James Sacouman, eds., *Restructuring and Resistance: Perspectives from Atlantic Canada* (Toronto: Garamond Press, 1990); and Michael Bradfield et al., *Economic Development: Alternative Policies/Atlantic Possibilities*, National Union of Public and General Employees, 1992.
108. See James Feehan, "Atlantic Provinces Economic Union: A Newfoundland Perspective" (Department of Economics, Memorial University, 23 July 1991). Unpublished paper.
109. *Standing Up to the Future: The Maritimes in the 1990s* (Halifax: Council of Maritime Premiers, 1989).
110. *Ibid.*, p. 3.
111. *Ibid.*, p. 16.
112. *Ibid.*, p. 6.
113. *Ibid.*, p. 13.
114. *Ibid*, p. 5.
115. Toronto Globe and Mail, 14 August 1993.
116. See *The 81st Session of the Council of Maritime Premiers* [press release], Moncton, New Brunswick, 17-18 June 1991.
117. For details, see *St John's Evening Telegram*, 30, 31 October and 2 November 1991.
118. For details, see Council of Maritime Premiers, "The Forum of Maritime Cabinets," 1992, Halifax, various policy position papers.
119. See *St John's Evening Telegram*, 11 March, 3 April, 14, 26 May, and 3 July 1993.
120. For details, see *St John's Evening Telegram*, 25 June 1994.

Chapter Four

1. Alex Netherton, "The Shifting Points of Politics: A Neo-Institutional Analysis," in Keith Brownsley and Michael Howlett, eds., *The Provincial State* (Copp Clark Pitman, 1992), p. 180.

2. Paul Phillips, "The Canadian Prairies — One Economic Region Or Two," in James N. McCrorie and Martha L. MacDonald, eds., *The Constitutional Future* p. 38.

3. *Ibid.*, p. 40.

4. J.W. Grant MacEwan, *A Short History of Western Canada* (Toronto: McGraw-Hill Ryerson, 1968), p. 73.

5. See Rand Dyck, *Provincial Politics in Canada* (Scarborough: Prentice-Hall, 1991), p. 375.

6. For details, see *ibid.* p. 373.

7. J. Arthur Lower, *Western Canada: An Outline History* (Vancouver: Douglas and McIntyre, 1983), p. 195.

8. Nelson Wiseman, "The Pattern of Prairie Politics," in Eli Mandel and David Taras, eds., *A Passion for Identity* (Toronto: Methuen Press, 1987), p. 366.

9. Gerald Friesen, *The Canadian Prairies* (Toronto: University of Toronto Press, 1984), p. 403.

10. *Ibid.*, p. 366.

11. For further details, see Thomas Peterson, "Manitoba: Ethnic and Class Politics," in Martin Robin, ed., *Canadian Provincial Politics* (Scarborough: Prentice-Hall, 1978), pp. 61-119.

12. J. Arthur Lower, *Western Canada*, p. 195.

13. Alex Netherton, "The Shifting Points of Politics," p. 178.

14. For details see Rand Dyck, *Provincial Politics in Canada*, p. 389-390.

15. Alex Netherton, "The Shifting Points of Politics," p. 181.

16. For details on socio-economic and political life in Saskatchewan, see John Richards and Larry Pratt, *Prairie Capitalism*; Christopher Dunn and David Laycock, "Innovation and Competition in Agricultural Heartland," in Keith Brownsley and Michael Howlett, eds., *The Provincial State*, pp. 207-42; S.M. Lipset, *Agrarian Socialism: The Co-operative Commonwealth Federation in Saskatchewan* (Berkeley: University of California Press, 1950); James Pitsula and Ken Rasmussen, *Privatizing a Province: The New Right in Saskatchewan* (Vancouver: New Star oks, 1990); David Smith, *Prairie Liberalism: The Liberal Party in Saskatchewan, 1905–71* (Toronto: University of Toronto Press, 1975); and Duff Spafford and Norman Ward, eds., *Politics in Saskatchewan* (Don Mills: Longman, 1968).

17. For further details, see David Laycock, *Populism and Democratic Thought in the Canadian Prairies* (Toronto: University of Toronto Press, 1990).

18. Rand Dyck, *Provincial Politics in Canada*, p. 394.

19. *Ibid.*

20. For further details, see Larry Pratt and John Richards, *Prairie Capitalism*, chaps. 5, 6, 7, 8, 10, and 12.

21. C. Dunn and D. Laycock, "Agricultural Heartland," p. 225.

22. See *ibid.*, p. 226.

23. Alberta experimented with both the Progressive Party, which was based on radical assumptions and a direct model of democracy, as well as the Social Credit party, which was more authoritarian, expert-dominated, anti-participatory and "plebiscitarian" in its approach. For further details on these very different approaches for dealing with economic and political problems and their historical significance, see C.B. Macpherson, *Democracy in Alberta*

(Toronto: University of Toronto Press, 1954); David Laycock, *Populism and Democratic Thought* (Toronto: University of Toronto Press, 1990); Peter Sinclair, "Class Structure and Populist Protest," in Carla Caldarola, ed., *Society and Politics in Alberta* (Toronto: Methuen Press, 1979); John Irving, *The Social Credit Movement in Alberta* (Toronto: University of Toronto Press, 1959); J.R. Mallory, *Social Credit and the Federal Power in Canada* (Toronto: University of Toronto Press, 1954); and W.L. Morton, *The Progressive Party in Canada* (Toronto: University of Toronto, 1950).

24. See Larry Pratt and John Richards, *Prairie Capitalism*, p. 164.
25. Nelson Wiseman, "The Pattern of Prairie Politics," in Eli Mandel and David Taras, eds., *A Passion for Identity* (Toronto: Methuen Press, 1987), p. 373. For further details on Alberta as a one-class and quasi-colonial society, see C.B. Macpherson, *Democracy in Alberta*. For an alternative view on the thesis that Alberta began as a one-class society, see Larry Pratt and John Richards, *Prairie Capitalism*, pp. 149-153.
26. See David Laycock, *Populism and Democratic Thought*, pp. 20, 70.
27. *Ibid.*, p. 23.
28. See C.B. Macpherson, *Democracy in Alberta*.
29. David Laycock, *Populism and Democratic Thought*, p. 208.
30. *Ibid.*, p. 214.
31. Larry Pratt and John Richards, *Prairie Capitalism*, p. 167.
32. Much of this paragraph was informed by an interview with a former cabinet minister in British Columbia who was involved in the field of intergovernmental relations.
33. For further details on the rise of provinces on the international scene see Douglas M. Brown and Earl H. Fry, *States and Provinces in the International Economy* (Berkeley: Institute of Governmental Studies Press, 1993).
34. See Ivo D. Duchacek, *The Territorial Dimension of Politics* (Boulder: Westview Press, 1986), chap. 3.
35. See Canada, *Dominion-Provincial Relations*.
36. Howard Leeson, "The Prairie Economic Council, 1965–1973" (Ph.D. Thesis, University of Alberta, 1983), p. 74.
37. See Howard Leeson, "Prairie Economic Council," pp. 73-94, and Gerry Gartner, "A Review of Cooperation Among the Western Provinces," *Canadian Public Administration*, 20 (Spring 1977), pp. 174-87.
38. See Howard Leeson, pp. 77-85.
39. *Ibid.* p. 77.
40. Ian McAllister, "Postwar Approaches to Regional Development: Some Comparisons Between the Industrial West and Third World Nations with Mixed Economies," *The Canadian Journal of Regional Science*, viii,2, p. 207.
41. *Ibid.*, p. 207.
42. For further details, see Premier Allan Blakeney, "Western Provincial Cooperation," in J. Peter Meekison, ed., *Canadian Federalism: Myth or Reality*, 3rd ed., (Toronto: Methuen Press, 1977); and *Proceedings of Prairie Economic Council*, Regina, Saskatchewan, 14 October 1965.
43. For examples of joint initiatives, see David Elton, "Federalism and the Canadian West," in R.D. Olling and M.W. Westmacott, eds., *Perspectives on Canadian Federalism* (Scarborough: Prentice-Hall, 1988), pp. 346-62.

44. See David Elton, *One Prairie Conference? Conference Proceedings and Selected Papers* (Lethbridge: The Lethbridge Herald, 1970).

45. For details, see B.L. Strayer, "One Prairie Province?," *Canadian Public Administration* xiii (Winter 1970), pp. 337-43; T.K. Shoyama, "Some Financial and Economic Implications of One Prairie Province," *Canadian Public Administration* xiii (Winter 1970), pp. 344-53; Ralph Hedin, "Economics of One Prairie Province," *Canadian Public Administration* xiii (Winter 1970), pp. 354-59; Gerry Gartner, "A Review of Cooperation Among the Western Provinces," *Canadian Public Administration* 20 (Spring 1977), pp. 174-87; and Eric Hanson, "The Future of Western Canada: Economic, Social, Political," *Canadian Public Administration* 18 (Spring 1975), pp. 104-120.

46. See Harry Strom, "The Feasibility of One Prairie Province," and W.A.C. Bennett, "Five Provinces for Canada," in David Elton, ed., *One Prairie Conference?*

47. Canada, Parliament, House of Commons, "Throne Speech," 29th parliament, 1st session, 4 January 1973.

48. For such evidence see Guy Benveniste, *The Politics of Expertise* (San Francisco: Boyd and Fraser Publishing, 1977); Colin Campbell, *The Super-Bureaucrats: Structure and Behaviour in Central Agencies* (Toronto: Macmillan Canada, 1979); Leslie Pal, *Public Policy Analysis* (Toronto: Methuen Press, 1987); and Hugh Heclo, *Modern Social Policies in Britain and Sweden* (New Haven: Yale University Press, 1974).

49. See Jean Marchand, "Regional and National Cooperation," *One Prairie Conference?*

50. For more details, see "Follow up on the Western Economic Opportunities Conference" (Calgary: Canada West Foundation, 1974).

51. Based on interviews.

52. Much of this paragraph draws upon interviews conducted by the author.

53. David Elton, "Federalism and the Canadian West," R.D. Olling and M.W. Westmacott, eds., *Perspectives on Canadian Federalism* (Scarborough: Prentice-Hall, 1988), p. 352.

54. There are several examples of cooperative initiatives between the four western provinces that came about as a result of Ottawa's attempt to corral the premiers and make them active collaborators in a new experiment in intergovernmental relations. For example, there have been many committees established to deal with such diverse topics as industrial development, foreign trade policy, a common electric power grid, grain marketing, transportation, research and development, the growing debt problem, and eliminating government duplication. It would be hard to deny the benefits of such discussions. For further details, see "Communiques From the Western Premiers' Conferences," 5-6 May 1977, 23 April 1980, 28-29 April 1981, 13-15 May 1985, and 30 May 1986; Western Premiers' Conference, "Report of the Western Finance Ministers," Lloydminster, Saskatchewan, 26-7 July 1990; and *Western Perspectives ... Time for Action: Reducing Interprovincial Barriers to Trade* (Calgary: Canada West Foundation, May 1989).

55. For more details, see Kenneth M. Curtis and John E. Carroll, *Canadian-American Relations* (Lexington: Lexington Books, 1983), Chap. 8.

56.   For further details on the evolution of closer ties between individual provinces
       and state governments, as well as premiers and governors in the regional/in-
       ternational domain, see Kenneth Curtis and John Carroll, *Canadian-American
       Relations*; R.F. Swanson, *Intergovernmental Perspectives on the Canadian-
       U.S. Relationship* (New York: New York University Press, 1975); Douglas
       M. Brown, Earl H. Fry, and James Groen, "States and Provinces in the
       International Economy Project," in Douglas M. Brown and Earl H. Fry, eds.,
       States and Provinces in the International Economy (Berkeley: Institute of
       Governmental Studies Press, 1993); Douglas M. Brown, "The Evolving Role
       of the Provinces in Canada-U.S. Trade Relations," in *States and Provinces*;
       James McNiven, and Dianna Cann, "Canadian Provincial Trade Offices in
       the United States" in *States and Provinces*; and I. Duchacek, "The Interna-
       tional Dimension of Subnational Self-Government," in *Publius*, 4, 1984.
57.   The Liberal Party of Canada, *Creating Opportunity*.
58.   See *Toronto Globe and Mail*, 15, 25, and 29 February 1992.
59.   "Prairie Integration: A Blueprint for Economic Renewal," conference organ-
       ized by Lloyd Axworthy, M.P., Winnipeg South-Centre, Winnipeg, 13-14
       February 1992, Province of Manitoba, Legislation Library.

Chapter Five

1.   Hershel Hardin, *A Nation Unaware* (Vancouver: J.J. Douglas Ltd., 1974).
2.   *Ibid.*, p. 50.
3.   *Ibid.*, p. 312.
4.   *Ibid.*, p. 314.
5.   *Ibid.*, p. 315.
6.   A.D. Scott, "Introduction: Notes on a Western Perspective," in Dickson
       Falconer, ed., *British Columbia: Patterns in Economic Political and Cultural
       Development* (Victoria: Camosun College, 1982), p. 178.
7.   For examples see Martin Robin, "British Columbia: The Company Province,"
       in Martin Robin, ed., *Canadian Provincial Politics* (Scarborough: Prentice-
       Hall, 1972), pp. 28-60; Stan Persky, "The Lotusland Agenda," in *Bennett II*,
       (Vancouver: New Star Books, 1983), pp. 250-63; R.M Burns, "British Co-
       lumbia: Perceptions of a Split Personality," in Richard Simeon, ed., *Must
       Canada Fail?* (Kingston and Montreal: McGill-Queen's University Press,
       1977), pp. 63-72; Stan Persky, *Fantasy Government* (Vancouver: New Star
       Books, 1989); Gary Mason and Keith Baldrey, *Fantasyland* (Toronto:
       McGraw-Hill Ryerson, 1989); and Margaret A. Ormsby, "The Spoilt Child
       of Confederation," in *British Columbia: a History* (Vancouver: Macmillan
       Company, 1971). For many, the phrase "spoilt child of confederation" and
       British Columbia have become synonymous. See, for example, R.M. Burns,
       "British Columbia and the Canadian Federation," in Patricia Roy, ed., *A
       History of British Columbia* (Toronto: Copp Clark Pitman, 1989), p. 156; or
       Donald Blake, "Managing the Periphery: British Columbia and the National
       Political Community," in *A History of British Columbia*, p. 176. These sen-
       timents, negative images, and traditions of extravagant rhetoric have deep

roots in the literature and have no doubt influenced the way people respond to issues raised by leaders in the province.

8.   There are many examples of such negative portrayals of British Columbian politicians. Ormsby, in describing relations between national and British Columbian officials in the pre-Confederation era wrote that, "Macdonald was swamped with appeals from his eager western supporters; almost everyone in British Columbia seemed to expect favours." Later on, Ormsby, in her description of political relations between Alexander Mackenzie and various leaders in the province after 1867, stated that, "His relations with provincial politicians were soon to leave him with the impression that British Columbians were a race apart, skilled in dissembling and adept at refusing to make plain statements of fact and candid declarations of policy." See Margaret Ormsby, *British Columbia: A History*, p. 253 and 261, respectively. As mentioned in Chapter Two, Robin Fisher decided to write a book on Duff Pattullo in response to all the negative commentary offered by eastern historians and the failure of British Columbian historians to counteract these old images. See Robin Fisher, *Duff Pattullo of British Columbia* (Toronto: University of Toronto Press, 1991), pp. x-xiii. Richard Simeon, in his analysis of what he sees as a poor record in defending provincial interests at intergovernmental meetings, singled out W.A.C. Bennett's personal style as being a significant factor. For details, see Richard Simeon, *Federal-Provincial Diplomacy* (Toronto: University of Toronto Press, 1972). Donald Smiley argued that the Social Credit leadership had "no vision, no plan, no real urge to remake society. In spite of its constant appeals to morality, Social Credit is at heart the pursuit of power divorced from purpose." See Donald Smiley, "Canada's Poujadists: A New Look at Social Credit," *The Canadian Forum* 42 (September 1962): p. 121. Walter Young and Terrence Morley referred to the W.A.C. Bennett administration as an "amateur government." See Walter Youg and Terrence Morley, "Te Premier in the Cabinet," in Terrence Morley *et al.*, ed., *The Reins of Power* (Vancouver: Douglas and McIntyre, 1983), p. 64.

9.   A.D. Scott, "Notes on a Western Perspective," p. 175.

10.   *Ibid.*, p. 174.

11.   *Ibid.*, p. 174.

12.   Until very recently, few academics or politicians would broach the topic of transnational interactions on ideas, culture, institutions, and patterns of economic and political development, mainly because there were many established taboos about not challenging the nationalist vision of Canada set out by established economic, academic, and political élites. Operating within the context where ideas, institutions, economies, and societies were for the most part organized on a national basis, there was great pressure to conform. As indicated by Cairns, "For its believers there are always elements of the sacred attached to nation-state. And the sacred is not to be approached casually, or in a purely calculating fashion." See Alan Cairns, "Ritual, Taboo, and Bias in Constitutional Controversies in Canada," *The Timlin Lecture Series*, (Saskatchewan: University of Saskatchewan, 13 November 1989), p. 11. Under these circumstances it is not surprising that political leaders would articulate visions that would call into question their patriotism. It is also worth noting

that the American-Canadian Borderlands Project was based on the need to challenge old ways of thinking and to defend the view that North America runs more naturally north-south than east-west, as specified by national boundaries. See Roger Gibbins, *Canada as a Borderlands Society,* Borderlands Monograph Series 2 (Orono, Me.: Borderlands Project, 1989). For further details on transborder associations and cross-border issues, see also Lauren McKinsey and Victor Konrad, "Borderland Reflections: The United States and Canada," *Borderlands Monograph*; Stephen J. Randall, Herman Konrad, and Sheldon Silverman, eds., *North America without Borders?* (Calgary: University of Calgary Press, 1992); Stephen Hornsby, Victor Konrad, and James Herlan, eds., *The Northeastern Borderlands*; and Joel Garreau, *The Nine Nations of North America* (New York: Avon Books, 1982).

13. For details on the geography of British Columbia, see John Bradbury, "British Columbia: Metropolis and Hinterland in Microcosm," in L.D. McCann, ed., *A Geography of Canada: Heartland and Hinterland* (Scarborough: Prentice-Hall, 1981), pp. 338-71. For a description of immigration patterns, see Jean Barman, "The West beyond the West: The Demography of Settlement in British Columbia," *Journal of Canadian Studies* 25, 3 (Fall 1990), pp. 5-18.

14. Terry Morley, "Politics as Theatre: Paradox and Complexity in British Columbia," *Journal of Canadian Studies*, 25, 3 (Fall 1990), p. 20.

15. This quotation is given in Terry Morley, "Politics as Theatre," p. 30. See David Elkins, "British Columbia as a State of Mind," in Donald Blake, ed., *Two Political Worlds* (Vancouver: University of British Columbia Press, 1985), p. 49.

16. See G.W. Taylor, *Builders of British Columbia: An Industrial History* (Victoria: Morriss Publishing, 1982); and John Bradbury, "British Columbia," pp. 338-371.

17. Jean Barman, *The West beyond the West*, p. 11.

18. For further discussion on party support patterns in British Columbia, see Donald Blake, ed., *Two Political Worlds*, Chap. 2; David Alper, "The Effects of Coalition Government on Party Structure: The Case of the Conservative Party in B.C.," *B.C. Studies* 33 (1977), pp. 40-49; T.M. Sanford, "The Politics of Protest" (Ph.D. Thesis, University of California, 1961); and Edith Dobie, "Some Aspects of Party History in British Columbia: 1871–1903," *Pacific Historical Review*, 1 (1932), pp. 235-51.

19. Edwin Black, "British Columbia: The Politics of Exploitation," in Dickson Falconer, ed., *British Columbia: Patterns in Economic, Political, and Cultural Development* (Victoria: Camosun College, 1982), p. 255.

20. See Margaret Ormsby, *British Columbia: A History*, p. 349.

21. See Patricia Roy, "Progress, Prosperity and Politics," p. 224.

22. For more details on the history of province-building under Premier McBride, see Margaret Ormsby, *British Columbia: A History*, Chapters 12, 13; P.R. Hunt, *The Political Career of Sir Richard McBride* (M.A. Thesis, University of British Columbia, 1953); and E. Patricia Roy, *"Progress, Prosperity and Politics: The Railway Policies of Richard McBride,"* B.C. *Studies*, 47 (Autumn 1980), pp. 3-28.

23. For details see Margaret Ormsby, *British Columbia: A History*, p. 346-365.

24. Patricia Roy, "Progress, Prosperity and Politics," p. 235.

25. As suggested by David Mitchell, *W.A.C. Bennett and the Rise of British Columbia* (Vancouver: Douglas and McIntyre, 1983), pp. 50-54, 57, and 58.

26. Norman J. Ruff, "British Columbia and Canadian Federalism," in *The Reins of Power*, p. 272.

27. For further discussion see Robin Fisher, *Duff Pattullo of British Columbia* (Toronto: University of Toronto Press, 1991), pp. 14-17.

28. *Ibid.*, pp. 14-16.

29. David Mitchell, *W.A.C. Bennett*, p. 52. See also Margaret Ormsby, "T. Dufferin Pattullo and the Little New Deal," *Canadian Historical Review*, 43, 4 (December 1962), pp. 277-97.

30. Robin Fisher, *Duff Pattullo*, p. 313.

31. *Ibid.*, p. 270.

32. For details, see Roger Keene and David Humphreys, *Conversations with W.A.C. Bennett* (Toronto: Methuen Press, 1980), pp. 30, 95.

33. R.M. Burns, "British Columbia," p. 163.

34. Paddy Sherman, *Bennett* (Toronto: McClelland and Stewart, 1966), p. 44.

35. See David Elkins, "Politics Makes Strange Bedfellows: The B.C. Party System in the 1952 and 1953 Provincial Elections," *B.C. Studies* 30 (1976) pp. 3-26.

36. S.J.R. Noel, "Leadership and Clientalism," in D. Bellamy, J. Pammett, and D. Rowat, eds., *The Provincial Political System* (Toronto: Methuen Press, 1976), p. 197.

37. According to C.B. Macpherson, in a plebiscitary democracy, "people give up their right of decision, criticism, and proposal, in return for the promise that everything will be done to implement the general will." See C.B. Macpherson, *Democracy in Alberta*, p. 233.

38. See "Presentation to Royal Commission on British Columbia Railway", University of British Columbia, Main Library, Special Collections Division, exhibits 172, 173A, 186, 256, 285.

39. See British Columbia, "Minutes of the First Alaska-Yukon-British Columbia Conference," (Victoria July 1960).

40. While Bennett rejected the two-nation theory, he endorsed the view that there were five economic zones or regions in Canada. These included Atlantic Canada, Quebec, Ontario, the Prairies, and British Columbia. For example, as far as he was concerned, the Pacific region should have the same number of senators representing its interests as the other four. Bennett's vision of Canada rejected the concept of two equal nations, as well as the principle of provincial equality. For further details, see British Columbia, "Proposals of the Province of British Columbia On the Constitution of Canada," December 1968; Ottawa, "Constitutional Conference," December 1969; and Canada, Federal-Provincial Conference, "Opening Statement of the Province of British Columbia to the Constitutional Conference," Victoria, 14-16 June 1971.

41. David Mitchell, *W.A.C. Bennett*, p. 394.

42. Lauren McKinsey and Victor Konrad, "Borderlands Reflections," p. 4.

43. Norman J. Ruff, "British Columbia and Canadian Federalism," in *The Reins of Power* p. 302.

44. See *ibid.*, pp. 292-95.

45. Canada, "Constitutional Conference Proceedings," Second Meeting, Ottawa 10-12 February 1969, p. 86.

46. Canada, "Opening Statement to the Constitutional Conference," p. 6.

47. For example, see Thomas J. Courchene, "The Community of the Canadas," (paper presented to the Belanger-Campeau Commission, School of Public Studies, Queen's University, Kingston, 1990).

48. Canada, *Open Statement to the 1971 Constitutional Conference*, p. 6.

49. Canada, *Constitutional Conference Proceedings*, (1969), p. 84.

50. *Ibid.*, p. 85.

51. *Ibid.*, p. 90.

52. See *ibid.*, pp. 139-40.

53. For details on Bennett's personalized approach to decision making, see Terrence Morley *et al.*, eds., *The Reins of Power* and Paul Tennant, "The NDP Government of British Columbia: Unaided Politicians in an Unaided Cabinet," *Canadian Public Policy* (Autumn, 1976), pp. 489-503.

54. John Langford and Neil Swainson, "Public and Quasi-Public Corporations in British Columbia," in O.P. Dwivedi, ed., *The Administrative State in Canada* (Toronto: University of Toronto Press, 1982).

55. See Richard Simeon, *Federal-Provincial Diplomacy* (Toronto: University of Toronto Press, 1972), p. 217.

56. *Royal Commission on B.C. Railway* 35 (1978) p. 4911.

57. *Vancouver Province*, 20 February 1954, p. 1.

58. *B.C. Government News*, January 1954, p. 4.

59. It is worth noting that Premier Bennett fully recognized the high costs associated with building physical infrastructures and developing sparsely settled regions, but he justified such an approach by making a direct comparison with nation-building and role play by the railway in defending the territorial interests of the country. See *B.C. Government News*, January 1954, p. 6.

60. "Presentation to Royal Commission on the B.C. Railway from W.A.C. Bennett," 6 September 1977, University of British Columbia, Main Library, Special Collections Division, exhibit 173A, pp. 2-3.

61. See "Presentation to Royal Commission from Ray Williston," September 1977, University of British Columbia, Main Library, Special Collections Division, exhibit 186, p. 2.

62. For more details, see Stephen Tomblin, "W.A.C. Bennett and Province-Building."

63. K. Rupenthal and T. Keast, *The British Columbia Railway - The Railway Derailed* (Vancouver: Centre for Transportation Studies, University of British Columbia, 1979), pp. 19-20.

64. For details on Bennett's quest to use transportation policy to defend his development priorities see "Presentation to the Royal Commission on the B.C. Railway from W.A.C. Bennett," 6 September 1977, University of British Columbia, Main Library, Special Collections Division, exhibit 173A.

65. For more information and analysis, see K. Rupenthal and T. Keast, *The British Columbia Railway*, pp. 116-17; and *Royal Commission on B.C. Railway*, vol. 1, pp. 24, 13, 75; vol. 2, p. 63, vol. 3, p. 132.

66. See Paul Tennant, "The NDP Government in British Columbia."

67. Norman Ruff, "British Columbia and Canadian Federalism," in *The Reins of Power*, p. 300.

68. *Ibid.*, p. 300.

69. Jean Barman, *The West beyond the West*, p. 295.

70. For further details, see Terry Morley, "Politics."

71. See Norman Ruff, "Leadership Autonomy and Federal Provincial Relations," Canadian Political Science Association Meetings (May 1981).

72. For further information, see Lorne J. Kavic and Gary Brian Nixon, *The 1200 Days: A Shattered Dream* (Coquitlam: Kaen Publishers, 1978), p.120.

73. *Ibid.*, 67.

74. See Lorne J. Kavic and Gary Brian Nixon, *The 1200 Days*, p. 104-105; Terrence Morley, *et al.*, eds., *The Reins of Power*, p. 283; and Larry Pratt and John Richards, *Prairie Capitalism*, p. 68.

75. See David Elkins, "British Columbia as a State of Mind," in Don Blake, *Two Political Worlds*, p. 55-56.

76. See Lorne J. Kavic and Gary Brian Nixon, *The 1200 Days*, p. 67.

77. Citation from Jean Barman, *The West beyond the West*, p. 325.

78. For an excellent discussion of these changes, see Terrence Morley, *et al.*, eds., *The Reins of Power.*

79. See, for example, D.V. Smiley, *Canada in Question: Federalism in the Eighties* (Toronto: McGraw-Hill Ryerson, 1980), p. 147.

80. For further information on the transformation that took place, see Allen Garr, *Tough Guy: Bill Bennett and the Taking of British Columbia* (Toronto: Key Porter Books, 1985); Warren Magnusson, *et al.*, *The New Reality: The Politics of Restraint in British Columbia* (Vancouver: New Star Books, 1984); Stan Persky, *Bennett II*; and Warren Magnusson, *et al.*, *After Bennett: A New Politics for British Columbia* (Vancouver: NewStar Books, 1986).

81. Michael Howlett and Keith Brownsey, "Politic Sector Politics in a Rentier Resource Economy" in Keith Brownsey and Michael Howlett, eds., *The Provincial State* (Mississauga: Copp Clark Pitman, 1992), p. 287.

82. Rand Dyck, *Provincial Politics in Canada* (Scarborough: Prentice-Hall, 1991), pp. 585-84.

83. For details, see British Columbia, *British Columbia's Constitutional Proposals: Presented to the First Ministers' Conference on the Constitution* (Victoria: Queen's Printer, 1978).

84. Alan Cairns, "The Politics of Constitutional Renewal in Canada," in Richard Simeon and Keith Banting, eds., *Redesigning the State* (Toronto: University of Toronto Press, 1985), p. 105.

85. See British Columbia, *Confederation for the Twenty-First Century: A Background Discussion Paper* (Victoria: Queen's Printer, March 1991).

86. See Rafe Mair, "Thoughts on Constitutional Position for British Columbia" in *Confederation for The Twenty-First Century: Discussion Paper On British Columbia In Confederation* (Victoria: Queen's Printer, 1991), p. 72.

87. Melvin Smith, *The Renewal of the Federation: A British Columbia Perspective* (Victoria: Queen's Printer, 1991), p. 53.

88. *Toronto Globe and Mail*, 4 April 1992.

89.   See *Toronto Globe and Mail*, 20 August 1992; and Canada, *Our Future Together: An Agreement for Constitutional Renewal* (Ottawa: Queen's Printer, 1992).

90.   For examples, see *Toronto Globe and Mail*, 19, 29 August 1992.

91.   For details, see "Memorandum of Cooperation Between British Columbia and Washington," December 1988-January 1989; T.B. Chadwick, "Hands Across the Border: The Pacific Northwest in Economic Partnership," *The New Pacific* (Fall 1989); P. Schell, "Bulldozing Borders," *The New Pacific* (Summer 1990); Charles Kelly, "Can Cascadia Manage Itself?" *The New Pacific* (Autumn 1992); Dori Jones Yang, "Magic Mountains," *The New Pacific* (Autumn 1992); Gordon Price, "Tale of Three Cities," *The New Pacific* (Autumn 1992); Editor, "The Power of One," *The New Pacific* (Autumn 1992).

92.   The globalization dimension of provincial policy making has spawned various cross-border environmental, economic, and political linkages. For example, the Pacific Northwest Economic region was approved by the legislatures of Alaska, Montana, Idaho, Oregon, Washington, Alberta, and British Columbia in 1991. Such cooperative arrangements are designed to provide the institutions necessary to pull the economic zone together, while ensuring that local state élites remain in control of future experiments.

93.   For more details on these and other issues facing Harcourt, see Brian Buchanan, "Brave New West," *The New Pacific* (Autumn 1992).

94.   See *ibid.*

95.   See "Environmental Agreement Between British Columbia and Washington," May 7, 1992; British Columbia, *Georgia Basin Commission Act*, 1990; and Alan F.J. Artibise, "International Georgia Basin-Puget Sound Sustainable Urbanization Project," December 11, 1992; and Charles Kelly, "Can Cascadia Manage itself?" *The New Pacific* (Autumn, 1992).

Chapter Six

1.   See Richard Simeon, *Federal-Provincial Diplomacy* (Toronto: University of Toronto Press, 1972).

2.   See *St John's Evening Telegram*, 27 November 1994.

3.   In Germany, interstate policies are coordinated among Lander through a system of "state treaties" that provide an effective mechanism for dealing with common problems. See *Approaches to National Standards*. A report prepared for the Government of Ontario by the Institute of Intergovernmental Relations, Queen's University, September 1991, p. 42.

Index